ALSO BY DORIS MUSCATINE

A Cook's Tour of San Francisco

A COOK'S TOUR OF ROME

A COOK'S

TOUR OF ROME

 by Doris Muscatine

ILLUSTRATED BY
Carolyn Cather

New York

CHARLES SCRIBNER'S SONS

To MOTHER

AND TO THE MEMORY

of FATHER

ℜ   *ACKNOWLEDGMENTS*   ℜ

W HILE preparing this book, I received help from many friends. They took me to their favorite restaurants and wineries, shared recipes, demonstrated cooking techniques, and answered questions with remarkable expertise. For their talents and their generosity, my warmest thanks go to Carlo Cipolla, Elena Servi Burgess, Barbara and Piero Pozzi, Carlo Jahn-Rusconi, Rita Benazzo, Emma and Angelo Servi, Amalia and Renato Torti, Sarah and Giovanni Pincherle, Catherine Feucht, Florence Casaroli, and Maria Strano. My husband, Charles, and children, Jeffrey and Alison, attacked numerous assignments of restaurant-judging and recipe-tasting without any signs of reluctance; elsewhere they demonstrated appropriate patience and encouragement, and for this I thank them dearly. I thank my husband, too, for his good-humored help with the manuscript. W. I. Follett, of the California Academy of Science, Dr. Horacio Rosa, of the Food and Agricultural Organization in Rome, Prof. J. E. Knott, of the University of California at Davis, the Giurloni Brothers, Distributors, the Ente Provinciale per il Turismo of Rome, and Giovanni Bentivoglio, of ENIT (Italian State Tourist Office), lent particular assistance with technical information. Roman restaurant owners and chefs, as the following pages amply testify, gave me the warmest cooperation. To them all, a toast in Sambuca con la mosca!

CONTENTS

I. INTRODUCTION   1

   Where Romans Eat And Drink   6

      MAP · WHERE TO FIND THE RESTAURANTS   20–21

II. THE RESTAURANT MENU   29

      MAP · WINES OF ITALY   84
      WINE CHART   85
      A NOTE ON THE RECIPES   90

III. THE RESTAURANTS   93

   1. *Characteristic Trattorie and Ristoranti*   99

      AL MORO   100
      GIOVANNI   106
      CHECCHINO DAL 1887   109
      CELESTINA   113
      ERNESTO   116
      TRATTORIA SILVANO PARIS   121
      ALFREDO ALLA SCROFA   124
      ALFREDO ALL'AUGUSTEO   124
      ALFREDO IN TRASTEVERE   124

CONTENTS

RISTORANTE CAMINETTO 128
TRATTORIA GALEASSI 131
CAMPANA 133
CAMPARONE 141
AUGUSTEA 145
ROMOLO 149
PASTARELLARO 154
RE DEGLI AMICI 157

2. *Ristoranti di Moda* 159

RISTORANTE RANIERI 160
HOSTARIA AL POMPIERE 162
PASSETTO 168
31 AL VICARIO 172
GIGGI FAZI'S HOSTARIA ROMANA 176
ANGELINO A TOR MARGANA 182

3. *Old-Style Trattorie* 187

MARIO AL LARGO PALLARO 188
OTELLO ALLA CONCORDIA 191
CHECCO ER CARRETTIERE 193
TRATTORIA IMPICCETTA
  "GIARDINO DEI POETI" 197
VINCENZO 202
TAVERNA MARGUTTA 207
DA GIGGETTO 210
PIPERNO A MONTE CENCIO 214
DA PALOZZO 216

4. *Elegant* 222

HOSTARIA DELL'ORSO 223
PALAZZI (CAMILLUCCIA) 230
CAPRICCIO 235

CONTENTS

GEORGE'S   240
CASINA VALADIER   244

5. *Seafood*   248

  AL MONUMENTO   249
  DA ANTONIO A SAN CALISTO   253
  RISTORANTE CORSETTI   257

6. *Tuscan Specialties and Game*   261

  LA FONTANELLA   262
  CHIANTI   264
  MARIO   267
  TOSCANA   271
  TULLIO   274
  NINO   277

7. *Bolognese Specialties*   281

  DAL BOLOGNESE   282

8. *Venetian Specialties*   286

  BATTAGLIA (TAVERNA ANTONINA)   287

9. *Pizzerie · Neapolitan Specialties*   292

  TEMPIO DI AGRIPPA   293
  PIZZERIA SANT'IGNAZIO   297
  RISTORANTE-PIZZERIA LA CAPRICCIOSA   301

10. *Atmosphere*   306

  DA PANCRAZIO   307
  TRE SCALINI   310
  DA MEO PATACCA   314

CONTENTS

IV. GLOSSARY · *Italian–English*   325

English–Italian   339

DIRECTORY OF RESTAURANTS   351

INDEX OF RECIPES   359

xii

A COOK'S TOUR OF ROME

I

INTRODUCTION

THERE is in Rome a zest, an earthiness, a *vivacità* that surround, excite, and thaw the Anglo-Saxon temperament. The Roman citizen breathes deep, and attacks life with gusto. When he cooks, serves, and eats, it is with the same capacity to enjoy that marks his other activities. "Romans are robust eaters and hearty drinkers, but they know how, when they are at table, also to capture the mood of festivity, to savour the conversation, to appreciate the company." [1] One of the ways to know Romans best is to meet them at dinner.

1. Bruno Rosai, "Cene a Roma," in *Romani a tavola, Almanacco dell'Accademia della Cucina*, 1962, ed. Luigi Volpicelli, Rome, 1961, p. 61.

2

The early citizen was at least as passionate about eating as his present day counterpart, to judge from Seneca's anecdote about the death of M. Gavius Apicius, a first-century epicure: "when, on counting his fortune, he found one day that, after having spent a hundred millions of sesterces mainly on food, he had only ten million sesterces left, and the prospect of starvation before him, he poisoned himself." [2] The Italian cuisine inherits venerable lessons and exotic tastes from the Greeks and Romans of antiquity and from the Orient (although I haven't heard lately

2. Apicius, *The Roman Cookery Book*, trans. by Barbara Flower and Elizabeth Rosenbaum, London and New York, Peter Nevill Limited, 1958, p. 12.

of anyone doing himself in over it). Apicius' haute cuisine cookery book records a lively skill with game and fish, a love of spices and wines, a dexterity with sauces, and an unabashed Roman appetite for anything edible.

Although today French and Italian cooking are not strikingly similar, Italy can justifiably claim the paternity of French cooking: tradition has it that the Florentine cooks of Catherine de Medici, whom she took along when she married Henri II of France, introduced the art to her court in 1533. But more than fifty years before this there had appeared in Latin a volume by the Italian scholar Platina, *De Honesta Voluptate*, containing five chapters of facts and recipes from the manuscript of a great Italian chef, Maestro Martino. This in turn found its way into Italian, German, and French translations, and had a substantial impact on early Renaissance cooking. Lord Westbury tells us: "Though never given the credit, Maestro Martino was in fact, for a period of nearly a hundred years, the Mrs. Beaton or Fanny Farmer of his day."

By the 17th century it was no longer de rigueur for the most important French kitchens to employ an Italian chef. The tide of influence flowed instead to Italy from the court of Louis XIV, a tide which finally subsided with the publication of P. Vincenzo Corrado's book, *Il Cuoco Galante* (1773), a treatise that rediscovered the traditions of Italian cooking, and promoted the feeling, Lord Westbury claims, "that French taste must be tempered with the fine products of the Italian soil and the good sense of Italian cooks." [3]

Today the Italian cuisine does not achieve the monumental sophistication, the elaborate and painstakingly contrived delicacy of the French, but what it lacks in subtlety it makes up in character and robustness, in a richness that is addicting but not cloy-

3. Lord Westbury, *Handlist of Italian Cookery Books*, Firenze, Leo S. Olschki, 1963, pp. xii, xv.

ing, satisfying but still enticing. "Cooking in Italy has, happily, remained an art, rather than become frozen into the rigidity of an exact science. One is even advised to cook a dish until the meat has become 'golden,' rather than instructed to roast it to a temperature of so many degrees for a stated length of time. This freer approach gives the art more individuality and life, and opens the door to interpretation and invention."[4]

This book is written in large part to open for the reader this avenue to the Italian world. It is to forestall the experience of Italy that many American travelers report: a steady diet of spaghetti and scaloppine, those being the only familiar, decipherable words on any menu. Such narrowness isn't fun, and it isn't fair to Italy. Nor is the spaghetti-and-scaloppine stereotype of Italian cooking limited to travelers. The depressing monotony of "Italian cooking" in America has also encouraged me to set down the impressions, experiences and recipes I collected during the times my family and I have lived in Rome. Besides thus serving as a guide for both travelers abroad and cooks at home, I hope it will provide vicarious pleasure for the armchair gastronome. It is meant, finally, as an expression of thanks to the Italian citizen himself for his warm embrace of strangers in his land.

4. Richard Hammond and George Martin, *Eating in Italy*, New York, Charles Scribner's Sons, 1957, p. 5.

Where Romans Eat and Drink

THE Eternal City abounds with places to eat and drink—bars and caffè, gelaterie, rosticcerie, osterie, birrerie, cantine, trattorie, ristoranti—dozens of them in every neighborhood, and a profusion in the downtown area. Weather permitting, and this means at the first pretense of spring, the sidewalks and streets suddenly

6

mushroom with tables, plants, lanterns and flower gardens. Music is almost everywhere. It is one of the most striking characteristics of Roman dining that music and food go together.

Strolling musicians and singers wander among the tables. Lately some rock-and-roll performers have made their appearance, with music and antics that are not the ideal aid to digestion. But most Roman minstrels still sing lovely old favorites like "Il Tango delle Capinere," "Signorinella," or "Come Pioveva"; or any one of the more recent popular songs, perhaps a winner at the song festival at San Remo. On request most singers can turn out Neapolitan dialect songs with the facility of a juke box full of quarters, but there the similarity ends. You will find yourself caught up in the persistence of their rhythm, and long afterward haunting snatches of their melodies will tease through your mind. Several restaurants have staff musicians, like the old tenor at Romolo in Trastevere, the youngsters with their guitars downstairs at Tempio di Agrippa across from the Pantheon (where on occasion a waiter can be persuaded to perform an aria or two), the singers at Da Meo Patacca, who are famous for regional songs, many of which they have recorded, and the talented professionals in places like the elegant Hostaria dell'Orso, where a guitarist and a pianist provide exceptional music in the bar and a tenor and orchestra serenade you at dinner.

Another feature characteristic of Italian eating is the atmosphere of leisure that surrounds it. There is never any rush. When you order a refreshment, you will get literally that: even the simplest demi-tasse brings with it a sidewalk seat in the sun, with unlimited lounging privileges. In the same way, dinner entitles you to linger indefinitely in the Edwardian elegance of a deluxe ristorante, or in sheltered ease under the grape vines on the terrace of a neighborhood trattoria. In fact, not only will you never be rushed from your table, but this leisurely atmosphere is so pervasive you will often find it difficult to get the check when you *are* ready to leave.

7

INTRODUCTION

It takes a long time to unwind, however, to the point of comfortably understanding "dolce far niente," particularly when you are pushed to the opposite philosophy by a tight, full schedule and a short space of time. The quick short orders of the rosticceria are tempting. Americans, accustomed to the speed and efficiency required to get their food jammed into them in time to make that two o'clock appointment back at the office, tend to be a bit fidgety during the usual Italian meal, for its several courses are cooked and consumed at a leisurely pace. After twenty minutes they are inclined to believe that the service is dragging, but it is only that the *ambiente* is different. You must come to an understanding with the custom rather than with the waiter. Since your meal is being cooked to order (the steam table being generally considered an abomination), it requires a good amount of time. It is not unusual to order your second course only after you have finished eating the first one. Planning ahead is not an Italian characteristic, though not through lack of foresight so much as in response to the weight of history and the reality of economics. It is sound procedure, by this logic, to handle things as they come. To anticipate the number of patrons who will dine in your restaurant on Tuesday is impossible, and so to cook up an arbitrary quantity of pasta in anticipation of an arbitrary number of guests seems foolish. Besides, the pasta will get soggy, and Italians like to bite through their spaghetti with feeling.

In practical terms, Italians don't plan their meals ahead, because until the recent but still unsteady prosperity, most households and many restaurants had no refrigeration. The centuries old custom of a daily market continues, with the reassuring result that the food served up at your restaurant table is fresh, no doubt purchased that very day. Some small trattorie occasionally send out on the spot for ingredients needed in the preparation of your order.

When you begin to function on the slower Italian rhythm you will discover that nothing much is lost—your schedule notwith-

8

standing—since this is the pace to which everything and every-body else is geared. And after a large midday meal accompanied by wine, you will not only begin to understand, but also to ap-preciate, the siesta. Though at first it may be hard, wine or not, to make yourself relax until 4:30 or 5 in the afternoon, a few fruitless attempts to get things done make it easier to succumb docilely to the Italian system. With almost the entire Roman population at rest until late afternoon, there is a certain futility in remaining abroad anyhow. You can't get your shopping done if the store is closed, and if you take the luxury of a late lunch and a siesta you'll be much more receptive during the midnight third act of the opera. With the exception of a few galleries and museums, everything in mid-afternoon is shut up tight, pad-locked, in fact, behind great iron grilles and shutters, the siesta hours (shorter in winter, longer in summer) responding to the weather like a thermometer.

Bars · (Caffè)

THE bar or caffè functions as a place for a light snack, as a meet-ing place and as a place to relax. It offers such a variety of appeal-ing nibbles and drinks that one can hardly pass them up. A Roman often takes his breakfast here—caffè latte or cappuccino, perhaps with a croissant or sweet roll. The constant hiss of the espresso machine announces immediate brews of coffee, steaming milk, and boiling water for punches and teas. There are available, besides, alcoholic beverages, often a large assortment of them, sweet pastry, and sandwiches. Most bars double as gelaterie and provide ice cream and other frozen wonders during the warm months of the year. Since Romans believe in the appropriateness of a food to the season, ice cream is, for them, strictly a hot

9

weather item. But some places, particularly fancy ones, provide summertime treats all year around, largely, I suspect, in answer to American taste, which in these matters is not seasonal.

Since the Italian breakfast is both early and light, it is customary to break the long stretch until lunch with a mid-morning stop at the bar for a coffee or aperitif; and it is often essential to calm one's appetite with a tramezzino or canapè (varieties of finger sandwiches) or a miniature pizza or flaky stuffed pastry, bubbling with cheese as it comes hot off the grill. By late afternoon, everyone feels the need of another refreshment, and you stop again to sip a vermouth and watch the tangle of the crowd as it knots and bunches along the avenues. With its umbrella-shaded seats and long icy drinks, the bar offers refuge from hot summer afternoons; when the chill and wet of winter penetrate your bones, a hot punch in a steamy caffè is the thing to thaw you. Most bars provide counters where stand-up patrons can save time, if they need to, and money. The same refreshments cost more with table service. You often pay by first purchasing a receipt from the cashier and then presenting it to the counterman with your order. One of the niceties of most Italian bars is straws made of real straw.

Among the hundreds of noteworthy bars that cater to Romans' between-meal eating habits, the best known is Doney's. At 145 Via Vittorio Veneto, it unfurls its flags and lines its tables along the sidewalks of almost an entire city block. There are large inside quarters too, but these do not provide comparable ringside seats for the perpetual parade of humanity outdoors. The Veneto is a swanky street that winds from the Porta Pinciana for several blocks through a section heavily populated with tourists. Besides a procession of caffè it is edged with luxury hotels, smart shops, and even the United States Embassy. The crowd that gathers here, to stroll, to stretch catlike in the sun, to check the entrances and exits of famous names at the Hotel Excelsior, is a fantastic conglomeration of people: characters of every nationality, complexion, attitude and pose, their origin labeled by the cut of their clothes or the rhythm of their walk. In this jumble of people, among the watchers and the watched, almost everyone takes on the temporary importance of a possible celebrity. Although this is fatally how Hollywood or Cinecittà might portray Rome, it *is* a part of Rome in fact, a part that is glamorous, gay, elegant, funny, nonchalant, snobbish, and always fascinating. While you watch from a table at Doney's you can obtain almost any drink, intriguing canapè, elaborate pastries, hamburgers and club sandwiches. The Café de Paris, Rosati, Al "cavallino rosso," Carpano, and the Golden Gate, flower-splashed and awning-shaded, add their color and facilities to the string of elegant cafés along this street. The Café de Paris, which vies with Doney's for first place, offers an extensive buffet and telephone service at your table. "Cavallino rosso" serves American breakfasts and replaces the old Strega bar, which made a reputation on real ice cream sodas, not an Italian confection by nature. The Golden Gate salutes California with a thoroughly Italian adaptation of the orange —filled with sherbet. (A more caloric orange, containing a mixture of frozen cream and candied fruit, is a specialty of the intellectuals' headquarters, the other Café Rosati, in the Piazza del Popolo.) Most of the Via Veneto places are on the expensive side, but you will enjoy them.

The Gran Caffè Berardo in the Piazza Colonna offers musical entertainment from six p.m. to midnight. One of the busiest bars is l'Hungaria in the Piazza Ungheria. It provides an inventive selection of grilled pastries and openfaced sandwiches, ice cream delights, imaginative confectionery and well prepared drinks. L'Hungaria turns out splendid frullatti di frutta, thick blends of fresh fruits, milk, sugar and crushed ice. But my favorite concoction, and one which this bar prepares exceptionally well, is the granita: a glassful of powdery sherbet-like ice, infused with a strong coffee, fresh lemon, or strawberry syrup, and, if you have given up on calories anyway, finished with an extravagant glob

11

of whipped cream. This ambrosia makes even a sticky hot day seem suddenly worth-while, and can be made easily at home: Heat two cups of water with four to six tablespoons of sugar (six are too sweet for me) for three or four minutes or until slightly syrupy. Add four cups of (prepared) very strong espresso coffee, mix well, and let cool. Freeze in the ice-tray of the refrigerator, stirring frequently to prevent it from forming a solid block. The freezing time varies, but never takes more than three hours. For lemon granita, substitute one cup of fresh lemon juice (six or seven lemons) and increase sugar to a scant half cup. For strawberry granita, make the syrup of one cup of water to one-half cup of sugar. When it is cool, add two cups of puréed fresh strawberries and the juice of one-half lemon. The coffee recipe serves six to eight, the lemon and strawberry three or four. Serve in a glass, topping the coffee and strawberry with sweetened whipped cream. One of my friends runs the finished granita through an electric blender before spooning it into the serving glasses, and reports that it improves the texture considerably.

Alemagna, at 181 Via del Corso, a deluxe downtown bar, offers settings of both animation and restraint by dividing its enormous interior into two compartments: an air-conditioned salon where voices hush, footsteps slacken, and mirrors reflect a calm pastel and silver decor; and a throbbing and efficient stand-up bar–pastry shop–ice cream parlor. Alemagna is a Milanese firm known for the quality and originality of its pastries and candies, which, like its competitor Motta, it markets throughout the Italian peninsula. Its Rome showcase, the large caffè on the Corso, offers these and more. Compositions of tongue, shrimp, smoked salmon, turkey breasts, sardines, hard-boiled eggs, capers and anchovies, glisten in their gelatine frames. Small casseroles of pastry crusts filled with mixtures of hams and cheeses, tomatoes and anchovies, and pizzette, the pocket-size editions of pizza, wait to be heated to order. The desserts are legion. Skilled chefs sculpt chocolate, nuts, ice creams and liqueurs into frozen and

baked compositions that are works of art. The Alemagna show-
room is a veritable museum of the confectionery world. Trays of
buttery cookies, petits fours, marrons glacés, chocolates, fudges,
hard fruit drops—even bite-size cocktail canapè—and all such
manner of alluring goodies dazzle the eyes. Instead of the orange,
Alemagna fills the lemon, the best, I think, of the frozen citrus
desserts. The most beautiful birthday cake my daughter ever had
was their creation: of pinks and sparkles, twirling tinsels, laces
and dustings of confectioner's sugar, it looked like a ballerina in
full whirl. In the same neighborhood, but in humbler surroundings, Giolitti (Via Uffici del Vicario 40; with branches at the
grand Casina dei 3 Laghi, Viale Oceania in EUR, and in the
Piazza Armellini) dispenses stunning desserts, excellent frozen
cream cakes and Rome's most fantastic ice cream concoctions.
If you can't make up your mind by the names, you can always
point out to the waiter some mile-high, eight-flavored sundae that
your neighbor is working his way through.

The Café Greco, 86 Via Condotti, opened its doors in 1760.
Its dark wood interiors, marble tables, and collection of faded
pictures preserve the feeling of another era. The maze of small
rooms reduces crowding, and charms you to linger in your semi-
private parlor. It is not surprising that many literati, among them
Goethe, Mark Twain, and Keats (whose house is nearby), have
found its atmosphere congenial. It was as appealing to painters as
to littérateurs; a painting that hangs in the National Gallery of
Hamburg shows a gathering of mid-nineteenth century artists clus-
tered around a Café Greco table. Certainly its most amusing visitor was Buffalo Bill in the company of several American Indians,
he in his fringed Western gear and they in their feathers. This in-
congruous group turns up in a photograph that the Café has for
sale, along with other postcards picturing celebrated visits. The
Café Greco is especially comfortable on a cold winter day. Its
steamy façade on the narrow Via Condotti invites you to seek
consolation inside, to warm luxuriously over a hot punch alla

livornese. To make this punch at home, preheat one small glass for each portion by filling it with boiling water. When the water is emptied out, put in sugar to your taste (usually one or two teaspoons), and a twist of lemon peel. Pour over it one very hot cup of strong espresso coffee, and approximately one tablespoon of rum (more if you like, but it cools the drink). Stir and serve immediately. In the bar a final jet of boiling water from the espresso machine insures the necessary high temperature, so if you find that the home brew isn't as scalding as a good punch should be, a few drops from the teakettle should set things right. If you prefer cognac to rum, it can be used interchangeably.

If you are a coffee drinker, there are several bars that are noted particularly for the excellence of their product, among them: the Peru, in Piazza Barberini; the Bar Pasticceria Roma (popularly called the Löwenbrau) at 82 Piazza Santo Eustachio; and Raimondi, at Largo Tritone 54–55, where Jamaican Blue Mountain blends are available. Although Italy does not particularly connote tea drinking, many Italians, influenced by their British associates, have taken up the habit with enthusiasm. In Babington's English Tearoom, at the bottom of the Spanish Steps, hatted and furred Italian ladies rendezvous, chattering over their tea and scones; Italian gentlemen stir their English Breakfast, Darjeeling or Formosa Oolong with a practiced nonchalance; and Italian children spread their jam properly on the toasted English muffins. The wicker of the chairs creaks cozily, and waitresses, an uncommon sight in Italy, round out the cheery picture in their starched uniforms, their perky apron bows following them around. The menu includes American banana splits side by side with the crumpets. Pancakes and waffles are among the specialties. Sundaes, bacon and eggs, familiar sandwiches and soups make Babington's a blessing for feeding small Anglo-Saxon children before the normally late hour of Italian dinner.

Two quiet bars are among my favorites. Canova maintains a world of calm and elegance just steps from the crush and clamor of the Piazza del Popolo. A series of tastefully furnished, intimate rooms leads to a hidden garden court fitted with gay umbrellas, that nestles snugly against the enormous wall of the Pincio Gardens. The other bar, which at lunch time converts to a full-scale restaurant, is in the courtyard behind the restrained and polished lobby of the Hotel Hassler-Villa Medici, at the top of the Spanish Steps. Surrounded by vines and flowers, you can sip your drink contentedly here and watch the lazy shadows play summer games across small terrace tables.

Rosticcerie

THE rosticceria, a cross between a delicatessen and cafeteria, serves quick, simple meals. Here dining is not an unhurried and lingering experience. Most foods are already prepared, and reheated if need be, rather than cooked to order. You often sit at long wall counters rather than at tables. American travelers, unaccustomed to an enormous repast and a fiasco of wine in the middle of the day, find rosticcerie appealing because of the efficiency and simplicity of one-dish meals, hot pastries, or grilled sandwiches. Rosticcerie are also reliable sources of cheeses, breads, cold meats, whole barbecued chickens, relishes, salads put up in little paper containers, and all such manner of supplies for an al fresco lunch on a driving trip or excursion. In most rosticcerie these days one comes across such items as Rice Krispies (but in Italy they "Pif, Paf, Pof"), packaged Crik-Crok (potato chips), pane in cassetta (packaged sliced sandwich bread) and sometimes even peanut butter. The first housekeeper we had in Rome, bent on surprising us and some friends who were stopping for a pre-dinner aperitif, fetched up a large tray of hors d'oeuvres. On tasting these handsome concoctions, we discovered

15

that under the prosciutto, salami, anchovies, and pickled mush-rooms there was a carpet of peanut butter procured from the local rosticceria, where she had been assured that this was a chic American delicacy.

Birrerie · Osterie · Cantine

BIRRERIE serve snacks and beer, and there are a few German and Austrian places in Rome that cook Bavarian and Viennese spe-cialties (described under Foreign Restaurants). Osterie and can-tine are unpretentious places where you can buy wine. You are welcome to bring your own food and join the other customers gathered at the rough tables and benches.

Trattorie

"IN Rome you go to dinner together. In other cities you go to the theatre together, to see a film together, to hear a concert together, even to cheer together at a football game. In Rome, however, the flavor of good company can't be divided from the taste of a good meal. . . . Everyone agrees that the table is the ideal place to meet for whatever reason, or more often, without any other reason. . . . It would be impossible for the myriad of trattorias—which spangle every street of Rome with surnames, diminutives, nick-names, some paired with robust occupational titles which range from *carrettiere* to *bottaro*—to keep going so steadfastly and splendidly without a local clientele, without an internal gastronomic tourism. . . ." [5]

The tradition of the Roman trattoria is unpretentiousness. Its atmosphere and cooking are plebeian rather than aristocratic, and the management, the kitchen, and the service are often a family affair. Its menu is studded with dishes that are the delight of the Roman populace: oxtails, lights, hearts, brains, pagliata. Its favorite salad is a mixture of wild greens and herbs. Its devotees feast on suckling lamb, fried codfish, cuttlefish, roasted mushrooms, and often crisp fennel or artichokes dipped raw into a cup of seasoned oil. Dishes come from its kitchen redolent of rosemary and wild mint, laurel and sage. There are flashes of hot red pepper in the spaghetti sauce, and cool draughts of amber Frascati wine to erase the bite. On Thursday there are gnocchi, on Saturday tripe ("giovedì gnocchi, sabato trippa"). The tablecloths, if not paper, will surely be dampish, with a faint and not unpleasant smell of laundry soap clinging to the linen. Sometimes a card game is in progress, the players and professional watchers drawn from the ranks of the neighborhood idlers, fittingly called poltroni, after the Italian word for easy chair. Every so often a dark-eyed child brushes through the beaded curtains to fill a liter bottle with wine for the family supper. In winter people keep their coats on, and a vendor, portable brazier slung from mittened hands, may shuffle between the tables selling hot roasted chestnuts. The family dog or a homeless cat generally waits patiently, hopefully, under someone's table.

There are, to be sure, more and more departures from this popular type of Roman dining room. The term trattoria no longer necessarily signifies simplicity, the menu less often features the full variety of butcher's products, the prices may have changed

---

5. Alfonso Vittorio Giardini, "A Roma si cena insieme," in *Roma a tavola, Almanacco dell'Accademia Italiana della Cucina*, 1960–61, ed. Luigi Volpicelli, Rome, 1960, pp. 13, 14.

upwards. But in the real trattorias, whether they have modernized their premises, added more sophisticated recipes to their menus, or started to employ outsiders as waiters, you will still find favorite Roman dishes well prepared, and a host who makes you feel like one of the family.

Ristoranti

IN general a ristorante is something more of an establishment than a trattoria: less folksy, more elegant in its decor, more extensive in its menu and more complicated in its cooking. There are several of great style, luxurious, expensive, and usually rewarding gastronomically. But to add confusion to these classifications, it must be said that some establishments, most of them very good, regard it chic to call themselves "trattorie," although they are fancier and more expensive than many a restaurant.

Atmosphere, often abetted with a heavy hand, is important to many restaurants in Rome, an inheritance from the propensities of the ancients, and from such forebears as a Roman aristocrat of the early 16th century, Agostino Chigi, who "entertained [in his Villa Farnesina] with fabulous luxury Pope Leo X, cardinals, ambassadors, artists and men of letters. . . . When he gave open-air banquets in a portico (now vanished) overlooking the Tiber, the silver plates and dishes were thrown into the river after every course; but prudence tempered ostentation, as a net was in position to recover them." [6]

Where modern Roman settings have not been enhanced by the imagination, it is often because the location itself is so re-

6. *Rome and Central Italy*, ed. L. Russell Muirhead, London, Ernest Benn Limited, 1956, p. 233.

18

markable. Ulpia, a deluxe restaurant that is noted for its cannelloni and tavern for after-dinner dancing, nestles at the edge of the ruins of the Forum of Trajan. The Domus Aurea Restaurant (Parco Colle Oppio) has a panoramic terrace overlooking the Colosseum, and the Roof Garden Restaurant of the Forum Hotel gives a view over the Imperial Forums. Il Fedelinaro (95 Fontana di Trevi) specializes in a view of the Trevi Fountain, as well as miniature fettuccine and an elaborate medallion of beef. There is even a restaurant set in the monumental ruins of the Baths of Caracalla, where opera lovers can attend to their appetites before enjoying an open-air presentation of "Aida" or "Tosca." The Hotel Hassler-Villa Medici on Via Sistina, just at the top of the Spanish Steps, offers its dinner guests the city's widest and handsomest view. Its rooftop dining room and terrace (glass-windowed for breezy weather) is one of the pleasantest settings for dinner that I know. The menu is large, expensive, and international but includes many special Italian dishes.

Probably the most unusual of Rome's restaurants is Il Fungo —The Mushroom—out in the new EUR quarter. This giant concrete structure, designed by Venturi as a water tower, still serves in that capacity. Mario del Monaco, a celebrated Italian singer, Fausto Simmi of the family that runs La Cisterna and the Villa dei Cesari, and the builder Carlo Rosa are partners in this enterprise. Their designer, Monardo, has turned the sixteen-floor high mushroom cap into a restaurant dining room (where snacks are served all day long), and its entry floor into an angled bar of more than usual architectural interest. On the fourteen floors in between, he has constructed "wine cellars," each devoted to a different country, and which the owners hope to place under the charge of its ambassador. In exchange for his gold entry key, he need only stock the place with the wines of his native land. The view from the top is exceptional.

Another of Rome's new bar and restaurant settings is in the Cavalieri Hilton, a colossal hotel high on Monte Mario, that is

19

WHERE TO FIND
THE RESTAURANTS

to Palazzi (36)

CITTÀ DEL
VATICANO

S. Pietro

Monte
Gianicolo

p.te
GARIBALDI

N

VIALE GIULIO CESARE

Pza C. di
Rienzo

VIA CRESCENZIO

Pza
Cavour

VIA D. CONCILIAZIONE

VIA DELLA LUNGARA

p.te
Margherita

p.te
Cavour

p.te
Vitt. Eman.

p.te
Aosta

p.te
G. Mazzini

p.te
Sisto

V. Garibaldi

50

Pza del
Popolo

8

6

35

12

12 45

44

34

22

30

48

Mte
Pincio

13

Pza
di Spagna

28

10

1

5 40

S.M. della
Pace

52

Pza Navona

51

7

33

Fontana
di Trevi

VIA DE

49

47

21

CORSO VITTORIO EMANUELE II v. PLEBISCITO

Lgo
Argentina

38 31

Pza Campo
dei Fiori

VIA ARENULA

4

43

42

46

16

23

3

5 29

S.M. in
TRAST. 39

19

41

20

VIALE DI TRASTEVERE

p.te
Garibaldi

54

18

Isola Tiberina

p.te
Cestio

p.te
Fabricio

p.te
Palatino

25 Teatro
Marcello

to Checchino (15

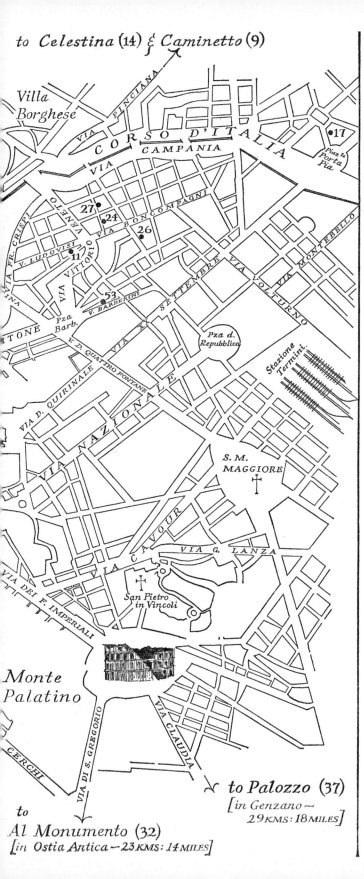

to *Celestina* (14) & *Caminetto* (9)

Villa Borghese

VIA PINCIANA

CORSO D'ITALIA

CAMPANIA

VIA

•17

Piaz. Porta Pia

VIA FR. CRISPI

VIA VENETO

VIA BONCOMPAGNI

27•

•24

26•

V. LUDOVISI

VIA VITTORIO

11•

53•

V. BARBERINI

VIA MONTEBELLO

VIA XX SETTEMBRE

VIA VOLTURNO

TRITONE

Pza Barb.

V. D. QUATTRO FONTANE

Pza d. Repubblica

VIA D. QUIRINALE

VIA NAZIONALE

Stazione Termini

VINA

S. M. MAGGIORE

VIA CAVOUR

VIA G. LANZA

VIA CLAUDIA

San Pietro in Vincoli

VIA DEI F. IMPERIALI

Monte Palatino

VIA DI S. GREGORIO

CERCHI

to *Palozzo* (37)
[in Genzano — 29 KMS : 18 MILES]

to
Al Monumento (32)
[in Ostia Antica — 23 KMS : 14 MILES]

KEY TO
THE RESTAURANTS
OF ROME

1   Alfredo alla Scrofa
2   Alfredo all'Augusteo
3   Alfredo a Trastevere
4   Angelino a Tor Margana
5   Antonio a San Calisto
6   Augustea
7   Battaglia
8   dal Bolognese
9   Caminetto
10 della Campana
11 Capriccio
12 la Capricciosa
13 Casina Valadier
14 Celestina
15 Checchino al Mattatoio
16 Checco er Carrettiere
17 al Chianti
18 Comparone
19 Corsetti
20 Da Meo Patacca
21 Ernesto
22 la Fontanella
23 Galeassi
24 George's
25 da Giggetto
26 Giggi Fazi
27 Giovanni
28 Hostaria dell'Orso
29 Impiccetta a Trastevere
30 Mario
31 Mario al Largo Pallaro
32 al Monumento
33 al Moro
34 Nino
35 Otello alla Concordia
36 Palazzi
37 da Palozzo
38 Pancrazio al Biscione
39 Silvano Paris
40 Passetto
41 Pastarellaro
42 Piperno a Monte Cenci
43 al Pompiere
44 Ranieri
45 al Re degli Amici
46 Romolo a Porta Settimiana
47 Sant'Ignazio
48 Taverna Margutta
49 Tempio di Agrippa
50 Toscana al Girarrosto
51 31 [Trentuno] al Vicario
52 Tre Scalini
53 Tullio
54 Vincenzo

a cross between a modern airport terminal and Marienbad. The facilities are numerous for quenching one's thirst or allaying one's appetite. The most interesting of these is La Pergola roof-garden bar and restaurant, with a terrace so vast as to be almost eerie, especially on a cool, moonswept night. A large crowd is instantly lost in its reaches, but the usual-size dance floor brings enough people reassuringly together again to let you know you are not alone. The music is Hawaiian, and the bar drinks exotic mixtures: Tropical Itch, Per Bacco, Roman Twist, and the Romulo and Remo. These come forth in an assortment of bar gear as elaborate as the Hilton's architecture, but including, on the simpler side, some stunning Venini glassware from Venice.

In the summer months, two deluxe open-air restaurants take full advantage of the usually balmy weather. The Belvedere delle Rose, far out on the Via Cassia (number 455), and the Casina della Rose, in the middle of the city in the Villa Borghese, present excellent food, dancing, and first-rate entertainment. The Belvedere is under the same management as the popular Via Veneto supper club, the Rupe Tarpea. Their best dishes are fine cannelloni and veal piccata. Another large establishment on a more modest scale that is particularly pleasant for outdoor summer dining is La Vigna dei Cardinali at 34 Piazzale Ponte Milvio. The specialties include chicken and baby lamb roasted on the spit, and live trout cooked to your pleasure. The present trend in summer dining is to drive out to the Roman Hills to one of a number of elaborate restaurants, several of which have Rome connections. Elio Cabala, on the Via Spinabella (a road which turns off the Via Appia Nuova just 21 kilometers from Rome) near Marino, is a restaurant and country club with summer cottages, swimming pools, and dancing, all under the intelligent direction of Tony Prantera of the celebrated Hostaria dell'Orso. The Villa Fiorio in Frascati boasts an eighteenth century garden, and serves an international cuisine at poolside. There are hotel accommodations and dancing as well, run with the refined touch of Vernon Jarrett of George's in Rome. At Castelgandolfo, the location of the Pope's summer residence, there is the Culla del Lago hotel and restaurant, a good place for lake fishermen, I'm told. During the hunting season La Pistamentuccia in Genzano is popular with lovers of small roasted birds or wild boar put up in a chocolate sauce.

But many other Roman restaurateurs have provided their own stage-sets. Perhaps the most remarkable of these is La Siesta in the Via Pontina past the EUR-Olympic area: a motel, large restaurant, bar, and pizzeria, overlooking a 500 meter track for Go-Kart enthusiasts, with grandstands for 1,500, and trackside seating for 2,000! If you feel like a turn around the course before your saltimbocca, there are lockers and dressing rooms, and karts for hire. At La Biblioteca (Largo del Teatro Valle 7), a subterranean restaurant under a Renaissance palace, the walls are lined with shelves and shelves of bottles. Giulio Cerroni, the director, tells me that when the restaurant started out in 1911 (under the direction of his father-in-law, Federico Raffi) it had none of the character of its present setting. Where there are now a string of rooms, an American bar, a tavern, and two orchestras, there was formerly a simple bottiglieria-ristorante, primarily the hangout of students from the nearby Università di Studi di Roma. It was they who referred to it as "the library" (La Biblioteca), saying, when they felt like passing a few hours in relaxation, "Let's go over to the library to study." The substitution of wine bottles for books is quite faithful to the original notion of the place. When I was last there, there was a rolling cart of fresh shellfish, and specialties of cannelloni, lasagne, tortellini in a cream sauce sprinkled with peas, a tegamino di vitella (veal and mushrooms in an earthenware pot), kid roasted Roman-style, and bass baked in a parchment bag. (The restaurant is closed from mid-June until mid-September.)

The Villa dei Cesari (Via Ardeatina 164) is a big and expensive place with a good dance orchestra and a setting vaguely

23

reminiscent of Imperial Rome. If you cannot resist being served by a bare-legged waiter decked out in an ancient Roman costume, this is the place for you. La Cisterna, in the Via della Cisterna, is a close relative—its proprietor is in fact the brother of the Villa's owner, and he is just as costume-conscious. His waiters prance about in 18th century red breeches. The Trastevere setting has a carnival air about it with its chains of lights strung over the street, and a whole orchestra performing (and it is the unique Roman restaurant in my experience that added a healthy charge for music to the bill). Its inner walls are gaily muralled and it does boast an authentic Roman well. At Apuleius on the Aventine Hill (Via del Tempio di Diana 15), you can dine aristocratically in a simulated first-century Roman house.

La Piazzetta (Via della Paglia 33, in Trastevere) turns indoors into outdoors by the installation of Persian blinds on the walls, plants climbing up to washing strung out of false windows, mattresses airing, and all such signs of a Trastevere piazza. Waiters wearing long black stockings, short velvet jackets, and brass scrolls bearing such medieval names as "Ariel," carry in the house specialty of fettucce alla strozzi (large egg noodles served with peas, mushrooms and meat sauce).

If you have an ear for Roman dialect, or better yet, a Roman friend, you may be amused by Cencio al Parolaccio. "Parolaccia" means "dirty word," but the English translation is unfair to the actual antics at Cencio. In the most outrageous Roman dialect the waiters and musicians ad lib, josh the guests and each other, and make spontaneous commentary on everybody, including the passing gentry. The words of familiar songs undergo remarkable changes, and the whole cast of characters invents stornelli (extemporized, generally bawdy songs) at the least provocation. Newcomers are always greeted by some well-aimed remark, and the menu, recited orally, always ends in a stream of off-color insertions. The waiter is likely to dump the silver in front of you

24

and with a wave of the hand make clear that setting the table is up to you, not him. If you ask for bread, he may toss you a piece. He will pause on his rounds to admire the handbag of an expensively dressed woman, "A little something from Porta Portese?" he will suggest, referring to the local flea market. A well-endowed woman may end up blushing, and characters out of the Dolce Vita set are always in for a bald ribbing. The remarkable thing is that this earthiness comes off with enormous good humor on all sides. The guests are continuously laughing, and those who blush do so with a smile. If the food is not extraordinary, everyone is too busy having a good time to notice it anyhow.

You can find plenty of color in almost any Trastevere trattoria. As one of our Roman friends remarked, the Trastevere quarter is really one big trattoria anyway. In this old section of the city across the Tiber, there is room for all kinds of eating places, with and without antics or costumes. Just walking around is part of the fun. Here you can lose yourself instantly in a maze of winding narrow streets, cobblestone passageways that snake between infirm houses strung together by their lines of clothes. Drying tomatoes and bobbing birdcages, parakeets and finches decorate their make-believe façades. The noise is constant: from Vespas and Lambrettas, automobiles and trucks, clomps of horses' hooves echoing against the stones, from voices speaking, shouting, shrieking in Roman dialect. In Trastevere nobody whispers. The first time we walked here my husband predicted, "Any minute now Cecil B. DeMille will step out and say 'Cut!' " If you should choose a simple trattoria, the chatter and gesticulation of your fellow diners will provide plenty of warm atmosphere. The fare is honest, the cost minimal, and the wine from the castelli cheering. A typically modest trattoria, Norcina in the Vicolo del Moro, may seat you in its cozy back courtyard under a summer sky that peeks through a trellised grapevine (and likely, above that, a line of wash). If you don't mind stares (after all, you pro-

25

vide reciprocal atmosphere) and butcher-paper table cloths, try the pizza and a litro of wine at Fontanone, behind the cascading fountain at the end of the Ponte Sisto.

Sprinkled through the city there are some foreign restaurants which deserve at least passing mention. Truly French restaurants are rare in Rome, but Moulin Rouge in Via Nomentana, and Les Escargots, a country inn at 46 Via Appia Antica, and a city branch at 34 Via Umiltà, feature several dishes cooked in the French manner. The Bouchées Caruso at Les Escargots are splendid; the proprietors won't reveal the recipe, because they claim they are related to the great Enrico Caruso whose favorite dish this was, and are vowed to secrecy. However, the recipe for green gnocchi comes close enough, with a sauce of butter, flour, and heavy cream. In the EUR zone, near the Palazzo dello Sport of Olympic fame, Enrico D'Avanzo has opened Samovar (Viale Oceano Pacifico 15), a Russian restaurant with plenty of the requisite minarets, caviar, and vodka. The Birreria Bavarese, Via Vittoria 47, offers German cooking and beer, folk music, and a predominantly young crowd. An Austrian beer hall, Birreria Viennese (also called variously Vienna Beer Garden and Wiener Bierhaus), dispenses its specialties at 21 Via della Croce. The Old Vienna restaurant and beer cellar (Via Degli Artisti 23) provides hi-fi dance music, and at the Birreria Albrecht (Via Francesco Crispi 39) the specialties are goulash, smoked pork, and Vienna sausage.

One of the liveliest foreign restaurants is the Hungarian Il Piccolo Budapest at 56 Vicolo dei Modelli near Trevi Fountain. The orchestra plays tzigane music, and the gypsy spirit is infectious. Another Hungarian locale, Tokay (Via Milano 10), is directed by Andrea Partos, a wartime pilot who spent some time interned in a concentration camp. Signor Partos recommends the strong Hungarian wine. Rachmil Tenenbaum, of Polish origin, and his Hungarian wife Sosannah, after four years in Auschwitz, married in Italy, and now make their life directing a Kosher restaurant

(Via Cavour 266) where the food is prepared in the Orthodox Jewish manner. Jerry's, at a subterranean Via Veneto address, (number 155, down one flight just opposite Bricktop's, which is one of Rome's most worth-while nightspots) is among several American-style restaurants, this one usually full of celebrities of the theatre. Jerry Chierchio, the American-born proprietor, was once a prize fighter. He has also opened a Polynesian restaurant, Luau, drawing on experience he acquired during some years in Hawaii. The Madison House (Via San Nicolò da Tolentino 76), the California (Via Bissolati 56), Rugantino's (Piazza di Spagna 46), Al "cavallino rosso" and the Manhattan Café (173 and 58 Via Veneto, respectively), and The Colony (Via Sicilia 45–47, behind the Excelsior Hotel) are other American restaurants that provide sandwiches, hamburgers, banana splits and such fare as consoles Americans away from home and satisfies Italians with a yen to do as the Americans do. The "cavallino rosso" is proud of its bacon-and-egg breakfasts, while the Manhattan Café (next to the USIS library) also serves salads and "drugstore" sandwiches, and provides as well a number of gliders to lull those in need of such comforts. The Colony has a far-reaching menu—respectable club sandwiches, corned beef and pastrami, lemon meringue pie, chocolate fudge cake, pancakes or waffles with syrup, broiled steaks with French fries and coleslaw, ham and eggs, hamburgers and hot dogs, American coffee—and excellent dry martinis.

On the exotic side, the Taverna Negma in Borgo Vittorio furnishes intriguing atmosphere and piquant cooking. The Libyan proprietress Stella (Negma means Stella or star) is married to an Italian, but where food is concerned her heart still belongs to her native land. To prepare such Arabian favorites as kuskus, kebab, and sciak-sciuka, she imports spices and special ingredients from Africa. Rome has several Chinese restaurants. One of the oldest, Shanghai, 29 Via Borgognona, was started by a couple of American soldiers after World War II, later was taken over by Sung John, a Hong Kong tenor who came to Italy to perfect his voice.

27

I found that Chinese food coupled with strolling Italian musicians was confusing. Other Chinese specialists are Tientsin (Via Capo le Case 55), China Garden (Via San Nicolò da Tolentino), and Hong Kong (Via Monterone 14–16 at Largo Argentina). Italo-Brazilian cuisine is the specialty of Il Tinello at 16 Via Porta Pinciana, and paella alla Valenciana and Spanish folk music are featured at Da Amato (Via Garibaldi 60, in Trastevere), and El Patio Andaluz (Via Aurelia Antica [Via Olimpica] 270).

II

THE RESTAURANT MENU

THE Italian menu, a mysterious document with infinite variations, cannot be studied simply. There is first off the handwriting (though some places, especially the fancier ones, do resort to typewriting or printing). The fine Spencerian hand has no relation to this undecipherable calligraphy. Further, there are innumerable categories of foods and courses, and each restaurateur has his own preferences for arrangement and terminology. Seafood or fish, for example, might be found under specialità; or under fried foods; or under soups, if it is clams or mussels steamed in broth, or a zuppa di pesce, which is really a stew anyway; or under pasta or pasta asciutta, if fish, such as tuna, is the

basic ingredient of a spaghetti sauce; or under antipasti if it is in salad form, or otherwise suitable to start the meal with; or under piatti espressi, a designation for dishes that are ready without further cooking; or under entrées, main courses; or even under a category labeled pesci, fish.

Generally the menu lists first the charge for bread and cover, "pane e coperto"; and then hors d'oeuvres, "antipasti"; soups and pastes, "minestre"; fish, "pesci"; meats and roasts, "carni" and "arrosti"; fowl, "pollame"; vegetables, "contorni"; salad, "insalata"; fruit, "frutta"; cheese, "formaggi"; sweet desserts, "dolci"; wines, "vini." If this seems reasonably clear, it is only because it is just half the story. There are many synonymous or variant labels, some as common as those above. The most confusing of these is the category of soups and pastes, which together constitute one course of the Italian meal, and are therefore sometimes listed together under one general heading, "minestre." When they are listed as separate items, soup comes under "minestra" or "zuppa," and paste is called "pasta asciutta" or "dry" pasta, that is, not in the soup.

It is not customary to list coffee, tea, milk or other beverages except acqua minerale, a sparkling mineral water which the Romans drink in quantity, often mixing it with their wine. Coffee, tea, and ice cream are usually brought in on individual order from the nearest bar, because many establishments have neither espresso machine nor freezer equipment, but there is always a bar a few doors away. Foods to be paid for according to the size of your portion, are followed by the abbreviations S.Q., "secondo quantità," or S.G., "secondo grandezza."

Like the menu, the Italian restaurant bill calls for special explanation. At the end of the meal, when you ask the waiter for "Il conto, per favore," a fascinating document arrives. In unbelievably crabbed handwriting, it shows an itemization of your dinner, charges for bread and cover, the small I.G.E. tax, and servizio, which is usually fifteen per cent. Although the servizio is included, it is customary, except in small places with meals at a fixed price (prezzo fisso), to give something more to the waiter. To check the bill carefully, item by item, as well as the total, is correct procedure, though this may be difficult for Americans to accept. It calls forth respect and demonstrates that you spend your money wisely; it shows that you care, an economically sound position. Rather than appearing to your Italian host that you are a mistrusting soul, you will seem wise and proper. Should you find an error on your bill, it need never be a cause for embarrassment, either to you or to your waiter. He will correct it with admiration. In a country whose economy is not as steady as ours, it is almost insulting to take too casual an attitude towards something so hard to come by as money.

But let's go back to the beginning of the meal and examine all the possibilities.

Hors d'Oeuvres · (Antipasti)

IF your appetite is hearty (an Italian does not ask, are you hungry; rather, do you have appetito) you should start with an antipasto. In fancy establishments the waiter appears with a kind of Italian smorgasbord on a wheeled cart, and you may pick from several dozen seafoods, relishes, cold meats and sausages, marinated masterpieces, salads, stuffed eggs, and the like. In simple places, the selection is made for you, and you receive a less elaborate assortment already arranged on your plate. A favorite way to begin a meal is with anchovies and fresh butter (otherwise it is unusual to get butter for your bread). The Italians at home often make a wonderful hot anchovy dip, bagna cauda, which Americans may find useful as cocktail party fare. Here is a popular version: Heat (but do not allow to boil) one-quarter pound of butter with six tablespoons of the best olive oil. Mince as thin as possible, or crush with a pestle, between six and a dozen cloves of garlic, depending on their size and your taste. Add them to the hot oil, keeping the temperature still below boiling, and leave for about ten minutes. Chop about 10 anchovy filets into fine pieces and stir into the mix. If you can get any white truffles, slice them thin and add just before serving the dip over a burner to keep it warm. The traditional things to dunk are raw vegetables cut into strips: fennel, spring onions, artichokes, mushrooms, celery, sweet peppers, cauliflower, cucumbers, radishes, carrots, cold cooked asparagus, etc. Although the Italians use this sauce

33

only for dipping vegetables, it is an excellent alternative to drawn butter for lobster, equally good poured over a fried filet of sole, a hearty baked halibut, or a broiled sea-bass, and peppy as a sauce for such hot vegetables as asparagus, cauliflower and broccoli.

Many seafood restaurants offer a marinated assortment, a kind of maritime salad. Clams and mussels, though sometimes served raw, are more frequently presented steaming aromatically, or baked on the half-shell. In the summer the delectable combination of cured raw ham (prosciutto crudo) sliced razor-thin, and cool melon or iced figs, is perhaps the best of all ways to start a dinner. The best of all prosciutto is the San Daniele del Friuli. Cooked ham, prosciutto cotto, is more plebeian, sandwich stuff. Another good antipasto is crostini, Florentine style: triangles of toast spread with a chicken liver-anchovy-caper paste. A whole order of the usual Roman crostini, rich in melted provatura cheese and anchovies, is a bit filling for a first course, and in fact, with a tossed salad on the side, is sufficient for a simple meal. While they wait for their supper, Romans like to munch on pieces of fogaccia, unadorned hot pizza crust, or a kind of garlicky toast known as bruschetto or bruschetta in Rome, but as schiena d'asino—ass's back—in other places. These bread slices are toasted first, then doused with oil and garlic. Many people omit the antipasto altogether or are beginning to substitute it for the heavier soup-pasta course.

Soups · (Zuppe)

Soups are plentiful, and at least as varied as the many types of *pasta* that float in them. Every restaurant offers a good broth (the best made from meat *and* chicken) with one or another variety of noodle or rice, but there are other rich and more complicated marriages of consommé. Places that make their own tortellini (small, delicately stuffed circular pastes), generally offer these not only with sauce but also "in brodo." Zuppa alla pavese is a nourishing broth that was invented by a peasant girl, so the story goes, when, on the occasion of the defeat of Francis I at the hands of the Spanish in the Battle of Pavia in 1525, it fell to her lot to fetch a bowl of soup for the prisoner king. She added an egg to it, thinking it might help to restore him. If you feel battle-weary, here is the recipe: heat up a pot of good consommé (either meat or chicken); meanwhile fry in oil or butter two or three small slices of French-type bread per portion; break an egg in each soup bowl, pour the hot soup over it, float the slices of bread around it, and sprinkle generously with grated Parmesan cheese. If you like your eggs done beyond a semi-raw state, poach them directly in the soup pot first.

A favorite Roman soup, stracciatella, also combines eggs and cheese, and is equally easy to make. For six portions, beat together three eggs, three tablespoons of fine flour, and three tablespoons of grated cheese. Add one ladle of cooled soup to the mixture, little by little. Bring the pot of broth to a boil and add the mixture, a bit at a time, stirring continuously with a fork. Boil gently a few minutes, and continue to stir until the "shreds" are cooked.

There are many simple vegetable soups, but the favorite is some version of the minestrone, a thick mingling of everything in season with rice, or shells or elbows of pasta, dried beans, and grated cheese. In the summer, Italians like this soup cold. There are highly prized soups in which clams and mussels plump open in their shells and add their fragrant juices to the aromatic broth of wine, garlic, marjoram and parsley in which they swim. The dextrous Italians use the half-shell as a spoon for transporting the seafood liquor. The glory of all fish soups, zuppa di pesce, is really a stew, better suited to the main course than to the beginning. It is an abundant mixture of fish, small whole ones, or

35

great meaty chunks, mussels, clams, octopus, scampi, cuttlefish, and shrimp, accented with red peppers, tomatoes, onions, and garlic, all steeping in fish broth and wine. For sensitive diners unaccustomed to the sight of members of the octopus family peeking out of their plates, the soup may be prepared without squid, cuttlefish or octopus, "senza calamare, seppia o polpo." But the soup will be much the better with them. And for that matter, have you ever really looked objectively at a lobster?

Pasta

THE invention and skill which Italians exercise in the creation of pasta dishes is staggering. By the 15th century, Platina's *De Honesta Voluptate* had already laid down rules for making maccheroni by hand, and after the invention in the early 19th century of a mechanical device for extruding spaghetti, rigatoni, and the like, the full range sprang into being.

Pasta, as well as rice or gnocchi, are always alternatives to soups; one never eats both at the same sitting. Italians generally dine on pasta asciutta at midday, and choose soup (to be sure, often afloat with noodles or other paste) for their suppers, although it is very upper class at any meal to skip pasta in favor of consommé. (However, sometimes it just indicates that your liver is acting up, a complaint traditional to all classes of Italian society.)

Rome's pasta specialty is fettuccine, regal egg noodles, most often tossed speedily with a good slab of butter and a generous heaping of finely grated cheese. Though rich, this dish is most impressive for its lightness and delicacy. The ritual of some fettuccine specialists, most notably Alfredo all'Augusteo, calls for a dramatic lowering of lights and a tossing of the noodles on gold fork and spoon with a motion that surely requires training in gymnastics and the theatre. Happily, the egg noodles, with or without ceremony, survive triumphantly. One restaurant lists them with affectionate pride as "maestose fettuccine al triplo burro." Fettuccine appear in other dress, sometimes adorned with meat sauce, or accompanied by mushrooms, prosciutto and peas laced together with butter and cheese. In other parts of Italy, they go by the name of tagliatelle, but do not always achieve the lightness of the Roman product.

Many people believe that each of the thousand shapes that make up the pasta repertory has a different and appropriate taste. Whether or not this is true, and it *does* seem so, the same basic dough, occasionally enriched with egg or spinach, goes into them all. The American child seems indeed underprivileged when you think that all he can turn up in his soup are the twenty-six letters of the alphabet. Besides the well-known lasagne, spaghetti, maccheroni and ravioli, Italian paste finds its way, in a variety of sizes, into shapes of shells, butterflies, bow-ties, little worms, seeds, elephant's teeth and wolf's eyes, stars, rings, wheels, pearls, hairs, feathers, ladders, and even just plain squares. Vernon Jarratt, the owner of George's, a patrician Roman restaurant, keeps a notebook on varieties of pasta, and there are now three hundred and forty-seven basic entries, not including local names, which would multiply into the thousands.

One whole branch of the family is distinguished by its stuffing. You can find filled agnolotti, capelletti, or tortellini, the last of which, according to legend, were modeled after Venus's navel. The most majestic are the cannelloni, square sheets of thin egg pasta rolled around a meat or cheese filling, tucked in a shallow casserole, covered with béchamel and tomato sauces, blanketed in grated cheese and baked until glazed and bubbling. When you find them in America, they are generally filled pancakes—quite another thing!

Although spinach does not have an obvious association with

37

pasta, it is used, together with ricotta cheese, in some of the lightest fillings (for example tortellini or ravioli di magro). More frequently it lends its tint and subtle flavor to the dough itself. One of the supreme Italian culinary accomplishments is lasagne al forno (or a richer version, vincisgrassi) especially good when made with green pasta. Some version of this dish is what Americans expect when they order lasagne (which is in itself only a type of noodle). The long wide lasagne are layered with a rich meat sauce, several cheeses, and a creamy béchamel. Neapolitan cooks at festival time prepare an animated lasagne al forno by enriching the recipe further with a layer of prosciutto and another of tiny well-flavored meatballs, polpettine.

Pappardelle, which are lasagne with fluted edges, are often served with a heavy brown sauce made from wild hare. Pagliata, veal intestine of very rich flavor (and not at all to be confused with ordinary tripe), makes a remarkable brown sauce for giant rigatoni.

The lively meat sauces originate in Bologna, a city noted for its gastronomical imagination. An Italian historian tells me that documents of the 14th century already describe "il vivere grasso che si fa in quella città," which is to say that the Bolognese have been eating well for a long time. Their meat sauces are really little stews, and you will find them listed on menus interchangeably as (pasta) al ragù or as (pasta) alla bolognese. The usual meat sauce contains a surprising number of ingredients: perhaps a mixture of veal, pork, and beef, the giblets and liver of a turkey, or the brains of a calf, simmered with carrots, celery, onion, tomato, garlic, oil, wine, a variety of fresh herbs, and sometimes a rich binding of cream sauce.

Bolognese sauce is often eaten with spaghetti, a paste which takes easily to any number of toppings. In fact, there is hardly a foodstuff that doesn't end up as part of a spaghetti sauce. There are some of deceptive simplicity, like olive oil and garlic, or tomato and basil. Clams couldn't be happier than when they are simmered in butter and oil, punctuated with spikes of garlic, blended with tomatoes, oregano, and fresh parsley, and sent steaming to the table over a heaping tangle of spaghetti. Mussels are treated in the same fashion; sometimes both shellfish are cooked together. One marine sauce mixes a wide variety of seafood, but it is not nearly as good, to my taste, as the garlicky clams or mussels. There are sauces based on prosciutto, onion, ricotta, mushrooms, anchovies, tuna fish, peas, truffles, mozzarella, parmigiano, pecorino, artichokes, and any number of rearrangements and blendings of these ingredients. Romans have two favorites: spaghetti alla carbonara and spaghetti alla amatriciana. The first mixes bacon, raw beaten eggs, pepper, oil, and cheese; the second, wine, tomato, onion, garlic, bacon, and tangy pecorino cheese. Here is a recipe for what is probably the ultimate combination, spaghetti with caviar.

SPAGHETTINI AL CAVIALE

1 lb. spaghettini (very thin spaghetti)
¼ lb. butter, melted

3 oz. black caviar (approximately)
juice of 1 large or 2 small lemons

Boil the spaghettini al dente in *lightly* salted water. Drain and turn into a warm serving bowl. Toss immediately with the melted butter and the caviar. Add the juice of one lemon, mix well, and taste. Add more lemon if needed. Serve immediately. Serves four.

Passatelli, crude squiggles made by forcing an egg-cheese-and-breadcrumb paste through a wide-eyed sieve or colander into a pot of waiting consommé, are another typical Bologna confection. These abbreviated spaghetti, reminiscent of spätzle and gnocchi, are prepared more often in the home kitchen than in the restaurant.

The Genoese, whose cooking, like that of many port dwellers, is spicy and lively, display their ingenuity with pesto, a sauce so named because it is mashed with mortar and pestle, blending into piquant intimacy fresh basil leaves, garlic, olive oil, Parmesan cheese, and often parsley and pine nuts. In Genoa, pesto traditionally accompanies trenette, a shoestring version of fettuccine, but it is at home with lasagne, spaghetti, and potato gnocchi as well, and is an inspired Genoese addition to the classic minestrone.

Americans are not always able to produce pasta that is as good as they find in Italy, even if they cook it expertly, because they often start with an inferior product. To obtain good results, you need—besides an *abundance* of briskly boiling water flavored with a good sprinkling of rock salt—pasta made from finely milled, hard grain (durum) wheat. The very best brand made in Italy, and the one to ask your grocer about, is from the Abruzzi firm of the Fratelli de Cecco di Filippo in Fara San Martino. The Italians simply ask for De Cecco. Other good names, and perhaps more widely available products, are Buitoni and Ronzoni.

Rice · (Riso)

RICE receives equal billing with pasta, particularly in the North. There are as many sauces and subtleties embellishing this basic grain as there are covering noodles. Romans are fond of giblets and rice, but certainly everybody's favorite is a risotto cooked in Milanese style, each mouthful hinting of the wine, chicken stock, sausage, and saffron with which it is infused. There exists a record of a similar risotto being served to an important personage who came to call at a 12th century Milanese monastery. Since rice at that time was a novelty and not yet under cultivation, the rare dish was served as a special dessert. There are all sorts of other

40

fine rice combinations: with seafood for example, my favorite one containing shrimp and wine; and a notable dish with sausage, truffles, peas, butter, cheese, and meat broth, one of the specialties that the old Roman restaurant Fagiano used to serve before it regrettably closed its doors. Sabatino di Giacinto, the proprietor of that venerable house, gave me his recipe. Melt one-quarter pound of butter in a large, deep frying pan. Cut up one onion in fine pieces and simmer gently in the butter. As the butter evaporates, add a few drops of water, cooking altogether about twenty minutes. Add water from time to time as needed. The onion should be reduced to an almost creamy consistency. Add one small pork sausage, ground or in small slices, brown a few minutes in the onion mixture, then add three cups of unwashed rice [since rice differs widely in quality, follow the recommendations on the package you use for the proportion of rice to liquid; the quantity given here makes six abundant servings]. Stir in well, mixing continuously, and cook for about five minutes. Add one quart of meat broth, mix once, cover tightly, and cook over the lowest possible flame for about fifteen minutes. Add another half quart of broth when the first broth has been absorbed, and continue cooking until the rice is just tender. Stir in a quarter pound of butter, one cup of cooked green peas, one cup of sliced, cooked mushrooms, one cup of Parmesan cheese. Mix in well and cook just long enough to heat through. At the very last moment, sprinkle with a handful of thinly sliced white truffles and grated Parmesan cheese.

Perhaps the grandest of all rice dishes is risotto alla Fregoli, named in honor of the Italian magician famed as a quick-change artist. Besides a pound of rice, the recipe for only six portions calls for butter, an onion, chicken livers, cocks' combs, prosciutto, lamb sweetbreads, dried mushrooms, white wine, Marsala, shelled peas, black truffles, broth, meat gravy, salt, white pepper, and grated Parmesan cheese.

Romans eat a great many rice croquettes, which they fill with

41

a good melting cheese that forms long strings in the eating, and which they aptly call supplì al telefono. About the best place to get these in Rome, although they are generally well prepared throughout the city, is the rosticceria Di Georgio Fratelli (Via S. Andrea Delle Fratte 13). Supplì make good snacks, or the first course of a dinner. Their manufacture is simple enough, and they come in handy as a way to use up leftover rice, which is the best kind anyway for their preparation. For about two cups of rice, beat one egg, and mix in well. Take a small amount of the mixture as a base, add a fifty-cent size slice of mozzarella cheese, and a small piece of prosciutto, or sausage, or a very little tomato sauce. Top with more rice mixture, and form into large egg-size croquettes by rolling in the palms of the hands. The stuffing must be completely tucked in. Roll each of the finished supplì first in flour, then in beaten egg, then in bread crumbs, and fry in a good amount of fine oil (if you have deep frying equipment, so much the better). Drain on paper before serving. When they are nicely browned outside, the cheese should be just ready to burst through.

Gnocchi

NOT every Roman restaurant offers yet another alternative to pasta asciutta, the incomparable gnocchi. There are several kinds of gnocchi, the two principal ones being of potato dough and of a semolino that resembles cream of wheat. The first type is boiled like pasta, then sauced or baked in layers with a rich gravy. The semolino variety, commonly called gnocchi alla romana, although not difficult to prepare, takes a bit more time, but produces such a splendid dish that it is worth the small labor. The cooked farina, enriched with butter and eggs, is spread to cool on a marble slab. After refrigeration has firmed it, it goes to the oven cut into small rounds generously spattered with dots of butter and drifts of cheese. There is a great division of opinion over which are the true Roman gnocchi, the potato or the semolino variety. Ada Boni, the undisputed Queen of the Italian kitchen ever since the publication of *Il talismano della felicità* in 1920, gives a recipe for potato gnocchi alla romana, but her instructions for gnocchi of semolino add no Roman label. Pellegrino Artusi (*La scienza in cucina e l'arte di mangiar bene*) gives what is called a "modified" version of gnocchi alla romana: flour, butter, gruyère, Parmesan, milk, and egg. He also gives the standard recipes for gnocchi di semolino, and di patate, with no further description of cooking style. Luigi Carnacina, whose enormous and lavishly illustrated volume *La grande cucina* has something of the dimension of an Italian *Larousse gastronomique*, gives recipes for gnocchi di patate alla romana (a typical Roman preparation that one must not confuse with the gnocchi of semolino that are served in restaurants, says he) *and* gnocchi di semolino alla romana (with no comment). Elizabeth David, although an Englishwoman, has written one of the best Italian cookbooks, *Italian Food*. In it she gives recipes for both kinds of dumplings as well as for cheese and spinach gnocchi, and wisely ignores the whole problem of Roman labels. One thing is certain, and that is that both gnocchi are excellent dishes, and that the "Thursday gnocchi" are the potato type. Other variations on this dumpling include corn meal, spinach, ricotta cheese, cream, and several combinations of flour with grated cheeses and eggs.

Meat · (Carni)

ITALIAN meat is uneven in quality, but no matter if it is not always tender, since good chefs pamper it until it is succulent.

Besides, the batticarne (meat-beater) is a standard piece of kitchen equipment.

Veal · (Vitello)

MILK-FED, very young veal is good in Italy and Italian cooks have a hundred intriguing ways with it. They prepare a simple roast of veal, but more frequently cook a rolled roast, stuffed with carrots, celery, prosciutto, and slices of hard-boiled egg. It is a household favorite in warm months especially, because the leftover portion, sliced, makes fine picnic fare the day after. For more epicurean tastes there is the Genoese specialty, cima. Minced sweetbreads, veal, brains, beaten eggs, and grated cheese, dotted with peas and slivers of artichokes, all well perfumed with marjoram, form the stuffing for a pocket of breast of veal. After boiling gently until it is tender, the cima rests for some time under a heavy weight in the refrigerator. The well-compressed loaf is served cold in slices.

The thin slice of veal, often pounded thinner, is the theme on which Italian chefs build their subtlest variations. Scaloppine (alternately called piccate), that delicate sauté that we know well in this country, takes on individuality at the pleasure of the cook, who may use white wine instead of Marsala, sprinkle it with a dusting of sage, or add razored slices of mushrooms, strips of pepper, or the ubiquitous tomato. The Italian gourmet orders his scaloppine al porto. Involtini, swelled out by the ham, cheese and vegetables they enclose, simmer brown in a rich stock. Uccellini scappati (or uccelletti matti), rolled veal birds, are cooked either in the oven or on the spit, sometimes interspersed with bay leaves and crusty oiled bread chunks. But the king of all these preparations is a Roman specialty, saltimbocca alla romana. Though not

44

complicated, it is a perfect blend of flavors, and as its name informs you, so luscious that "it jumps in the mouth."

Grilled veal chops, served with a wedge of lemon, provide a good follow-up after a first course on the rich and caloric side, and are usually better than the misnamed bistecca di vitello. However, if your appetite and curiosity get by the pasta unimpaired, a costolette al cartoccio, a cutlet baked in a paper bag together with ham, onion, mushrooms, peas, and who-knows-what, is one of the best of the veal dishes. Ossobuco, another Roman favorite, transforms marrow-filled cuts from the shin bone into a hearty meal by braising, browning and saucing. Breaded veal cutlets are sometimes baked with cheese or tomato sauce, and there are many kinds of stews. You can be sure that almost any dish based on vitello will be good.

Lamb · (Abbacchio)

ABBACCHIO, suckling lamb, is exceptional in Rome. It lends itself well to roasting, and is often turned on the spit until it is crusty. Strong suggestions of garlic and rosemary herald its approach. It can be dressed up with truffles and oil, or anchovies and red wine, and is often stewed alla cacciatora.

Beef · (Manzo)

BEEF in Italy is likely to be a good deal tougher than we are accustomed to, whereas the milk-fed veal and abbacchio are more delicate. Vitellone, a two or three year old fellow who hasn't yet

45

formed work muscles, is something in between veal and beef: no longer delicate, not yet full-flavored, but at least chewable. Tuscany raises good beef cattle, so that a bistecca alla fiorentina will always turn out to be a broiled T-bone of reasonable quality. There is no Italian ritual comparable to our rare, medium-rare, medium, medium-well routine; no branding irons, wooden markers, or other symbols indicate that this is John's steak and he wants it rare but not too rare. A grilled steak is served rare, al sangue, as a general practice. If you like it better done, you can inform the waiter that you do *not* want it al sangue or that you do want it ben cotta, well-cooked (but this is not necessarily the equivalent of well done).

Bistecca di manzo is another thing entirely. It is indeed a beefsteak but often very thin and tough. Filetto is just what its name implies, and is tender whether it originated in Tuscany or not. Tournedos alla Rossini, an international favorite usually served in the deluxe restaurants, have a layer of pâté de foie gras and a winey brown sauce. Rosbiffe (or rosbif) sometimes turns out to be more of a pot roast, but all'inglese tells you that it is cooked in the venerable way. You can order boiled beef, but the Italian manzo bollito or manzo lesso comes with a spicy green sauce, or oil and salt, instead of a heap of cabbage. Several good stews, spezzatini, stufato (or notably, stufatino alla romana: beef simmered in red wine with onions, garlic, bacon, and tomato), appear on menus, but hamburger is usually available only in establishments that specialize in American foods. A Roman favorite, and it is very good indeed, is oxtail stew, coda alla vaccinara.

Pork · (Maiale)

MODERN Romans are fond of pork and so were their ancestors. Here is an ancient recipe for suckling-pig à la Flaccus:

Prepare the piglet like a boar, sprinkle with salt, and put in the oven. While it is cooking put in the mortar pepper, lovage caraway, celery-seed, asafoetida root, fresh rue; pound, moisten with *liquamen* [or *garum*, the ancients' most important seasoning sauce, manufactured from the salted flesh and entrails of small fish such as anchovies, sprats, and red mullets, ripened in the sun, then strained], blend with wine and *passum* [a sweet cooking-wine, prepared from sun-dried grapes]. Bring to the boil in a saucepan with a little oil. Thicken with cornflour. When the sauce is cooked pour over the pig, pound celery-seed to powder, sprinkle over, and serve.[7]

Modern Romans make any number of good pork sausages, one of which, cotechine, cooked with lentils, is the real Roman New Year's dish. Arista, pork roast garlanded with rosemary and garlic, is often turned on the spit, like the porchette, whole roasted porkers stuffed with a fieldful of herbs and garlic, that are the traditional meat of the carnival. Each family that has prepared a roast sets up a makeshift sandwich shop, the porker propped high to tempt everyone's appetite, the rolls and round breads stacked in mountains by its side, each ready to contain a slab of mouth-watering meat. As the day goes on, the porkers diminish and finally disappear, for they are hard to resist. In Rome they make their appearance at the Trastevere festival of "Us Others," the Festa Dei Noantri. In a blaze of illumination, the "real" Romans celebrate it for eight boisterous July evenings. The Trasteverini transform the Viale Trastevere into a circus, a toy market, an art gallery, a luna park, the midway of a great show. The entire quarter beyond is alive with contests, folk singing, theatre, dancing, parading, and general hilarity. There are fireworks and sometimes boating contests on the Tiber. Crowds crush along the streets and jam double or more the usual number of sidewalk tables and chairs. The air takes on the sweet fragrance of the wines from the Roman castelli, which appear and disappear by

7. Apicius, *The Roman Cookery Book*, p. 211.

the barrelful. The consumption of roast porkers defies statistics, and a comparable number of red watermelon slices fill the stands and stomachs of the Trasteverini.

Except for the carnival porkers and bacon, pork is otherwise limited to the cool months, when it is available in a wide variety of sausages, as roasts, cut into substantial chops that are cooked on the grill (ai ferri), or occasionally braised in the form of ribs. Italians like the flavor of fresh lemon with their meat, and pork chops, braciole di maiale, are customarily garnished with a wedge or two, a practice that is much more appetizing than serving them up with applesauce.

Variety Cuts · (Frattaglie)

VARIETY cuts find wide use in Italian kitchens, and we would do well to take up some of their established recipes. None that I know of needs the two days of preparation or the dashing use of Calvados required for French tripe à la mode de Caen. But Italian cooks are equally inventive with their tripe dishes. Trippa di bue alla romana, after cooking gently for many hours in a vegetable liquor, sometimes with prosciutto added, comes from the kitchen lavishly seasoned with grated cheese and chopped fresh mint, an herb that Romans use widely and unexpectedly. Another part of the intestine, the pagliata or pajata, is one of the best of variety parts because of its giblety juices. It is grilled or roasted, and in a sauce for rigatoni, it is one of my favorite dishes.

Cold boiled tongue, like boiled beef, is traditionally accompanied by a piquant green sauce (salsa verde). Mixed fry Roman style, fritto misto alla romana, may include artichokes, sweetbreads, brains, veal cutlets, zucchine, liver and heart. There are many recipes for kidneys, sweetbreads, and heart, and liver appears on every menu. I find it hard to choose between the widely cooked Venetian specialty, liver and onion sauté, and fegatini di pollo alla salvia, chicken livers with sage (a real Roman would throw in a few cocks' combs with the chicken livers). Here is a recipe for calf's liver and onions that was given to me by the former owner of the Trattoria Gallinaccio:

FEGATO ALLA VENEZIANA

for each portion:

2 tbsp. onion in small slices	laurel
olive oil	1 tbsp. white wine
¼ lb. calf's liver	1 tbsp. vinegar
salt and pepper	

Brown the onion in a skillet, add the liver cut in small strips, salt and pepper, and a sprinkling of crushed laurel. [If you use fresh, use it sparingly, since the flavor is penetrating.] When the meat is browned on one side, and about half done, turn it and add the wine and vinegar. Cook quickly until these are consumed. Serve immediately. You can substitute heart for the liver.

The omnivorous Roman also eats calf's head, feet, tail and ears; and often the spleen, pancreas, spinal cord, and marrow, a capacity he inherits from his forebears. Apicius gives recipes for cow's udders, sterile cow's wombs, and capon's testicles.

A modern Roman favorite is the coratella, made from lamb parts, and so delicious as to have brought forth at least one ode on its preparation.

L'abbacchio ci fornì la coratella
che noi mettemmo subito in padella.
Fu lì che cuore, fegato e polmoni,
tagliati a pezzettini, incominciarono
a cuocer vivamente e sfrigolarono
in un soffritto dai dorati toni. . . .

> The suckling lamb furnished the coratella
> that we put immediately in the frying pan.
> There the heart, liver and lights,
> cut into little pieces, began
> to cook briskly and sizzled
> in a sauce of golden vegetables. . . .

"But where are the Roman artichokes?" suddenly asks the poet, thinking of the recipe of an expert cook. "They are thrown in the pan, tender and fresh, giving life to the meat no matter how exquisite it may be, and deserving a medal and a diploma for a flavor that is found only in Rome." [8]

Game · (Cacciagione)

THE hunting season, besides being dangerous—this is the time to abandon the field picnic—is the source of some very unusual cookery. Although you can eat your wild boar roasted, you will be doing what the Romans do, and have been doing since ancient times, if you order cinghiale with a sweet and sour sauce of vinegar, chocolate, pine nuts and prunes. Hare is similarly cooked sweet and sour, agrodolce, or marinated in a spicy concoction of red wine before being transformed into a sturdy main course or a sauce for lasagne. Capretto, suckling kid, makes as fine a roast joint as anyone could desire, and though not a wild beast, is often coupled with game on the menu. If you are not thrown off by the rather alarming sight of small spitted birds traveling their circular course above the embers, heads flip-flopping, you will share another taste known to ancient Rome. The birds are skewered with fresh sage leaves and alternating crusts of bread brushed with oil

8. Luciano Folgore, "La coratella coi carciofi," in *Romani a tavola*, p. 95.

and garlic. Besides duck, guinea fowl, and pheasant in appropriately spirited sauces, a modern Roman diner has the choice of an
aviary that includes woodcocks, bullfinches, ortolans, quail,
thrush, lark, snipe, figpeckers, partridge, wood pigeon, squab, and
dove, and to which his forebears could have added ostrich and
flamingo. During the hunting season, the roads are crowded with
more than the usual hodge-podge of two-wheeled vehicles, a veritable motorcade of men dressed for the hunt, guns strapped
across their backs, mufflers wound nose-high against the cold,
each astride a Vespa, Lambretta or motorcycle, weaving perilously
through the traffic. It is no wonder, judging from the crowd of
hunters, that the hunted turn up with such abundance on Roman
tables.

Fowl · (Pollame)

THE most popular chicken dish is pollo alla diavola, broiled
chicken. Like so many successful recipes, chicken in the style
of the devil has numerous variations—pan-broiled, oven-baked,
or charcoal grilled. At least one man has based his reputation, and
in this case, his name on this excellent dish, the "Chicken Man"
of La Villetta, a trattoria in Trastevere. Some of my friends swear
that the little trattoria in the Piazza in Piscinula serves the best
—and least expensive—devil's chicken of them all. Neither roast
chicken nor turkey is commonly stuffed with bread, but sometimes with ham, fennel, chestnuts, sausage, olives, and truffles.
Turkey breasts, breaded and sautéed golden, trimmed with a generous scattering of truffle wafers, or smothered in mushrooms,
ham and melted cheese, appeal more to Italian tastes, and I
must add, to mine too. I also like the small unstuffed chickens,
anointed with oil and perfumed with rosemary, that are baked

51

in the oven or turned on the spit. Since most kitchens have small ovens, householders often send turkeys to the bakery for roasting in an oven that is large enough to accommodate such a big bird. (Most Italian stoves, I was surprised to discover, consist of an oven and burners, but no broiler, in spite of the popularity of broiled foods. There are numerous top-of-the-stove grills that work reasonably well but make a hideous mess. Restaurants are generally better equipped.) Every restaurant has boiled chicken, pollo lessato, because Italians who want to eat delicately consider it the lightest possible meal. In the summer many restaurants offer chicken salad. A rare place or two specializes in chicken or pheasant baked in clay, pollo (or fagiano) alla creta.

Fish · (Pesci)

THE ancient Romans adored fish, and the manner of cooking it was of the utmost importance to them. The Emperor Domitian is reported, in fact, to have once convened the Senate in order to decide on the best way to prepare sturgeon (they voted unanimously for a sauce piquante). The modern Romans inherit this enthusiasm, but fishing yields less than it used to. Some Italian fishermen have taken, illegally, to bombing their catch—and incidentally, blowing up all the young fish in the area, thus cutting down even more on future supplies. There is still a reasonable selection on restaurant menus, but prices are gradually climbing. Some Roman restaurateurs offer fish from the Adriatic, which are more highly prized than their Tyrrhenian relatives. But fish come to Rome from closer points: Fiumicino, the port of the capital; Ostia, the ancient port; Anzio, rebuilt since the war, the gleam of its new buildings sparkling along the sea. Lake fish come from such waters as Bracciano to the north; from Nemi, also notable because two ancient Roman boats were recovered there (and unfortunately burned in 1944 by the Germans); and from Albano, an old crater near the summer residence of the Pope.

Restaurants specializing in fish set up a daily display which, on a miniature scale, reproduces the gaudy color and gaiety of the market. Here, in clamorous juxtaposition, lie giant orange prawns, marbly brown and gold eels, purple octopus, smoky squid; goldfish, mullet and grayling flash silver and copper, their iridescent armor glancing in contrast to stony clams and black clusters of mussels. A bewhiskered catfish, barbio, or a toothy dentex, dentice, await the oven and the grill. Occasionally the stare of a knobby red lobster punctuates the tapestry of colors. Your waiter may suggest a freshly caught ombrino or spigola, and fetch it from the display for your approval before sending it to the kitchen. The chef may roast it whole or steam it in bianco, a simple bouillon sometimes delicately infused with spices or dotted with parsley. This method underscores the natural flavor of the fish and retains all its juices. Fish is never overcooked in Italy, and species that are dry by nature are rescued with oils or sauces. Fish are baked, grilled, poached, fried and stewed, frequently combined with anchovies, herbs, white wine, garlic, such fresh vegetables as celery, tomatoes, peppers, onions and mushrooms, or even, as in this unusual recipe for acciughe ripiene, with cheese:

FRESH STUFFED ANCHOVIES

2 dozen fresh anchovies	breadcrumbs
1 oval of mozzarella	olive oil
parsley	lemons

Split the anchovies down the belly by inserting the thumb in the opening and running it along to the tail. Pull out the bones, all in one piece, clip off the tails, wash the fish and pat dry. Set aside. In a flat casserole or baking dish, put enough oil to cover the bot-

53

tom, and sprinkle with breadcrumbs. Open each fish flat. Put one slice of mozzarella, slightly smaller than the fish, on twelve of the fish. Cover, sandwich-style, with the other twelve fish. Line the pan with the stuffed fish. Sprinkle with breadcrumbs, chopped parsley, and a light dusting of salt. Add a good amount of olive oil, enough so that the fish are well bathed in it. Put to bake in a moderately hot oven for fifteen to twenty minutes, or until the breadcrumbs are a fine golden color. Squeeze lemon juice over the fish, and serve with additional lemon wedges. Serves four.

Codfish, a national favorite, usually come from the market salted and dried flat, though often the storekeeper stocks them in fresh water, saving the cook many hours of preliminary soaking. (They must soak a minimum of eighteen hours.) When these baccalà are ready for cooking, numerous recipes apply. Olive oil is a traditional ingredient, and anchovies, capers, black olives, garlic, and parsley go well with this strong flavored base. The final preparation is often preferred cold, and is in great demand on fast days. Sole, sogliola, a great delicacy of the Roman table, is best served in a simple butter sauce, alla mugnaia. It is one of the few fish recognizable to Americans, many of the others being not only foreign to our eyes, but brutish as well. The rospo, no relation to a frog, although his name might mislead you, seldom displays his ugliness in the showcase. He turns up beheaded and skinned, and not in the least bit alarming. The grilled tail, coda di rospo, is a delicacy. The San Pietro is another ugly fellow, but delicious.

Tiny two-necked clams, vongole, make one of the best sauces for spaghetti. Like mussels, cozze, they pop up in antipasti, marinated in happy combination with other fruits of the sea; they make a rich dish of soup, and as a topping are frequent ingredients, along with shrimp, of a Roman concoction, fish cooked in a paper bag. Not far south of the city, along the hillocked beaches edged by pines, you can often see solitary fishermen, trousers rolled thigh-high, rhythmically trudging the shallows, their clam gear raking the bottom for these little delicacies.

To an Italian, the octopus family brings shivers—of delight. Squid, crusty and golden, though often served solo, may join periwinkles, shrimp, tiny crabs in edible shells, and a small whole mullet or goldfish in a mixed fry. The toasty circlets of squid resemble nothing more startling than a platter of French fried onion rings. Romans adore squid cooked in a tomato, wine, and garlic sauce with plenty of fresh peas. Most recipes for squid and cuttlefish (calamari and seppie) are interchangeable. Octopus, polpo, is a tougher customer, and takes more cooking. This beast is often prepared whole, after appropriate cleaning and a resounding beating to break the fibers, covered over with water and oil and seasoned lightly with salt, pepper, tomato and parsley. Tightly sealed in the pot, he must simmer a couple of hours over a low flame. When the cover is removed the kettle reveals an unrecognizable creature, which has been likened by one Italian writer, in rather flowery prose, to a rosy giant chrysanthemum floating in an exquisite broth. Since his metamorphosis included a great deal of tenderizing, the octopus must be served from the same pot; a transfer might cause him to lose his shape completely. Quarter-size baby octopi find their way into marinated salads, fish soups, and best of all, into hot oil, to be fried delicately. They are as common a sight as the crunchy mounds of tiny fried white bait.

The Italian taste for seafood readily accommodates sea snails, sea urchins, sharks, rays and eels, including morays and lampreys, which the ancients kept, as well as consumed, by the pondful. Modern Romans add rays and eels to their fish soups, and make one of their principal Christmas dishes of eel (capitone) roasted with oil, vinegar, wine, garlic and laurel. Lobsters (crayfish) appear in fewer culinary variations than other crustaceans, perhaps because they are so excellent boiled. Not every restaurant serves them, and they are expensive. Large prawns, scampi (Danish lobsters), and a Roman delicacy, mazzancolle, tempt my appetite much more. How divine they are, buttery in their shells straight off the grill, or plump with cognac, wine, and tomato sauce!

At one sitting, a good zuppa di pesce will introduce you to a wide assortment of marine life and to a distinguished culinary accomplishment. This stew balances not only texture, color and shape, but spice and perfume. Its aroma assaults your nostrils before it is half out of the kitchen; its oranges, reds and whites, silvers and greens, dance before your eyes; the red pepper, garlic and saffron dazzle your tongue; and the chunks of fish, loops of squid, bumps of clams, crescents of prawns, juicy from their winey bath, speak to your soul. The exact ingredients depend on the day's catch—exchange being characteristic of Italian cooking, and to me, one of its fascinations.

Snails · (Lumache)

No good Roman would forego his platter of snails on the Festa di San Giovanni. Every June 24th, when the city celebrates the day of St. John the Baptist, the stewpots bubble with these tiny creatures soaking up a purée of tomatoes, oil, garlic, and anchovies, scented with freshly chopped mint. The very best snails feed on grape vines, and I suppose a real connoisseur can tell a Frascati snail from a Genzano one. Before Parioli became a fashionable residential quarter, its fields yielded a considerable snail harvest. These plump fellows, from what then was called l'Acqua Acetosa, were considered next best to their vine-fed relations. Ada Boni's recipe for snails cooked Roman-style recommends a good dash of hot red pepper along with the other ingredients. The traditional accompaniment is rough homemade bread in thick slices.

Eggs · (Uova)

EGGS, the mainstay of breakfast in America, find their place in the Italian menu at lunch or supper. Sold in the market individually, since only a foreigner would buy a dozen at a time, there is no need for protective crates. The vendor simply wraps them in newspaper, which the buyer adds to all the other supplies already swelling her shopping bag. There are several qualities, the highest grade, uova da bere, eggs for drinking, being those that Italians are fond of sucking raw from the shell, although some prefer boiling them a minute or two. They cost a few lire more, but these are, to my taste, the ones for cooking too. The frittata or omeletta can be an hors d'oeuvre, or a fine light supper entrée, the perfect choice to follow a rich and heavy paste. For that matter, it can include the pasta, as it does in this recipe for frittata di pasta: Beat together four eggs. Add salt, pepper, and four tablespoons of Parmesan cheese. Heat abundant oil or butter in an omelette pan, and pour in the egg mixture. When the bottom begins to set, mix into the top about two cups of whatever leftover pasta you have, and cook until almost set. Fold the near half over towards the center with a spatula. Tilt the pan away from you to help fold the far half inward. A smart tap on the handle will make it fall into place. Hold the serving dish over the pan, and quickly flip the omelette, folded side down, onto the dish. If you want to be really fancy, sprinkle with grated cheese and dots of butter and slip under the broiler until it browns. You can also serve the omelette straight out of the cooking pan.

If your preference in eggs is for fried, poached, boiled or scrambled, you can ask the waiter to bring you uova fritte, in camicia or affogate, sode (hard-boiled), alla coque (soft-boiled), or strappazzate. However, not every waiter is familiar with a poached egg, so don't be surprised if you get a quizzical look instead. Eggs alla russa, devilled eggs with salmon or tuna, capers, gherkins, mayonnaise and often a casing of gelatin, are one of several varieties of cold eggs served in antipasto form. They add decorative accents to spreads of sausage, cheese, kippers and olives, breadsticks, crusty rolls and glistening relishes, in the windows of delicatessens and rosticcerie.

Vegetables · (Contorni)

MANY greens strange to our tastes turn up in Italian markets. After cooking they are often served cold, with a dressing of oil, sometimes oil and vinegar or lemon juice, that sets off their pungent character. It is worth trying them, not for their novelty alone, but for their tart flavor, which complements perfectly entrées of broiled meat or grilled chicken. Broccoletti di rape, the best of these, can be found in this country among oriental produce as Gai Choy, or can be closely approximated by using turnip greens. Romans cook it frequently over low heat with garlic and oil, covered to steam in the vapor of the washing water that clings to it. They also boil it, then season it with oil, lemon, salt and pepper.

More exotic vegetables, like the roots of the scorzonera, or viper's grass, find their way onto Italian tables, but not with the frequency common to spinach, asparagus, peas, or beans. Romans add pine nuts and raisins to spinach. They cook wild green asparagus more often than the larger cultivated white variety, and in January an early field type as thin as a match stick, with flavor more pronounced than any of the others. The forebears of the famous petits-pois, Italian peas, were introduced to France in the 16th century. Roman peas are today the best on the Italian market, and the combination with prosciutto and onions, an established favorite, brings out their flavor with conviction. Beans come long and thin, short and thick, brown, white, rose, and green, as well as fresh or dried, and one large, farinaceous type, lupini, is a common nibble, to judge by the numbers of street vendors who put them up in paper cones. Romans cook fava beans with bacon, but in the spring they eat them raw with pecorino cheese. Fagiolini a corallo, string beans and tomatoes, taste as gay as they look. And fagioli con le cotiche, a real Roman favorite, is an exuberant combination of cooked dried beans, pork rind, tomatoes, ham bones and chunks of meat, onion, garlic, fresh basil, oil, rosemary, and parsley.

Cauliflower grows purple in some regions, but its regal color fades, unfortunately, when it is cooked. Fresh picked, it makes as gorgeous a sight as you will ever see, layered into a mosaic on the back of a Neapolitan cart, weaving and bobbing behind a donkey on the way to market. Beets, chard, broccoli, the best of which is grown in the outlying Roman castelli, carrots, and Brussels sprouts find a place on the Italian menu. Cabbage is abundant in the fall and winter months. The chestnut displays its versatility in candies, desserts, and vegetable dishes, and is a traditional accompaniment to many kinds of game. One of the best ways to use chestnuts as a vegetable is to make this simple purée, purè di castagne:

Make slits in one pound of chestnuts and put them in a pan in a hot oven until the skin begins to brown and crisp. Peel off the skins as soon as you can handle them. Put the peeled chestnuts to cook in two cups of chicken broth along with a stalk or two of celery. When they are tender (twenty minutes to half an hour), put them through a vegetable mill [or for modern kitchens, purée in a blender]. Add as much of the broth as is needed to make a light purée. Return it to the stove, add a good lump of butter, salt, pepper, and *sugar* to taste, and stir over low heat until well blended. An un-Italian but thoroughly agreeable addition is a tablespoon or two of sour cream or heavy cream along with the butter. This dish goes splendidly with game, pork, chicken, and turkey.

Italians consume the Jerusalem artichoke, topinambur, and fennel, finocchio, which is as good raw and crisp at the end of a meal as cut into a salad, or cooked buttery soft as a vegetable. The topinambur, scraped, cut into pieces, and boiled in salted water until tender, can be used like a potato, or served cold with a sharp French dressing. Truffles, tartufi, extravagantly adorn almost everything. Potatoes often roast along with the meat and pick up a tinge of rosemary and garlic. Italians are not the meat-and-potato eaters we are, for they consume their carbohydrates sufficiently in the form of pasta. But many entrées strongly suggest a potato accompaniment, and whether or not you have just polished off a portion of lasagne, tortellini, or fettuccine, you may not be able to resist the crispy patate fritte with your abbacchio. The following recipe, Pollo alla Rita, manages to use both rice and potatoes in one dish. It was given to me by a Roman friend and excellent cook.

Quarter one small chicken and brown it in a mixture of butter and oil to which you have added a clove or two of minced garlic, a sprinkling of rosemary, and some chopped parsley. As soon as the chicken is colored, add a glass of broth or water to keep the chicken from becoming dry, and continue to cook gently.

Bring two cups of water to a rolling boil, add one tsp. salt, and when it boils briskly again, add one cup of rice. Cover, lower heat, cook twenty to thirty minutes or until the water is absorbed. Turn into a colander and pass immediately under cold water. Put the rice into a large low casserole, add a good lump of soft butter and a little juice from the cooking chicken. Mix well and spread over the bottom. Over the rice put one piece of prosciutto cotto (boiled or baked ham) for each portion. On each slice of ham put one quarter of the chicken. Sprinkle around the chicken one-half pound of mushrooms that have been sliced and cooked in butter, and sprinkled with salt, pepper, and chopped parsley. Over this sprinkle French fried potatoes, made by slicing two medium potatoes in pencil-thick pieces, and immersing them in hot oil until golden. (Drain on paper, and salt before adding.) The final touch is two cups of medium béchamel sauce well laced with grated Parmesan or Swiss cheese. Bake in a moderately hot oven until it begins to brown nicely.

Corn on the cob exists mainly for Americans. Once a house guest gifted us with ears of sweet, small-kerneled white corn, which he found through an advertisement in the Rome-published American newspaper (it caused a sensation in our kitchen, and the excellent woman who cooked for us, who could prepare a corn meal polenta of grandeur, preferred that we ourselves cook these simple cobs, for fear that she might ruin them); on another occasion in a chic Trastevere restaurant, I ate golden corn roasted, but it was unpalatably dry and tough. I have never seen it elsewhere in Rome, except in advertisements for a few specialty markets and restaurants. Corn meal (polenta) is another story. It is a standby, and is even more common in the North.

Mushrooms, tomatoes, peppers, eggplants, and squash star in Roman vegetable cookery. These vegetables earn acclaim as dishes in their own right. Their flavor dominates and mingles with the meats, cheeses, herbs and breads that form their stuffings. Picked in gaudy variety, mushrooms are often large enough for filling or baking, one per person. A jumble of these colorful umbrellas in the raw, their ruffles, fringes, and spots casually creating an autumn harmony of creams, buffs, oranges, and browns, signals and invites from the doorway of many a trattoria. Perhaps the most excellent mushroom in Italy is the boletus edulis (porcini), and it is used as well in its dried form. Another special genus, amanita Caesarea (ovoli), adds a brilliant orange color to restaurant and market displays. The button mushroom in various sizes is excellent and less costly than the porcini or ovoli, but not nearly so distinguished in flavor. Mushrooms have their own special merchants in large markets; otherwise the Italians order them through butchers, poultry dealers, or game sellers. Among

61

the many fine mushroom dishes that Italians concoct are funghi trifolati, thin vertical slices sautéed in oil, mingled with garlic and parsley, and crowned with lemon juice and a ball of butter mashed with anchovies. Roasted porcini, perfumed with garlic, and bathed with oil and butter, cost more than many an entrée on the restaurant menu, and when knowledgeably cooked—still firm and incredibly delicate—they are worth every lira. Perhaps the most distinguished and unusual mushroom dish is raw mushroom salad. There are several variations on it, some made with ovoli and gruyère cheese, some with porcini and truffles. The best that I have ever tasted was at Signor Bolfo's Palace Hotel in Pavia, and his chef, Signor Dellafiore, was kind enough to give me these instructions:

> Take one pound of mushrooms—about two-thirds porcini, one-third champignons (cultivated button-type). Pick only the freshest and most healthy specimens [a button mushroom is really fresh when the head and stem are still joined, concealing the gills]. Select a small size, more or less uniform. Clean with a damp cloth, and remove the stems. [Never soak mushrooms in water; they will absorb it like a sponge.] Slice the caps in thin, vertical sections [using a truffle cutter, if your kitchen equipment, like Signor Dellafiore's, happens to include such specialized items]. Slice in very thin slivers one white truffle from Alba. Mix all together in a bowl. Squeeze over the mushroom and truffle slices the juice of one large lemon. Mix salt and pepper according to your taste with three tablespoons of olive oil and pour over the salad. Toss lightly and leave for about fifteen minutes in a cool place or in the refrigerator before serving. This quantity should make four people very happy.

Though it seems hard to believe, tomatoes were once unknown in the Italian kitchen. Scholars differ widely on the exact date of their appearance. The earliest possibility is the late Middle Ages, when a religious carried back seeds from China, according to one account. More probable is the theory that they were introduced in the 17th century from South America, the place where tomato sauce may well have been invented. Whatever the date, the early 19th century has been called a turning point in Italian cooking, because it was then that the tomato captured the popular fancy, and invaded the cuisine. It certainly turns up nowadays every place: stuffed with rice and tarragon, sliced cold (and often green) into salads, puréed into all kinds of sauces (the pear-shaped variety makes superb purées). Tomatoes, green peppers, and white onions unite in a patriotic sautée alla bandiera, combining the red, white and green of the Italian flag. In Rome this same dish is called alla romana. Peppers frequently swell with subtle stuffings, and are devoured, like their filled tomato companions, either hot or cold. My favorite pepper dish, one with a tantalizing flavor, is peperoni sott'aceto. Sweet red peppers roast over charcoals, the flame of a stove, or in the oven, until their skin is blackened and loose enough to remove without inordinate difficulty. When they have been skinned and seeded they are cut into strips, salted, and put to soak in garlic and vinegar, and often olive oil, which, if used in quantity, changes the preparation to peperoni sott'olio. Jars of very good (unroasted) peppers in vinegar are available in delicatessens and most groceries. Zucchine take on flavor from a meat filling, and often come with a tomato and cheese topping. But baking is only one of many tricks that Italian chefs play with this delicate squash. Its absorbent nature attracts tastes of olive, garlic, and cheese when it is sliced and simmered to a tender turn, and it crisps brown and succulent when it is fried. Melanzane, eggplant, holds a prominent place in Italian cooking. Besides being fried, baked, sautéed and roasted, it combines successfully with capers, tomatoes, anchovies, cheeses, olives, mushrooms and all manner of other ingredients. Perhaps the two most common dishes, whole meals in themselves, are melanzane alla parmigiana and melanzane alla romana. The first recipe calls for layers of eggplant, tomato sauce, Parmesan and mozzarella cheese, the whole baked to a bubbly consistency; the second alternates eggplant with to-

63

mato sauce, meat sauce, and mozzarella, a hefty variation on the classic theme. One of the best eggplant recipes, called caponata, comes from Sicily. You can make it as an hors d'oeuvre this way:

> Sauté one eggplant, diced but not skinned, in a good amount of olive oil until golden, then set aside. Sauté one large sliced onion and two stalks of coarsely chopped celery until they become translucent and the onions begin to take on color. Add two cups of tomato purée or solid pack tomatoes, and cook until the vegetables are soft. Add the eggplant, a tablespoonful or two of capers, a dozen chopped black olives, a small whiskey glass (1 oz.) of vinegar, one tablespoon of sugar, and salt and pepper to taste. Mix together well, correct the seasonings if necessary, and cover and simmer about one-quarter hour. Store a day or more in the refrigerator before using.

The Sicilians traditionally include fried baby octopus, boiled lobster, shrimp, hard-boiled eggs, artichokes, asparagus, and smoked tuna eggs for a garnish, but they generally consume the dish as a main course. The Siracusans prefer the simpler form, without tomatoes, but with the addition of a small amount of grated chocolate.

The king of Roman vegetables is the artichoke, which in this region is blessed with a characteristic uncommon to its species elsewhere: it can be eaten in its entirety. Romans prepare their carciofi alla romana, stuffed between the leaves with fresh mint, garlic and oil and steamed tender in the vapors of a dry white wine; alla giudia, plunged whole into deep fat and cooked until the leaves curl, and the plant opens like a blossom, crisp, brown-tinged, and eminently edible; and alla manticiana, cooked on the grill. Whether or not Americans can reproduce these delights depends on the local availability of small artichokes, those with the choke still undeveloped. But even so, ours are not as tender or as flavorful as the Roman ones. Cardi or gobbi, another member of the thistle group, also appeal to Italian appetites. The an-

cients consumed stinging nettles, but only, as recommended by
Apicius, for therapy.

Salad · (Insalata)

BECAUSE vinegar might spoil your taste for the wine, salad generally comes at the end of the meal. Italians often like their
greens raw, unadorned but for olive oil and a touch of vinegar.
Menus list green salads, mixed salads and special salads. The
first combines whatever lettuce and other leafy green plants came
from the morning market; the second adds to the greens whatever the whim of the chef dictates, and for this reason is often
called insalata capricciosa. Special salads might contain firm
green tomatoes in an oil and vinegar dressing (red tomatoes are
more usually for cooking); radicchio, a curly red-leafed plant of
the radish family, similarly flavored; puntarella, spiky, green, and
pungent, dressed with chopped anchovies, garlic, oil, and lemon
juice (for the hearty eater); and other such manner of raw vegetables. Salads alla russa have a mayonnaise dressing and a generous mixture of cooked vegetables; they are generally considered
antipasti. Italian markets and many restaurants offer rughetta, a
small and pungent green that is not available, as far as I can discover, in this country, even though it has long been popular in
Europe under the name of rocket plant. It lifts any salad above
the ordinary, and is one of the necessary ingredients of the real
Roman salad, the misticanza. This assortment of perfumed herbs
and piquant grasses has a great deal more character than the mere
tossed green salad. Its leaves and spikes are the smallest and ten-
derest from the fields, and add to the salad all the freshness of a
country garden. Romans sometimes add such vegetables as

fennel, radishes, and tomatoes, but the fragrant greens are lively enough without any additions. Until a century ago, every convent and monastery gave space and time to its garden, a good portion of which nurtured ingredients for the misticanza. Roman poets have written widely on its merits.

Italians are very fond of raw vegetables dipped in a seasoned olive oil called pinzimonio. They dunk celery, fennel, radishes, and small tender artichokes, but raw mushrooms, peppers, carrots, and cucumbers are equally good. I have even seen an Italian recipe for lemon-bathed avocados, halved and stoned, but left in their skins, filled with pinzimonio and served with a spoon for scooping.

Dessert

THE Italians have no one word for dessert. They customarily end a meal with cheese, fruit, or nuts. Dolci, sweets, are reserved for special events: holidays, anniversaries, birthdays and name-days (of equal importance). This is a general habit, but of course not a rigid one. And sweets are consumed in quantity between meals.

Fruit · (Frutta)

FRUIT is good all over Italy. It bursts with ripeness, and the sweet juices confirm the marvelous reputation of the Italian sun. Although its appearance may be marred by slight markings or irregularities, these do not detract in the least from its superior flavor. Fresh tree-ripened fruit in season arrives at your table like so many blooms in a bowl. Since you wash the fruit yourself, it is generally afloat, or accompanied by a separate dish of water. The restaurant charges you by the piece. In the cooler weather, nuts and dried fruits often come along. Since an Italian diner never eats with his hands, he attacks even his apple or pear with knife and fork. He peels it, quarters it, removes seeds and stem with the assurance, speed and skill of a surgeon. Any waiter can skin an orange in one twirling motion, the peel spiraling away in a long ribbon of gold. Before presenting it to you, he finishes up by cutting whole slices, arranging them in slightly overlapping sections, and sprinkling them with sugar crystals or drops of liqueur. Certainly the best of all oranges is the magnificent ta-rocco. The meat of this Sicilian blood orange is an intense purple-red, surely the royal blood of the citrus family. Mandarin oranges are excellent, but grapefruit, I found to my surprise, is rare, and when available, small and not of exceptional quality. Many Ro-mans have never heard of it. But no matter, for fruits which *we* lack either in quantity, or altogether, grow in abundance. Enor-mous orange cachi, persimmons, herald the fall season. Loquats, medlars, pomegranates, and cactus pears from Sicily enliven the fruit bowl. Bananas come from Africa, are a state monopoly like salt and tobacco, and are price-fixed and costly. Peaches, plums and apricots, as well as magnificent grapes, though certainly no rarity to any of us, will surprise you by their consistency and per-fume. It is a common sight to come upon a Roman holding a heavy bunch of muscats under the trickle of a public water spout, or in the shower of a fountain, and consuming them, dripping and succulent, on the spot. Romans like plums, and irreverently call one purple variety "nun's thighs." Raspberries and straw-berries come to the table fresh, but the blackberry family seems to end up in the jam jar. Long-stemmed cultivated strawberries equal the size of plums, but their wild cousins from the woods, fragolini dei boschi, are delicate and tiny. Their subtle and exotic flavor stirs yearnings, after the season is over, that are hard to

67

dispel. What a treat they are, glistening with the amber of Aurum, a cordial that adds its orange flavor without masking the distinction of the berries. But they are even better dressed with lemon juice, and most exquisite mixed with just the right amount of vinegar. If your taste coincides with mine, you will order berries with less sugar than the Italian sweet tooth requires.

Melon that is the offspring of crossbreeding and scientific calculation does not exist in great variety. Unlike most other fruits, which come at the end of the meal, muskmelon or cantaloupe, melone, generally starts a dinner. Traditionally it is served with prosciutto and is as good a beginning as a meal can have. Figs are served in the same manner. Slices of watermelon and cantaloupe on ice brighten the summer scene in Trastevere, where vendors sell them from sidewalk stands. In winter, the air is heavy with the irresistible aroma of roasted chestnuts, whose seller huddles against the cold over his brazier glowing red with coals. Fresh coconut, in strips, is sold both at sidewalk stands and on the beaches, where the vendor, barechested and bronzed, his feet hardened against the hot sands, carries his wares in a bucket of cold water. Olive, peanut, and mussel salesmen offer him seaside competition.

Italians pour liqueurs on their fruit with a generous hand. They put kirsch on pineapple, and a peach often ends up sliced and well sugared in the last glass of dinner wine. Every menu lists macedonia di frutta, fruit cup. The Italian trick is simply to add maraschino to the diced fruits, and to serve the dish very well chilled. Pears and apples baked in white wine are a pleasant way to end a dinner.

Cheese · (Formaggi)

SHEEP, goats, cows, and buffalo give their milk for Italian cheeses. The variety is large and appealing, and each region has its own specialties, or local names for many common types. Fontina, a mildly tangy Piedmont cheese, makes an exceptional fondue when cooked in the following manner: For four portions, cut three-quarters of a pound of fontina into dice, put these in the top part of a double boiler, and cover with a half glass of milk. When you are ready to make the fondue, mix in four beaten egg yolks, and add a good lump of butter. Heat over boiling water, stirring with a wire whip or wooden paddle. Add salt (gingerly: the cheese is often salty) and pepper (white, if you have it) and continue cooking until the mixture is thick and creamy. Divide immediately among separate serving plates, or pour into one large dish, and cover with raw white truffle slices. Serve with toasts or chunks of French bread. Parmigiana, used widely in its grated form both in and on a staggering number of dishes, is splendid eaten whole, a fine companion to wine, and, according to Italian belief, an aid to the digestion besides. The best is called (in Rome) grana; it improves with age, and should not be overlooked in this ungrated form. Several soft and mild cheeses, bel paese, certosino, and stracchino, are spreadable, and indispensable for picnic sandwiches. They form a fine base for salami or ham with strips of roasted red peppers. Provola, a buffalo cheese, and provolone, made from either buffalo's or cow's milk, are equally good smoked or sweet. The Italian version of Swiss cheese, groviera, has a fine nutty character. A wedge of gorgonzola, sharp, green-veined, and creamy, contrasts well with fresh fruits, especially pears. Mozzarella, famous as a cooking cheese, is pleasant eating, too, and is often sprinkled with a good grating of black pepper. It is best when made from buffalo milk and in

69

all the Naples area the roadside is strung with signs proclaiming veritable mozzarella di bufala. Here and there in the fields one can see the herds of these strange beasts, but they are not so plentiful any longer. Neapolitan pizza undoubtedly achieved its fame because of the superior flavor of this buffalo cheese. Fior di latte, a cow's-milk mozzarella, has a milder flavor. Italians produce a most delicious unsalted cream cheese, mascherpone, light but not airy, sold in bulk, and available only in the cool weather. They prefer it as a dessert with sugar, jam or fruit, and sometimes mixed with sugar and coffee. The Romans have their special favorites. Ricotta, an unsalted cottage cheese made from ewe's milk, is the basis of many fillings for pasta and pastries, and finds wide use all through Italy. Pecorino romano, a sharp sheep's milk cheese, is grated over soups and sauces, adaptable wherever parmigiana is at home, and in Rome usually used instead of it. Provatura, a very fresh buffalo milk product, is similar to mozzarella, but creamier. These days it is getting hard to find. Romans like caciocavallo, which bears a strong resemblance to provolone. Butter is not a common Roman spread, though fancy restaurants serve it without the asking. The ancients never even made it, although they were fond enough of cheese.

Sweet Desserts · (Dolci)

SWEETS in Italy are a very special thing. There are those peculiar to holidays of importance, such as the Easter cakes baked in traditional forms, and taken with a bit of wine in the caffè. At Christmas time all of the pasticcerie, bars, and caffè, as well as the corner groceries, put in stocks of panettone, a Milanese specialty of rich brioche bread baked with candied fruits and raisins. The various firms put it up in fancy portable packages, rope-handled, a size for every family. Romans have their own Christmas favorite, pangiallo, a cake abundantly studded with raisins, pine nuts, candied orange peel, almonds and spices. At summer festival time, the Romans fry special cream puff-doughnuts and fritters, fritelle or zeppole di San Giuseppe, at sidewalk stands to sell hot and sugary to strolling merrymakers. Then and during the Christmas celebration in Piazza Navona, they set up counter candy factories and turn out torrone (nougat), ribbon candies, pine nut confections, and all manner of other wondrous sweetmeats. The dessert or dolce, just like all Italian cooking, shows marked regional preferences. The most elaborate of all sweets are Sicilian, and many are available in Rome, including cassata alla siciliana, a rich ice cream and candied fruit concoction; a Sicilian cheese cake of ricotta, grated chocolate, candied fruits and cake; cannoli, a similarly exotic Sicilian mélange of cottage cheese or custard, chocolate and candied fruits, swelling out of a crisp, chocolate-dipped cone; and torrone, the Sicilian version of which contains nuts and candied fruits baked into a confection so sweet that it makes my teeth ache just to think of it.

Italians are fond of puddings, whips, and rich purées of all kinds, but, to judge from the frequency of its appearance on their menus, fondest of all of crema caramella, or caramel glazed custard. Zuppa inglese combines custard with cake well doused with rum or liqueur, and can be made according to the following recipe: Make vanilla custard in the top of a double boiler by adding one cup of sugar gradually to eight well beaten eggs. When well blended, add one quart of warm milk, a little at a time. Stir continuously, and cook until the pudding thickens. After a minute or two, remove from the stove (stirring all the while) and add one teaspoon of vanilla. Use spongecake, lady fingers, or any soft light cake. Cut the cake into three layers of about three-quarters of an inch thickness. Place the first layer on a large platter and sprinkle generously with rum—about one-third cup. Pour half of the custard over it, top with the second

71

layer, repeat the process, add the third layer, and sprinkle with a final one-third cup of rum. Pour one-half a pint of whipped cream, beaten with one teaspoon of vanilla, over the top. When using lady fingers instead of cake, it is better to arrange them in a mold or soufflé dish, standing them around the edge as well as layering them. To add interest, and the Italians usually do, spread each layer of cake or lady fingers with jam before adding the custard, or sprinkle with candied fruits, also decorating the top. Sometimes this dessert contains chocolate custard or zabaglione instead of the classic vanilla cream, and I have had it with a strong Marsala flavor.

Zabaglione, no stranger to us, is the best of all the whips, a creamy froth of warm egg yolks, sugar and Marsala. The abundant chestnut, puréed and mounded to a peak, gets a snowy topping of whipped cream in faithful resemblance to Monte Bianco, from which it also takes its name. Here is the recipe: Bake one pound of chestnuts that have been slit along one side in a hot oven for about ten minutes, or until the skins are crackly enough to take off. [If you prefer boiling, this is acceptable procedure, too, though I find it is more tedious to remove the skins.] Put the shelled chestnuts in a sauce pan, cover them with milk, add a piece of vanilla bean, and boil gently for about twenty minutes. Drain, saving the milk but discarding the vanilla bean, and put through a sieve. (If you prefer to use liquid vanilla flavoring, add now.) Add one cup of powdered sugar and enough of the milk to bind the purée to a consistency of about mashed potatoes. Force through a pastry tube with a medium size opening, letting the spirals of chestnut fall into a cone-shaped mound. Refrigerate at least two hours before serving with a topping of heavy cream whipped with vanilla and sugar. [Alternative method: Add a sugar syrup to the mashed chestnuts, along with a lump of butter. Use two-thirds cup of sugar to one-quarter cup of water.]

Roman punch, a fanciful concoction of citrus sherbet, meringue and rum, originated, according to Samuel Chamberlain,

72

as an aid to the digestion of gargantuan Edwardian meals, and was served *before* the roast.[9] George's in Rome serves an Elizabethan syllabub that rivals Roman punch. They whip up dry sherry, brandy, cream, lemon juice, egg white and sugar and refrigerate this mixture for half a day before serving it in the tall narrow glasses that have been traditional for centuries.

Although Italians at home or in the bar delight in amaretti, almond macaroons, and such hard cakes as panforte, a nut and candied citrus cake from Siena, they derive most pleasure from the gooey, rich and alcoholic desserts that many restaurants provide. My very favorite is this ambrosial mixture of chocolate, coffee, and orange, Torta Emma Servi:

Cream six ounces of softened butter with about one cup of sugar [best, I find, to use confectioner's sugar]. Add the yolks of four eggs, one at a time, mixing in well. Then blend in one-half of a one-pound can of chocolate syrup (such as Hershey's) and two tablespoons of instant (powdered) coffee or coffee syrup. Line a pie pan with Saran wrap or wax paper. Cover with lady fingers cut in half lengthwise, or any plain cake cut about one-half inch thick. [Altogether you will need about eight ounces of lady fingers.] Pour over them a good sprinkling of Grand Marnier or Cointreau [brandy or any other liqueur can be substituted], and one half of the chocolate mix. Add a second layer of lady fingers or cake, repeat the process, and finish with a topping of lady fingers and liqueur. Cover with a sheet of Saran wrap, and then a lid or plate that fits within the edges of the pie tin. Cover with heavy rocks, an iron, or other suitable weight, and refrigerate over night. When ready to serve, invert the cake onto a serving platter, and top with one half pint of whipped cream seasoned with vanilla.

Deluxe restaurants often add to what is already quite a production by exhibiting their dolci on a rolling cart that draws your

9. Samuel Chamberlain, *Italian Bouquet*, New York, Gourmet, 1958, p. 557.

eye like steel to a magnet. Many restaurants limit themselves to one or two specialties, and some of the small trattorie never serve sweets at all.

Ice Creams · (Gelati)

ITALIAN ice cream, though equally smooth, is less creamy than ours, really something in between ice cream and sherbet, but it gains in this way a more refreshing and less cloying character. In the extreme it can be too watery, or too synthetic, but usually the flavor captures faithfully and fully the personality of whatever fruit or other ingredient is its essence. Chocolate is absolutely dreamy—smooth but not overly sweet—and gianduia is the best chocolate of them all. Vanilla, on the other hand, is distinctly poor. Do not miss pistacchio, or nocciole (hazelnuts), or limone, which, of the many exceptional fruit flavors, to my taste is supreme. Most bars and gelaterie sell cones in the warm season. You can avoid making a painful decision by buying a gelato misto, a cone or dish that holds a one-scoop sampler of three flavors dabbed with whipped cream. More and more bars are selling frozen oranges and lemons filled with sherbet. You can always order ice cream in restaurants, whether or not it appears on the menu, because it is so easily portable from the nearest bar, and for some restaurateurs more economical than an investment in equipment to keep it refrigerated. The fame of several places derives partly from some glorious concoction of their own, such as Tre Scalini's tartufo: chocolate ice cream surrounding a plump maraschino cherry, riddled with chunks of whole chocolate, and mounded with whipped cream. Corsetti, otherwise noted for the artful cooking of fish, presents a distinguished

74

grande coppa mista, a pyramidal structure of ice creams, with a great chimney of a rolled wafer.

Beverages · (Bevande)

ROME alters American drinking habits. Italians prefer wines and aperitifs to hard liquor; vermouth or Campari replaces the cocktail. You will rarely see an intoxicated Italian, even though no meal is complete without wine. The wine that accompanies lunch or dinner is available in restaurants in flasks of a quarter, a half, or a full litro—a little more than a quart. In some homey places, wine is sold "a calo": you pour from a full bottle, but you pay only for the amount you drink.

Although the cocktail party is not yet common, it is gaining ground, because, as one Italian culinary expert puts it, it does solve the problems of modern social life in a practical way.

Italians favor not only white, red, quinine, and dry vermouth, but a mouth-puckering assortment of aperitifs, in particular bitter Campari, of a gorgeous red color and slightly medicinal taste. Gaspare Campari, who invented it, was an Italian Horatio Alger. At fourteen he left his small country village with very little money, a small amount of schooling and a great desire to make his way in the world, starting in Torino. He chose to seek his fortunes as an apprentice behind the bar of a caffè-liquoreria. There, among the absinthes, wines and herbs, he learned and recorded notebooks full of formulae, for it was the practice in the mid-1800's for each caffè to manufacture its own beverages. His work was extremely successful, and he eventually became proprietor of his own place in Milano, in the gallery near the great cathedral. He and his family prospered there, and he invented

75

the two Campari drinks which brought him fame, the bitter and the cordial. After his death, the by now dynastic operations under the direction of his sons brought forth a third beverage, vermilion Campari-soda, an aperitif that Italians down as frequently as Americans consume Coke.

Several other aromatic infusions share this popularity. Alchermes, a heady carmine beverage, take its hue from cochineal. China, quinine, turns up under various labels, not only in elixir form, but mixed with bubbling water or vermouth. If your taste runs to the bitter, there is also the tonic Fernet Branca; Rabarbaro, a rhubarb derivative; and the dark Cynar, made from artichokes. But like olives, these Italian beverages often demand an acquired taste.

The Piedmont region produces today many vermouths with renowned labels: Martini and Rossi, Cinzano, Gancia, and Carpano, whose founder invented this brew of wine and herbs in the first place, and whose spicy Punt e Mes is one of the best beverages around. It is common practice to order vermouth by brand, for example, "Un Martini, dry," you say to the waiter. But if you are an American you may receive instead a dry martini, which the waiter knows is your national preference anyway. And since even martini *cocktail* drinkers sometimes tolerate una buccia di limone, the twist of lemon peel that combines so happily with straight vermouth, it gives no clarifying clue to order it. Conversely, when you do want a martini cocktail, you may end up with straight vermouth. Therefore, in general, it is wise to order specifically; to state whether you want dry or sweet, vermut or cocktail, with ice, with lemon peel, with seltz. I have heard Americans successfully get a vermouth by ordering a martini, "*senza* gin" (without gin). When an Italian wants a cocktail, he is likely to order a Negroni, a mix that he can also drink in long form if seltzer water is added. Just as American gin drinkers have their uncompromisingly different recipes for martinis, Negroni

76

lovers share no common formula. Basically, the drink consists of equal parts of gin, bitter Campari, and sweet vermouth, with ice and a lemon peel. But this quiet equilibrium invites experiment. Equally good, and milder, is this aperitif invented by Renato Torti: Mix two ounces of Cinzano Bianco (Cinzano white vermouth), one-half ounce of Carpano Punt e Mes, and one dash of gin. Pour over ice and serve with a twist of lemon peel. Another "mixed" drink that has created some little vogue during the hot Roman summers is cold champagne poured over an icy crushed peach.

Both American-style cocktails and Scotch are available in Italy, and usually inexpensive. The same goes for brandy. The robust Italian Vecchia Romagna is a real bargain, but not for delicate palates. The most potent and inexpensive brandy, grappa, is distilled from pressed grape skins, has quite a kick, and goes well in coffee, caffè corretto. Italians drink a lot of beer, of which there are several fine native labels on the light side. Birrerie dot the streets of every town, and in Rome there are several Bavarian beerhalls.

Aurum, an orange liqueur with an amber brilliance, is the Italian Triple Sec. It is fine over fresh fruits, particularly wild strawberries and pineapple. Strega, a blend of citrus extract and many herbs, bewitches as it should, for its name means "witch." But legend tells us that the witches who brewed the original concoction were really beautiful damsels in disguise. A second of its charms is the superstition that those who drink it together will always stay together. Italians also manufacture excellent mint liqueurs, and a variety of anise-flavored alcohols. Many hosts, including restaurateurs, present Sambuca to their guests at the end of the meal. In Rome, this cordial is served with a few coffee beans afloat in the glass, and is called Sambuca con la mosca (Sambuca with the flies in it).

Wines · (Vini)

ITALIAN wines generally offer no serious competition to their French neighbors. This is not to say that there are no good Italian wines, but none is as majestic as some of the pressings across the border. The great wines of Piedmont, however, are exceptional, and a few reach the heights of the fine French vintages. But it is one of the sad facts of Italian wine production generally, that owing to understandable economic pressures, wine aging as practiced by the most revered Piedmont vintners is a luxury that few others can afford. In fact, a good part of each year's output goes at once to the table, and often in the restaurant you drink grape juice that is still fermenting—making your stomach rumble, your head heavy, and your knees giddy. The taste may be a hint of what a good wine it might have been a few years hence, had it matured tenderly in wooden casks in the meanwhile. The quality of Italian wines would certainly rise considerably if they were made more often in the venerable manner: aged first in the barrel, and then in the bottle.

Many bottled wines are aged at least in the glass, so that if you are seeking out the best ones, you can be guided by the date on the bottle. In general, a wine should have a minimum of three years' maturation; the finest Barolo should be drunk only after ten, and the best Chianti after six. Since some of the Italian wines lose their quality during transportation (though not most of the really good ones), you are often better off with a naive and fruity local wine drawn from the barrel and served in a carafe than with the bottled reminiscence of a sophisticated but fragile product from another district. But often so-called "local" table wines are doctored and fortified—and the freshness and charm of the product are lost. By sampling locally, you will taste wines that are variously flinty, sweet, raisiny, perfumed, and dry, from which on occasion some unheralded flask will yield up a real surprise, as did a white wine I once drank in Assisi. However, unbottled wines also have the disadvantage of uniqueness, so that, on subsequent visits it is not likely that I shall ever obtain exactly the same refreshment that Assisi once offered me. Vini comuni cost very little, a surprising twenty-five to fifty cents a quart, so experiment takes only a small investment. You can order them in any size carafe that suits you, and the simple ritual that has been established is to enjoy them without fuss. Both reds and whites are served chilled or at room temperature, they seem equally at home with meat, fish and fowl, and Italians do not consider it irreverent to add water or sparkling mineral water in quantity.

Although the vini comuni are in general unreliable for serious wine drinkers, in the average Rome restaurant the white wines from the Roman castelli, the neighboring towns south and east of the city in the foothills of the Apennines, can be a pleasant exception. Frascati, a golden perfume, doesn't stand up well even the few miles distance to the capital, but it fills more Roman flasks than the wines from Nemi, Albano, Grottaferrata, Castelgandolfo, Genzano, Velletri, or Marino. The Rome winery Maccarese produces a white Maccarese, red Fregene, and Castel S. Giorgio Rosé, which you may want to sample when in that area, although they are not generally as successful as the wines from the Castelli.

If you have the opportunity to make the short trip to Frascati, you will discover its wine at its virginal, unadulterated best, straight from the cellar of any one of a number of cantinas. These wine cellars, with rough wooden tables and benches, and a jumble of drinkers downing cool glasses of amber refreshment, are numerous wherever wine is produced, and you may take your lunch along to accompany the flask of wine you buy. Genzano produces good white and red wines, slightly bubbly and wondrously refreshing, and worth the trip to taste. Another good excursion in the environs of Rome is to the wine festival in Marino, a boisterous and rollicking autumnal celebration. Bands bleat, grapes hang in gargantuan festoons, townsfolk parade, shimmery and gimcracky carnival booths line the square, wine spews from the fountain for all to drink freely, and the whole population chants and trumpets, cacaphonous in honor of the Grape.

A few districts product most of the noteworthy Italian wines, and Piedmont is in a class by itself. This district produces the very best reds, a number of them distinguished. It makes, besides, the Italian vermouths, and—perhaps more famous—sparkling Asti Spumante, Italian champagne. This bubbling wine is available either sweet or dry; the best is probably Cinzano Brut, which for around two dollars a bottle will add its festive sparkle to any occasion.

As to the reds, the king of them all is Barolo. It is a velvety, deep red wine that ages evenly and becomes in maturity a rich and full-bodied elixir, the only Italian wine that can compete with a good Burgundy, and the kind of wine to be drunk on special occasions. Nebbiolo is another noble pressing that comes from the same grape. It has just a trace of sweetness, and gets its name—which literally means fog—because the fruit is allowed to ripen in the late, foggy days of the season. In the old days, Piedmont aristocracy traditionally served Nebbiolo at the end of the meal, in front of the open fire, and it still seems most enjoyable at the finish of dinner. For everyday drinking, the Piedmontese choose heavy, full-bodied Dolcetto, or Grignolino, a light wine which is near to a rosé in character, and, as the Italians say, "beverino"—eminently drinkable. Barbaresco, another heavy, full-bodied red, does not have the luster of Barolo. Gattinara doesn't achieve the heights of Barolo either, but in the best years it can reach the same class. Like the Barolo and Dolcetto, it is excellent with game and roasts. For more ordinary drinking, three lesser wines from Piedmont do well: Barbera, Carema, and Freisa. The first two are rough, the last bubbling.

Outside of Piedmont, the wines are of a lesser quality, but there are several worth pointing out. The hills near Verona have borne grapes far back in history according to evidence unearthed by modern excavators, who found grape pits in bronze age dwellings; and, in dwellings of the iron age, pits that are the very same as of today's classic European wine grapes. From the province of Veneto-Euganea comes a duo of good reds, Valpolicella and Bardolino—smooth, clear, and especially refreshing in hot weather. The same province produces Merlot, good with beef and game; and the pale but sunshiny Soave, a nice dry white. There is also a rare, dry, hard-to-obtain Pinot Grigio, and some sparkling wines, such as Prosecco.

Wines from the Trentino area are generally very good, and highly reliable. Santa Maddalena and Lago di Caldaro, light colored, dry reds, can be drunk with most lighter meats and entrées, and are good hot-weather wines. There are two very good whites from this region: a Riesling and a highly aromatic Terlano.

Tuscany gives us Chianti, familiar to all in the roly-poly straw-covered containers. Wine doesn't age well in those bulging glass flasks, so the superior Chianti vintages are matured first in wood, then finished in glass bottles of regular design. The output is very large and not all of the wines under this label are uniformly palatable. The southern state of Puglia sends large shipments of stout red wines to fortify northern products, but the blend is not always smooth and genial. To be certain that you are buying the characteristic wine you anticipate, look for either a black rooster or baby emblem on the bottle. The best Chianti, red or white, bears one of these labels: Ricasoli (Brolio and Meleto), Antinori, Serristori (Machiavelli and S. Andrea). Tuscany produces several other creditable reds, of which I have sampled and found pleasing the Montepulciano, and many sweet dessert wines.

Another large district for wine production is the island of Sicily. The luxurious blend, Marsala, is only one of several dessert wines, some of them heavy enough to be considered almost liqueurs. Corvo di Salaperuta, red or white, is a notable example of the dry Sicilian dinner wines.

Almost all of the other Italian states cultivate grapes and produce acceptable pressings, with the possible exception of regions like the Abruzzi and Molise. Calabrian wines are generally fresh and naive, and there are more creditable vintages from other districts worth trying when you come across them: Cinque Terre from Liguria, a golden wine of rich flavor that matures well (and the real Cinque Terre is difficult to find elsewhere in Italy); Grumello, Sassella, and Inferno, three good reds, unsophisticated but pleasant, and easily found in Rome, from the Valtellina of Lombardy; Frecciarossa St. George, a generous rosé (not to be confused with Fressiarossa Grand Crux, a red with a slightly acid taste) also from Lombardy; the Marches' Verdicchio, a dry white that is worth buying for its lovely bottle alone; Umbria's excellent Orvieto, in a straw-covered flask like that of ordinary Chianti (and since this sunny white wine is a stable traveler, you can buy it with assurance when you see it on the menu); and a sparkling red from Emilia-Romagna called Lambrusco, unfortunately among the poorest of travelers, so not to be drunk outside of its own province. Campania produces several wines of more than passing value, such as the romantically if somewhat sacrilegiously named Lacrima Christi (Christ's tears); Falerno, an heir of the Roman Falernum; a number of tender and fragrant Ravello wines put out by the Caruso family (who also own a fine hotel and restaurant on the very top of the Amalfi peninsula); and good whites of steady quality from Ischia and Capri—possibly hard to come by. In Rome you may come upon a wine from nearby Montefiascone with the improbable name Est!Est!!Est!!! There are red and white varieties and sweet and dry, not all of equal caliber. Although the wine loses little through shipping, it may take several samplings to discover a bottle whose quality supports this story told about it. One Cardinal Fugger, a German with an immense passion for wine, always lodged when traveling in whatever inn offered the most palatable vintage. On his way to Rome he dispatched in advance a servant whose function it was to taste the local offerings and mark the best station by chalking "Est" on the door. When he came to Montefiascone, the servant was so signally impressed that he chalked Est!Est!!Est!!!, the name now attached to the wine of Montefiascone. The Cardinal so well concurred in his servant's judgment that he never reached the Holy City, but stayed on in Montefiascone, where some say he finally passed away from an over-abundance of Est!Est!!Est!!!

WINE CHART

AFTER sampling some of the superior Italian wines, you may want to purchase and store a variety of them for use in your own home, particularly to complement Italian cooking. The following chart should serve as an introduction at home and abroad to some of the most interesting wines, aperitifs, and after-dinner drinks. There are a few simple rules to bear in mind for successful home wine storage: avoid light, vibrations, and strong odors; maintain a constant temperature (best around 55°), and tilt the bottles slightly downward to keep the corks moist. Whites are seldom lively after four or five years, and wines with a low alcohol content spoil more easily than those with more.

WINES OF ITALY

SWITZERLAND

Gattinara
*Carema
PIEDMONT
*Freisa
*Barbera
‖Moscato d'Asti
*Nebbiolo *Grignolino
*Barbaresco †Cortese.
‖Asti-Spumante
*Barolo
*Dolcetta

*Inferno
*Grumello
*Sassella
LOMBARDY
*Frecciarossa St. George

†Terlano
**TRENTINO-
ALTO ADIGE**
*Santa
  Maddalena
Lago di Caldaro
†Riesling
**VENETO-
EUGANEA**
‖Recioto
*Valpolicella
*Bardolino
†Pinot Grigio
†Soave

‖Prosecco
**VENEZIA
GIULIA**
*Merlot

LEGEND
*—RED AND ROSE WINES
†—WHITE WINES
‖—DESSERT WINES

L I G U R I A
‖Cinque Terre

EMILIA-ROMAGNA
*Lambrusco

*Vino Nobile
di Montepulciano
TUSCANY
‖Vino Santo
*Chianti

SAN MARINO

†Verdicchio
MARCHE

†Orvieto
UMBRIA

**ABRUZZI
& MOLISE**

LATIUM
★ROME
†Castelli
Romani

‖Aleatico

CAMPANIA
ISCHIA ISLAND
ISLE OF CAPRI
†Capri
*Lacrima Christi

PUGLIA

LUCANIA

SARDINIA
‖Vernaccia

T Y R R H E N I A N   S E A

CALABRIA

LIPARI ISLANDS
‖Malvasia di Lipari

M E D I T E R R A N E A N   S E A

‖Marsala
†*Corvo di Salaparuta
SICILY

ISLAND OF
PANTELLERIA

Y U G O S L A V I A

A D R I A T I C   S E A

NAME	DISTRICT	COMMENTS	PRINCIPAL PRODUCERS
Barolo	Piedmont	Heavy, velvety, full-bodied; best after 10 years; Italy's most distinguished wine.	Fiorina, Flli Borgogno, Gabri, Mirafiore, Einaudi
Nebbiolo	Piedmont	Heavy-bodied, perfumed, trace of sweetness; perhaps best at end of meal.	same as for Barolo
Dolcetto	Piedmont	Heavy, full-bodied, good for general table use.	same as for Barolo
Gattinara	Piedmont	Heavy, full-bodied, matures excellently.	Spanna
Barbaresco	Piedmont	Heavy, full-bodied, lacks the finish of Barolo, matures more quickly.	Fontanafredda
Barbera Carema	Piedmont	Strong, full-bodied, but rough; young wines best for general table use.	Flli Borgogno
Grumello Sassella Inferno	Valtellina, Lombardy	Lively, full-bodied, best well aged; readily available in Rome.	Negri
Merlot	Veneto-Euganea	Good with beef.	Kettmeier, Kuppelwieser, Cantine Sociali di Portogruaro (Venezia)
Chianti	Tuscany	Lively, full-bodied, improves with age; drink only aged, bottled wines for roasts and game.	Antinori, Barone Ricasoli's Brolio and Meleto (less fine), Serristori's Machiavelli and S. Andrea
Vino Nobile di Montepulciano	Tuscany	Dry, velvety, ages well.	Giannini, "EVI"
Corvo di Salaparuta	Sicily	Dry, even, generous.	Duca di Salaparuta

NAME	DISTRICT	COMMENTS	PRINCIPAL PRODUCERS
Grignolino	Piedmont	Smooth, light-bodied, delicate, good young.	Flli Borgogno
Freisa	Piedmont	Strong and dry; uneven when young; can be used with roasts if well aged.	Mirafiore
Lago di Caldaro	Trentino-Alto Adige	Dry; available on Wagon-Lits.	Kettmeier
Santa Maddalena	Trentino-Alto Adige	Dry, good in hot weather; excellent when well-aged.	Lechthaler, H. Lun
Valpolicella	Veneto-Euganea	Even, rich, good with roasts if well-aged.	Bertani, Bolla
Bardolino	Veneto-Euganea	Lusty, dry, drink young.	Bertani, Bolla
Lambrusco	Emilia-Romagna	Light, fruity, sparkling red; very poor traveler—do not drink outside of its province.	Cantina Sociali di Sorbara
Lacrima Christi, red	Campania	Well-balanced, better with age.	Giuseppe Scala, Flli Antonio
Frecciarossa St. George	Lombardy	A superior rosé from Pavia; adaptable to all light foods.	Azienda Agricola Frecciarossa (Odero)

Fish Wines · white

NAME	DISTRICT	COMMENTS	PRINCIPAL PRODUCERS
Soave	Veneto-Euganea	Dry, good body.	Bertani, Bolla
Orvieto, dry	Umbria	Straw-covered bottle; delicate; good traveler, drink anywhere.	Papini, Antinori, Mirafiore
Cinque Terre, dry	Liguria	Aromatic, excellent when well aged; small output; generally hard to find.	Casa Ansaldo
Lacrima Christi, white	Campania	Smooth, dry, light.	Giuseppe Scala, Flli Antonio, Gancia (sparkling)
Capri	Campania	Light color, delicate, aromatic, hard to find.	Giuseppe Scala
Cortese	Piedmont	Golden-green, dry, aromatic; drink young.	Brovia, Fontanafredda
Verdicchio	Marches	Dry, rounded, delicate, best when well aged.	"Staphilus" of Bertelucci e Fantone
Corvo di Salaparuta	Sicily	Dry, classic.	Duca di Salaparuta
Pinot Grigio	Veneto-Euganea	Dry, smooth, not easy to obtain.	Tenuta Santa Margherita
Riesling Terlano	Trentino-Alto Adige	Very good, dependable wines; Terlano aromatic.	Carli

Ordinary Table Wines

Castelli Romani	Latium	Golden, aromatic; often adulterated outside their own towns; poor travelers; drink only in Rome area.	
Chianti · flasks	Tuscany	Hardy red, ample white, above average table wine.	black rooster or baby crest

NAME	DISTRICT	COMMENTS	PRINCIPAL PRODUCERS
Asti-Spumante	Piedmont	Made from muscat grapes; sparkling; gay and inexpensive.	Cinzano (Brut), Gancia, Mirafiore, Zoppa
Cinque Terre, sweet	Liguria	Hard to find; best well aged.	Casa Ansaldo
Prosecco	Veneto-Euganea	Dry, usually sparkling, often served with fish.	Ruggeri
Marsala	Sicily	Many varieties, including chocolate cream, egg, and almond; ages excellently; widely used in cooking.	Pellegrino, Rallo
Recioto	Veneto-Euganea	Plain or sparkling; red or white.	Bertani
Moscato d'Asti Passito	Piedmont	Sweet, smooth.	Mirafiore
Vino Santo	Trentino-Alto Adige	Mellow, sweet, golden; ages well.	Ricasoli, Serristori, Antinori
Aleatico	Various regions but particularly good from Puglia	Light red; rich, sweet flavor; improves with age.	Antinori
Malvasia di Lipari (and various Malvasia wines from other areas)	Sicily	Produced from dried grapes on the island of Stromboli; golden, sweet, harmonious bouquet.	Fratelli Beccaro
Vernaccia	Sardinia	Golden, full-bodied; ages well; can be used with light meals as well as desserts.	"Vinalcool"

APERITIFS

NAME	COMMENTS	PRODUCERS
Bitter Campari		Campari
Campari Soda		
Vermouth	Classic: sweet or dry.	Carpano, Cinzano, Cora, Gancia, Martini e Rossi
Punt e Mes	Bitter vermouth.	Carpano
Cynar	Aperitif with artichoke base.	Pezziol
Fernet	A bitter bitter.	Ferrero, Branca
Ferro China	A quinine-iron tonic.	Bisleri
Rabarbaro	Derived from rhubarb.	Ramazotti

LIQUEURS & BRANDIES

NAME	COMMENTS	PRODUCERS
Strega liqueur	A blend of citrus and herbs.	Alberti (Benevento)
Vecchia Romagna	A fruity, lively, and inexpensive brandy.	Buton
Cordial Campari	A bitter cordial.	Campari
Maraschino	A sweet cherry cordial; widely used on fruits, but a refreshing drink.	Drioli, Luxardo
Anisetta	A cordial based on sweet anise.	Meletti
Sambuco or Sambuca (con la mosca)	An anise-flavored cordial (with whole coffee beans afloat).	Tuoni & Canepa
Grappa	Fiery and inexpensive, resembles French marc.	Occhino, Andrea Da Ponte, Bortolozzi
Aurum	Orange based, golden cordial.	Aurum Distillery

A NOTE ON THE RECIPES

ROMAN restaurateurs and chefs have been most generous in sharing their recipes with me. Together these recipes make up a selective but basic Italian cook book, including most of the favorite Roman dishes. A few of the ingredients, such as pagliata, may be difficult to obtain in this country. Where this is the case and a substitute is suggested, it will produce a good result, though somewhat different from the original. The following general culinary suggestions may prove helpful:

Unless otherwise noted, wherever prosciutto is specified, it refers to prosciutto crudo, raw Italian cured ham. Italian markets, specialty shops, and fancy delicatessens are usually reliable sources in this country, but should you have difficulty finding it, substitute cooked ham or Canadian bacon.

Where a recipe calls for Italian clams (vongole) you can use tiny Japanese canned clams with great success—usually a closer approximation of the delicate Italian bivalve than a husky though live American fellow. Mussels are often unobtainable fresh in the United States, or at least they are limited by season. But they come canned either in or out of their black satiny shells—the former an aesthetic necessity for the fish soups—from such gourmet specialty houses as Les Echalottes, 373 Campgaw Road, Ramsey, New Jersey (mail order catalogue available).

Fresh herbs are easy to grow in a small amount of space; however, half the amount of dried herbs will be an acceptable substitute in most recipes. The exceptions are dishes calling for fresh sweet basil (notably the pesto, or the minestrone with pesto added), and those requiring fresh sage leaves.

The pasta used in testing these recipes was all made from durum hard grain wheat. If you have to use another type, there may be some slight difference in cooking time (and taste). Buitoni, Ronzoni, and De Cecco brands are satisfactory pastes, and

90

most Italian markets have loose pasta of good quality. For other makers, check the label for contents.

Tomato sauce in these recipes means homemade tomato sauce in the Italian sense, pomodoro passato: strained stewed tomatoes, carrots, onions, celery, and seasonings. American canned tomato sauce is a sharper, stronger thing, so it would be better to substitute puréed canned tomatoes when you don't make the sauce yourself. On the other hand, where tomato *paste* is called for, if you use an Italian brand it will be considerably stronger than its American equivalent, used in these recipes.

Ricotta, the Italian cheese made from unsalted ewe's milk, has a flavor and texture quite different from American cottage cheese, which it resembles and which can serve as its substitute when ricotta is not available.

The exact duplication of some of the wild mushroom recipes will be possible only for well-trained mycologists; but the substitution of cultivated species for porcini and ovoli will give excellent dishes in themselves, and be far safer than practicing mushroom hunting on an amateur basis. If fresh mushrooms are unavailable, dried mushrooms usually add more flavor to sauces and stews than do the canned variety, which should be reserved for more delicate dishes.

Where grated Parmesan is needed (and where not?), you will obtain much better flavor by grating a hunk of good cheese fresh on the spot than by relying on packaged, pre-grated products. For pecorino, substitute Parmesan.

For broth, substitute bouillon cubes or stock bases mixed with water.

Use good ingredients, only the best quality herbs and spices, and as fine a cooking wine as you can afford. The flavor of the dish you are making can reflect only what goes into it.

There are several things to note about the making of pasta. Because of the difference in the hardness of the wheat used in various flours, the absorption of water in the dough varies, the kneading and rolling out become a matter of judgment, and the cooking time changes. Use hard grain flours if they are available. The recipes in this book will give you the general rules and measurements, but if the dough seems too wet—or not wet enough—it will be because of the difference in the basic ingredients. The best advice about learning to make good pasta is to practice until you have the feel of the dough and can make slight adjustments accordingly. If you know someone who makes her own noodles, it is very instructive to watch the process before trying it yourself. In making egg dough, you can substitute one or two egg whites instead of one whole egg (per batch). The addition of a little olive oil to the dough keeps the pasta from sticking when it cooks.

Whether you make your own pasta or buy it ready-made, the best way to tell when it is cooked al dente—still very firm—is to taste a piece. Italian cooks always use an abundance of boiling water to which they add rock salt—easier to regulate than the table variety. When the pasta is done, stop the cooking instantly by adding a glass of cold water to the pot. *Never* rinse cooked pasta, but drain immediately, then mix at once with butter or a bit of the sauce. When boiling lasagne or cannelloni which will undergo additional cooking later, remove from the water, plunge into a bowl of cold water, and spread on towels to drain. When cooking ravioli or gnocchi, always keep the water just at a boil, rather than racing it as for the other pastes, and when they are finished scoop them out with a large slotted spoon; otherwise they may break. One final precaution: Italians eat a large portion of pasta as a first course; the quantities given in this book are for first course portions, Italian style. If you prefer your pasta in smaller quantities, as an accompaniment to the main dish, cut down the recipe proportionately.

III

THE RESTAURANTS

EXPLORATION and discovery add dimension to dining. To stumble, hot and dusty, from a long walk over uneven terrain, into an unpretentious dining room where a flask of cool Frascati materializes at a word, to unwind and unbend as you study the menu and debate with yourself whether to have gnocchi or cannelloni today—this is the mood and context of appreciation. You will find plenty of opportunities to experiment in Rome, for cozy

94

eating places are tucked in every wrinkle of the city's face. However, the pleasures of new discovery notwithstanding, there are a number of Roman restaurants that you should make a point of seeking out. In the section that follows I would like to describe some of the best restaurants in the city. I have included most for the quality of their cooking, though there are a few where the atmosphere is more interesting than the food. I include the

venerable establishments that have been heard of frequently before, if their current performance still merits a listing. I tried each
restaurant anonymously, paid my own way, and accepted no form
of compensation for any of the listings in this book.

I have arranged the restaurants in a number of categories which
I hope will be useful to the reader, although such distinctions are
never clear-cut, nor do they preclude a certain amount of overlapping. For readers who want a simplified guide for a short stay
in Rome, one restaurant from each category will give a good idea
of the whole range of Roman eating places. Among them, you
can sample Roman specialties, game and fish, and regional dishes
from other parts of Italy; you can dine in humble quarters, in
some of Rome's loveliest piazzas, or surrounded by patrician
decor in veritable palaces. With these as a starting point, you can
enlarge and enrich your gastronomic acquaintance with the city
by embellishing from the whole list.

If you plan a meal in a particular restaurant, it is wise to check
ahead to be sure it is open; in the deluxe places a reservation is
usually a necessity. The alphabetical directory at the back of the
book gives addresses and telephone numbers. Unless otherwise
noted, the dinner prices (including table wine and service) fall in
the inexpensive to moderate range by American standards: that
is, $2 to $5. I do not list hours nor weekly or yearly closures because these can be so irregular as to make a directory thoroughly
unreliable. Most restaurants close one day of the week, but it
varies all through the city; many restaurants close for varying pe-
riods of time during the summer (August being the most popular
month because of the Ferragosto holiday), but the exact dates are
generally decided annually; such changes in other seasons as may
be necessitated by further vacations, remodeling, or illness are
often announced at the last minute by a scrawl on the back of a
menu tacked to the door. Daily hours are not uniform either,
though in general restaurants—except for the supper-club variety,

and a few very fancy places—serve both lunch and dinner, the former being the Roman's larger and more important meal. Though Romans like to eat late, most restaurants begin serving lunch around noon time, and dinner by about seven-thirty in the evening. But if you dine at these early hours you may find the scene dull. For animation with your fettuccine, it is best to arrive later.

The only requirement for a Roman meal is a lively appetite and a generous capacity for enjoyment. At the end of your dinner, when the host asks "Ha mangiato bene?" ("Have you had a good meal?") I hope you will be able to reply, "A Roma, si mangia sempre bene!"

1. Characteristic Trattorie
and Ristoranti

A LARGE group of restaurants shape the basic character of Roman eating out. Not different in nature or tradition from simple trattorias, they have nevertheless responded to the cosmopolitanism of a great city in discernible ways. Many grew out of humbler establishments, often enlarging their premises, brightening and refurbishing, extending their menus, and producing cooking that

99

became a shade more complex. Others started out as modern restaurants, but their owners, coming from the old family-style tradition, retained its warm and familiar approach. In atmosphere, these restaurants range from such unassuming premises as Campana and Romolo to the bustling modern dining room of Augustea and the handsomely appointed interior of Ernesto. There are fancy guest books here and there; you can often have your picture taken by a wandering photographer; and at some of the "Alfredos" there is a bit of ceremony over the noodles. But in spite of such occasional, citified touches, all of them manage to retain some of the basic unpretentiousness of their heritage.

℘ AL MORO ℘

AL MORO's recipes follow instructions handed down practically unchanged for three generations. Today's generous and communicative host, Mario Romagnoli, is a grandson of the original owners who established their trattoria almost seventy years ago. Following their tradition of handing the business on from father to son, Signor Romagnoli is presently transmitting to his son Franco the secrets and skills of the family kitchen which he learned from his own father.

Although Al Moro is not much more than a coin's throw from the famous Trevi Fountain, it is so well tucked away in its adjacent small street that one can easily pass it by. But it is worth searching out, even though it does not beckon to the customer with the gaudy enticements of its Trevi neighbors. This is also the neighborhood of the Piazza Colonna, the hub of modern Rome's commercial and political activities and the center of one of Rome's old quarters. Here in old Roman days, in fact to the very palazzo that today houses Al Moro, Roman citizens trekked to pay their "balzelli," the equivalent of present-day taxes—which, as Signor Romagnoli sagely points out, "ossillano tutti i contribuenti del mondo," "are a cross for all the world to bear." Ancient Romans, by way of securing the legality of documents, including tax receipts, affixed to them a stamp (a tradition that modern Romans carry on with exasperating faithfulness). The word for these stamps, "bollette," gave the Via delle Bollette its name.

What was in ancient times the principal entrance to the tax building is today the second of two Al Moro dining rooms. There are still in evidence two well conserved ancient granite columns, complete with capitals, and two Roman capitals besides. The traffic of government officials still exists too, for the Italian Parliament is close by, and today's clientele includes many ministers and parliamentary personnel. A good number of journalists, attorneys and professional people from all over Italy also gather here.

The menu of Al Moro is a guide to many of the specialties of Roman cuisine, but here they are cooked with a difference. Signor Romagnoli is very proud—and he should be—of that special something that makes his cooking stand out above that of so many trattorie. In sharing many of his recipes with me, he said, most apologetically, that he must keep secret in some cases a few small tricks and additions that the family has guarded so long and so jealously. Who can blame him when the results are so satisfactory?

The first of the recipes from the kitchen of Al Moro is a pasta specialty, spaghetti alla Moro. "Gentile Signora," Signor Romagnoli told me by way of introducing this fine dish, "Lei aveva mangiato in molti locali di Roma e in speciale modo in Trastevere, i spaghetti alla carbonara, i quali sono molti lontani dai spaghetti alla Moro." "Kind lady, you have eaten in many places in Rome, and particularly in Trastevere, spaghetti alla carbonara, but that is a far cry from our spaghetti alla Moro."

SPAGHETTI ALLA MORO

1 lb. spaghetti	2 tbsp. butter
6 strips very lean bacon	2 eggs
2 tbsp. olive oil	grated Parmesan cheese
dried hot red pepper	

Put enough spaghetti for four portions into abundant boiling water. In a frying pan place six strips of *very* lean bacon cut into little narrow strips. [In Moro's kitchen they measure 1½″ by ½″.] Add about two tablespoons of olive oil, and either a little paprika, or as they do at Moro, "peperoncino rosso, come facciamo noi a Roma"—"dried hot red peppers, as we make them in Rome" (not quite as sharp as our cayenne). Continue cooking until the bacon is browned, add two tablespoons butter, and when it has melted, remove from the fire. When the spaghetti is cooked al dente, drain and put in a large warm serving bowl. Beat two eggs well and add immediately to the spaghetti, mixing very quickly; pour the bacon mixture over the pasta, sprinkle generously with grated Parmesan cheese, and serve—and eat—immediately, lest the egg become amalgamated. [If you allow your portion to remain cooling sadly before you until everyone has been served, the dish will lose its character, as is the case with so many foods. The Italian habit, which strikes us as rude at first, but quickly proves to be the only rational approach, is to begin eating as soon as the food is set in front of you.]

Scampi alla Moro is a simple and delicious dish in which we can substitute prawns for the delicate Italian shellfish. According to our host, this is "un piatto di grande effetto e di molto figura," "a dish of great effect and impressiveness."

SCAMPI ALLA MORO

½ lb. scampi or prawns per portion	salt and pepper
	fresh lemon juice
olive oil	butter

Cut the shellfish in half lengthwise, leaving them in their shells. De-vein under cold running water. Arrange them in a flat pan or baking dish with a little olive oil, and season with salt and pepper. Cook them in a 375° oven for 10–15 minutes, watching them carefully so that they do not overcook. When they are pink and done through, pour over them fresh lemon juice, enough to flavor each one, and dot liberally with butter. Return to the oven for five minutes to absorb the lemon and butter bath and serve immediately. [At Moro's they prepare squid in exactly the same manner with great success. If you try this substitution, double the cooking time for squid of about three ounce size (five or six to the pound). You can also vary the basic recipe, whether you use prawns, scampi, or squid, by sprinkling on any of a number of minced herbs or garlic, according to your mood. Both white wine and cognac add a richness that is agreeable.]

POLLO ALLA DIAVOLA
(Chicken alla Diavola)

1 young chicken of not more than 3 lbs.	salt and pepper olive oil

Halve a young chicken, season it with salt, pepper, and olive oil, and put it in a frying pan. Cover it with an iron or aluminum lid that is smaller than the circumference of the pan so that it rests directly on the chicken. On the lid place a bowl or pot full of water to act as a weight. Cook over a *slow* fire for 20–25 minutes, or until the underside is well browned. Turn and continue cooking until the second side is brown and the second joint is tender (about 20 minutes more). [Signor Romagnoli likes to serve his pollo alla diavola accompanied by an insalata capricciosa, a salad whose exact ingredients depend on what was gathered in the fields, and on the whimsy of the cook. I sometimes add fresh rosemary and a touch of garlic to the seasonings of the chicken.]

Porcini (boletus edulis), wild brown-capped mushrooms, cost dearly in their season, but are still used frequently in Italian cooking. They are available dried all year around. So great a variety of

103

mushrooms grow wild or under cultivation in Italy, that the seller in the local market place is a specialist who deals in nothing else. Some mushrooms flaunt ruffled combs to rival any cock's; others resemble a sponge; and even those that grow in an expected shape and color may, in some varieties, reach proportions that would shield a good sized elf. Signor Romagnoli has a recipe of the utmost simplicity for a porcini delicacy that you will be able to reproduce even with cultivated mushrooms. Although Italians generally peel field mushrooms very carefully, you will only need to scrub the cultivated variety. Here is Moro's recipe:

FUNGHI PORCINI AL FORNO
(Baked Wild Mushrooms)

1 lb. large mushrooms	¼ cup olive oil
3 large cloves garlic	salt and pepper
6 wooden toothpicks	fresh chopped parsley

Use the largest mushrooms you can find; the Italian dish uses porcini often 3 or 4 inches across. Scrub with a rough brush or cloth until clean and smooth. Remove the stems and save for another purpose. Place the mushroom caps, cap-side down, in a baking dish. Cut three large cloves of garlic in half and thread these pieces on six toothpicks. Place these in the pan among the mushroom caps. Pour ¼ cup of olive oil over the mushrooms so that each mushroom is anointed and the bottom of the dish is moistened. Adjust the garlic pieces so that they are immersed in the oil. Sprinkle with salt and pepper. Put in a 400° oven for 5 minutes. Baste carefully with the garlic-flavored oil and return to the oven for 5 minutes or until they are cooked. Before serving, discard the garlic and sprinkle with freshly chopped parsley. Makes four generous portions. [I find that the large hothouse mushrooms I use require about ten minutes additional baking time. For an elegant platter, prepare these mushrooms the next time you broil steak—filets or other individual cuts are best—and when the steak is ready, arrange it on a warm dish, put a large dab of butter and one sprig of a fresh herb like marjoram or rosemary on each portion, and pour the mushrooms and their juice over all.]

CARCIOFI AL PINZIMONIO
(Raw Artichokes and Dipping Sauce)

At Moro you can eat a splendid appetizer called carciofi al pinzimonio, crisp raw artichokes with a sauce of olive oil, salt and pepper for dipping. This dish depends not only on the Roman artichoke but on its crisp second growth. Even if you are fortunate enough, as are some Californians, to be able to obtain young and tender produce that can be eaten immature, choke and all, it will not substitute raw for its Roman counterpart. In this country, the pinzimonio can be used with steamed artichokes, or as a dip for other uncooked vegetables such as celery, fennel, radishes, or peppers. Wash well whatever vegetable you choose, cut in dip size pieces and sprinkle generously with lemon juice. Keep cold until ready to serve. Arrange on a platter around a cup containing the pinzimonio, made of one cup of the best olive oil, salt, and pepper, either freshly ground black, or the grated dried red variety.

FRAGOLINE ALL'ACETO
(Wild Strawberries with Vinegar)

If you have the kind of wine vinegar that Moro does, this is one of the most delicious of all ways to prepare fresh strawberries. When the tiny wood berries are in season, Moro dresses them (or the big, cultivated variety) with a splash of mild vinegar and lots of sugar. Well mixed, the berries repose for at least several minutes, better a half hour or more. They should be served slightly chilled. No trace of vinegar taste remains, only the intensified perfume of the strawberries. [Experiment with a few berries and the best mild vinegar you can find to work out the proportions for this recipe.]

GIOVANNI

THE first thing that strikes you at Giovanni's small restaurant is the number of fond reunions between travelers, who return with steadfast devotion, and the large family that runs the place. There are handshakes all around, and everyone exchanges affectionate reminiscences. The Sbrega family, headed by father Giovanni, holds all the positions from chef to cashier. Wife and brother are in the kitchen to help Papa, and his sons and daughters scurry through the small room or out to the few sidewalk tables, fetching up steaming platters of home-made pasta, crusty roast abbacchio, or freshly sliced peaches mixed with just the proper amount of lemon juice and sugar. Daughters Lilli and Gabriella can point out the day's specialties in charming English or French. One of the brothers is an accountant when he isn't carrying trays at the restaurant (he speaks French and English, too). Giovanni began work as a cook's helper in a Rome restaurant when he was thirteen years old. From that time on he had a passion to cook. He never uses cook books—and never has, says he—but has learned everything through apprenticeship coupled with a bit of experiment and a good deal of natural talent. After many years he managed to save enough to start up the small restaurant in the Via Marche. That was some thirty years ago. Basically the place hasn't changed. The accommodations, though up-to-date, are quiet and modest. No Sbrega has ever felt the temptation to emulate his swanky Via Veneto neighbors.

The menu runs to unsophisticated dishes that are especially good because everything is home-made and market-fresh. The pasta is always light and well sauced. Among Giovanni's specialties are fish from the Adriatic, where only the best fish get caught; a splendid roast abbacchio; and cannelloni. Here are his recipes for each of the specialties:

106

SOGLIOLE AI FERRI ALL'ITALIANA
(Grilled Sole, Italian Style)

Use one sole per portion. Clean the fish thoroughly, strip off the black skin from the back, wash, pat dry, and dredge with flour. Pour or brush a little olive oil on the grill, and place the fish on it, cooking until it takes on a clear golden color. Serve with lemon wedges.

ABBACCHIO ARROSTO
(Roast Lamb)

Signor Giovanni advises that the very best cut of lamb for this dish is that quarter which comprises the loin and kidney up to the first ribs. It should be milk-fed, and therefore very tender. We do not have the equivalent meat in the United States except in a few areas with large Italian populations, where local butchers offer baby lamb at a premium.

Wash the lamb well, pat it dry, and place it in a roasting pan. Sprinkle it with salt, a little olive oil, and three ounces of butter cut into three pieces—one at each end, and the third at the center. Put it into the oven, preheated to 475°, and roast it for at least 45 minutes. During this time, baste the meat well every five or ten minutes with the oil, butter and pan juices. [The addition of garlic and rosemary will give a more robust flavor.]

PATATE ARROSTE
(Roast Potatoes)

To roast potatoes along with the meat, wash and peel one potato per portion. Slice into two-inch pieces, the width and thickness of French fries. Use a roasting pan large enough to accommodate both meat and potatoes easily. Place the potatoes in one part, the meat in the other. Sprinkle the potatoes with oil, salt and pepper, and dot generously with butter. Turn and baste them three or four times during the cooking so that they brown evenly. If you add garlic and rosemary to the meat, sprinkle some on the potatoes, too.

CANNELLONI AL FORNO

filling:

½ lb. veal browned in butter
   or oil
2 tbsp. butter

5 tbsp. grated Parmesan
   cheese
nutmeg

béchamel sauce:

2 tbsp. butter
2 tbsp. flour

1 to 1½ cups milk
salt

tomato sauce: (2 or more cups)

oil and butter
1 onion, chopped
1 carrot, chopped
1 stalk celery, chopped

3 cups fresh tomatoes, in
   chunks
fresh basil
salt and pepper

pasta:

2½ cups flour
2 eggs

salt
water

seasoning:

4 tbsp. grated Parmesan cheese

FILLING: Put the cooked veal through the food chopper, add the butter, Parmesan cheese, and a good grating of nutmeg. Mix together until well blended, and put aside.

BÉCHAMEL SAUCE: In a saucepan melt the butter, add the flour a little at a time, mixing well, then the milk (prewarmed), mixing continuously. Cook about ten minutes until you obtain a smooth, thick sauce, and the flour is well cooked.

TOMATO SAUCE: To the pan in which the meat cooked, add a little oil and butter, and sauté in it one chopped onion, one chopped carrot, one chopped stalk of celery. Add about three cups of fresh tomatoes in chunks, a little fresh basil, a clove or two of minced garlic, a scattering of parsley, and salt and pepper. When it has reduced to a thick sauce after about two hours of simmering, strain it through a coarse mesh.

PASTA: Make a dough of the sifted flour, eggs, a few drops of water as needed, and the salt. Work it well—for at least ten minutes. Roll it out into thin sheets, and cut these into rectangles of three or four inches. Let them dry on towels for about twenty minutes. Put a very large pot full of salted water to boil, and when the water races throw in the squares, a few at a time. When they rise to the surface, let them cook another minute or two, then scoop them out with a draining spoon. Dip them at once in a pot of cold water, then set them side by side on a damp cloth to drain. Distribute the meat filling, a little on each rectangle, and roll them up like little tubes. Butter a large shallow casserole or baking dish, place the filled and rolled squares side by side in it, bathe them with the béchamel sauce and the tomato sauce. Dot here and there with dabs of butter and sprinkle grated Parmesan cheese over all. Bake in a moderate oven for fifteen to twenty minutes. Serve immediately. This makes twenty-four small cannelloni or eighteen slightly larger. Serves six. [This is the simplest of the cannelloni recipes in this book.]

CHECCHINO DAL 1887

CHECCHINO, one of Rome's great trattorie, is located in the midst of a strange quarter. Just across the square is the city's slaughter house, il mattatoio, which accounts for the restaurant's alternate name, Checchino al mattatoio, as well as for some of its specialties. Not far off is the antique Aurelian wall. Close by rises the ancient Pyramid of Cestus, one of the best preserved and also most startling of Rome's antiquities, a sepulchral monument to the Roman tribune who died several years B. C. Next to the

Pyramid spreads the Protestant cemetery, where Percy Bysshe Shelley, John Keats, his artist friend Joseph Severn, Goethe's son, and Tolstoy's daughter lie less ostentatiously commemorated.

In Roman times storehouses for oils and wines lined the Tiber's banks from the slaughter house to the Aventine, and one spot became the dumping ground for the broken clay storage vessels. Its name, Monte Testaccio, in fact derives from the mound of potsherds, which eventually reached mountainous size: over 100 feet in height and some 900 yards around. About 900 A. D. the inhabitants discovered that the terracotta mountain possessed characteristics very well suited to the storage of wine: it maintained a fairly constant temperature, no matter how uneven the actual heat, warming in the winter and cooling in the summer. They began excavations for a series of caves, which by papal decree came into private ownership around 1600. The kitchen, canteen and dining room of Checchino are partly excavated from the original clay caves. During the Middle Ages this same area was a favorite site for jousting and tournaments.

The trattoria, a relative newcomer to the locality, began operations in 1887 as the Trattoria dell'Olmo, a name suggested by a huge and prospering elm tree nearby. Its first directors were the great grandfather, then the grandmother, of the present owner. During her reign, Sora Ferminia's specialties made the place famous. She handed the business on to her son, Francesco Mariani, who gave it his nickname, Checchino. Today Francesco's red-bearded son Sergio manages the business end of things and Sergio's mother takes charge of the kitchen.

The restaurant is the seat of the Academy of Italian Cuisine, which honored it with a diploma for excellence in cooking in 1958. A year earlier the Italian Chamber of Commerce bestowed on it a gold medal. It is no surprise that the guest book should be brimming with signatures—some of them illustrious—nor that Signor Mariani should have on hand a collection of appreciative letters from Checchino patrons as far afield as Australia, Japan,

110

Germany, England and Ethiopia. In the guest album Elsa Maxwell enthused, "Checchino!! a wonderful dinner, a wonderful place, a charming patron! Thank you!!" Although the hosts are delighted with the number of celebrities who swell these lists, they are most proud of those diners who are, as Signor Mariani explained to me, "simpatici clienti . . . . . . sconosciuti, non noti, ma veramente buongustai che danno tanta soddisfazione." —"Most congenial clients . . . . . . unknown, not famous, but truly connoisseurs who give us much pleasure."

Checchino's raised hearth provides a cheerful winter blaze, and its terrace is refreshing in the summer. Its cooking is traditional Roman, and the best of its kind. Here is the place to try such typical fare as rigatoni con pagliata, coda alla vaccinara, trippa alla romana, abbacchio alla cacciatora or alla romana, carciofi alla giudia, animelle di vitello ai ferri, and pollo alla diavola. And you will be surprised at the reasonable cost.

Signor Mariani has kindly given me the recipe for the tender oxtail alla vaccinara, and also the secret of his superb pagliata.

CODA ALLA VACCINARA
(Stewed Oxtail)

1 fat oxtail	tomato sauce [optional]
3 tbsp. lard and olive oil	6 small stalks white celery with
1 onion, chopped	leaves
2 cloves garlic	fistful of pine nuts
a few cloves	2 tbsp. raisins
salt and pepper	½ oz. or 2 tbsp. grated bitter
½ glass white wine	chocolate
2 cups stewed plum tomatoes	

Select a good fat oxtail, wash it well, and cut it into discs. Blend about 3 tbsp. lard and olive oil and heat in a heavy-bottomed skillet. Add the oxtail. When it is brown (remember to turn it continuously) add the chopped onion, two buds of garlic, a few cloves, and salt and pepper. After some minutes, add the white wine, and cook

111

for fifteen minutes longer, covered. Add the stewed tomatoes, simmer for an hour longer, then cover with hot water (mixed with a bit of tomato sauce if you like), cover the pot tightly and simmer very slowly for 5 to 6 hours, until the meat falls away from the bone. During this time, take some white celery, remove any stringy pieces, and boil the stalks with the leaves on until soft. Reserve until the oxtail is cooked. Then take a little of the gravy of the oxtail and mix it with the drained, boiled celery, a fistful of pine nuts, the raisins, and grated bitter chocolate. Bring to a boil and after 5 minutes pour it over the oxtail. Blend and serve immediately. [The number of portions depends on the size of the oxtail you get. The sauce will serve eight. Three-quarters of a pound of meat per person makes a reasonable serving—about three medium discs or two large.]

RIGATONI CON LA PAGLIATA
(According to the old recipe of Sora Ferminia,
cooked this way at Checchino since the late 1800's)

[Pagliata, also written pajata, is tripe, but not the honeycomb variety. It is the part of the intestine that contains juices of indescribable flavor, close to that of the giblets of fowl, though far richer. It is most difficult to obtain in the United States, and neither the texture nor the flavor of ordinary tripe can substitute for it. This recipe may be made using giblets, and the result, though it will bear only a pale resemblance to the original, will nevertheless be very good.]

1 lb. pagliata, the tubular intestine of beef
3 tbsp. olive oil and lard
1 onion, chopped
1 clove garlic
salt and pepper

a few cloves
½ cup dry white wine
2 cups stewed plum tomatoes
2 tbsp. tomato paste
1 to 2 lbs. rigatoni
Parmesan cheese

Skin the pagliata, cut it in pieces of about eight inches without severing one piece completely from the other. [Or, better, ask the butcher to skin it and tie the sections into doughnut-like pieces, easier to work with than the partially-cut variety.] In a heavy copper skillet put a mixture of 3 tbsp. olive oil and lard. Keep the fire moderately high and after the fat has melted add the pagliata. It is indispensable to turn the pagliata continuously until it is brown. A few seconds before the end of the browning, add one chopped onion, one clove of garlic, salt, pepper, a few cloves, and the dry white wine. Cover the pot and continue to cook over a high flame until the wine is almost all absorbed. It is important to uncover and stir frequently, lest it become crusty.

Having reduced the sauce, add two cups stewed plum tomatoes. Lower the fire (keep the pot always covered), and after a half hour of cooking, add a little tomato paste. The complete cooking takes around three hours.

When the pagliata is ready, boil rigatoni (1 to 2 pounds, depending on the quality and your appetite) until just tender (al dente), which should take about fifteen minutes. Drain, return to the fire, add a good sprinkling of grated Parmesan cheese and a little sauce, stir gently, and heat through. Turn them out steaming onto a hot platter, pour the pagliata and its sauce over the rigatoni, and serve at once. Makes four large servings.

[To substitute giblets, use ¼ lb. per serving.]

CELESTINA

PARIOLI is a comparatively new and upper bracket quarter of Rome, close to the main downtown area. Its streets still contain a number of pleasantly faded umber walls alternating with the swanky new white ones, but its iron-railed balconies are giving way to modernistic decks and flower-filled pent-house terraces. Wash still flies defiantly from some balconies, but in most cases it hangs discreetly on the rooftop clotheslines preferred by Parioli managements. Maids in this neighborhood seldom beat the bed-

113

ding over the window sills or the rugs over the railings, and shouting is reserved for only the most urgent situations. The United States Ambassador's large, walled estate is one of many diplomatic residences, and the Villa Borghese, with its gardens, hippodrome, museum, and zoo, borders one side of the district. The great Etruscan museum, the Villa Giulia, as well as the modern art museum, are also in the neighborhood, so even though the modish streets and modern markets are less lively than many other sections of the city, you may often find yourself spending time in Parioli.

There is a pleasant and moderately priced restaurant, Celestina, on the broad Viale Parioli, where the walks of the avenue are ample enough to provide it with a whole summer dining terrace. When it started there some forty years ago, the open countryside surrounded it; now its neighbors are shops and markets, and the chirp of the bird and the cricket has yielded to the din and rumble of modern traffic. The proprietors, who were born in the province of Romagna, where some of the best of all Italian cooking originates, haven't changed their ways a bit. They believe in personal supervision, and ever since they opened Celestina they have taken care of their customers as if they were part of one big family.

Romagnola cooking is characteristically well seasoned, often rich and melting with cheeses. Celestina's menu has a few samples of regional dishes, most notably green lasagne baked creamy between layers of sauce and blankets of cheese, and cotoletta alla bolognese, a breaded veal cutlet glorified with a cover of ham and runny cheese. The pasta here is delicate and well sauced. The tortellini, little stuffed rings of paste, generally served at Celestina in broth, are as good as you will find. The egg noodles are usually served with one of the rich meat sauces characteristic of the Bologna region. Celestina turns out a particularly crisp chicken alla diavola, and a classic dish of saltimbocca alla romana, one of the recipes Luigi Rodriguez has kindly given me.

114

SALTIMBOCCA ALLA ROMANA

per portion:

about 3 ounces young veal	olive oil
½ to 1 sage leaf	lump of butter
1 slice prosciutto	Marsala [optional]
wooden toothpick	

Cut the veal into very thin slices, remove all fat, and pound to tenderize if necessary. Cut these slices into rectangles and place on each one at least half a leaf of sage and a thin slice of prosciutto cut the same size as the veal rectangle. Attach the sage leaf and prosciutto to the veal by threading a wooden toothpick through them. Do not use any salt in this recipe. Cook gently, veal side down, in a little olive oil. When the veal is browned, turn the saltimbocca so that the prosciutto can brown. When it is a good color, add a generous lump of butter. Serve the meat with the sauce poured over it. For a richer dish, add a little Marsala after the butter melts.

UCCELLINI SCAPATI
(Veal Birds)

1 lb. veal, cut into very thin slices	1 sage leaf for each veal slice
salt and pepper	several slices of bacon
1 slice of prosciutto for each veal slice	butter
	broth

Pound the veal slices well. Season each slice with salt and pepper, cover with a slice of prosciutto and a leaf of fresh sage. Roll up each seasoned veal slice into a sausage shape, and thread these on small skewers, with a piece of bacon in between each roll. Melt a good lump of butter in a frying pan larger than the skewers, and set the veal in it to brown. When they have taken on a good color, add a few drops of broth from time to time, and continue cooking for about a half hour, or until tender. Serve covered with the gravy and

115

surrounded by puréed potatoes, into which, besides the usual butter and cream, you can mash a spoon or two of grated Parmesan cheese. Serves six.

[The Italians often adapt this recipe to the broiler. It is usual to thread chunks of French bread along with the veal birds and bacon, and to anoint the whole with oil or melted butter, mixed with a bit of white wine if you like. Another variation is the addition, in either recipe, of a slice of mozzarella cheese along with the sage and prosciutto.]

ERNESTO

SIGHTSEERS, though they frequent Ernesto's general neighborhood, often overlook the Piazza dei Santi 12 Apostoli where the restaurant is located. It is close by the Corso, the long avenue that runs from its far end in the Piazza del Popolo into the famous Piazza Venezia. This square boasts one of Rome's most beautiful buildings, the Palazzo Venezia, which Mussolini occupied during his regime and from whose balcony he often harangued the crowds. It also houses what is known as the "wedding cake," a monstrously ornate monument to the second Victor Emanuel. But the fanciest thing in the square has nothing to do with architecture. The traffic policeman, mounted on a podium in the middle of the piazza, swoops, arches, pirouettes, and gesticulates, and although his studied motions are completely incomprehensible, the mere crook of a wrist sends terrifying streams of traffic rushing headlong hither and yon.

Just out of this bustle is the quiet Piazza dei Santi 12 Apostoli, characteristic of the city during the reign of the popes. In those days the strangely elongated square was a very upper class residential neighborhood, filled with the palaces of some of the most famous of Rome's princes: Odescalchi, Barberini, Palestra, Co-

116

lonna. The most patrician building of them all was the Colonna palace on the eastern flank, so grand that it incorporated the church of the Santi Apostoli with no more effort than that of a mother hen taking a chick under her wing.

Number 49 at the end of the square was for more than two hundred years a comfortable inn, especially noted for its Est!Est!! Est!!! Nowadays it is the pleasantly modish restaurant Ernesto, a haven for game lovers and enthusiasts of good cooking generally. Ernesto Cavicchia, the proprietor for well over twenty years, has managed to keep the scale intimate, the walls stacked high with wine bottles against handsome dark wood paneling, and the buffet laden with all kinds of goodies. More recently he has opened Ernesto alla Cassia (Via Oriolo Romano 59, tel. 32 26 15) about five miles out of town on the Via Cassia Nuova. It is constructed on a spacious scale, has a generous outdoor dining area for the warm months of the year, and an excellent, price-fixed, several-coursed dinner no matter what the season.

Among the specialties at Ernesto's in town are bucatini alla amatriciana, long thin macaroni sauced according to a traditional Roman recipe with bacon, onions, tomatoes, and sharp pecorino cheese. Spaghetti alla carbonara, another Rome favorite, is tossed with bacon, raw beaten eggs, and grated Parmesan cheese. Ernesto makes delicate cheese cannelloni, filling the squares of egg dough with a mixture of ricotta, brandy, egg, and a sprinkle of parsley, before baking them with béchamel and tomato sauces, gobs of butter, and a generous spread of cheese over the top. Another specialty is rigatoni all'ammiraglia, large tubes of pasta dressed with an assortment of seafood. Ernesto makes fine cozze al gratté, plump mussels baked with a crust of seasoned breadcrumbs; and a spirited insalata di frutti di mare, mixed seafood, greens, and celery tossed in a nippy oil-and-vinegar dressing. His country-style omelette, frittata alla burina, encloses an assortment of sautéed vegetables, and is delicious served cold.

117

In the winter season, Ernesto's menu sends game lovers into ecstasies. Wild boar simmered in a sweet and sour sauce harks back to ancient Roman tastes. The ancestral recipe combined honey, mustard, vinegar, dates, and pine nuts. Ernesto puts his boar to simmer in vinegar and pine nuts, too, but he adds chocolate and prunes to his sauce. This dish is for adventurous souls, and nobody will be offended if you order your boar just plain roasted instead. Partridge and quail are cooked with crusty bread chunks, pheasants and the long-beaked woodcock with polenta, and wild duck lends its flavor to the rice that accompanies it.

Ernesto has given me three recipes, each a specialty of the house.

INSALATA DI FRUTTI DI MARE
(Seafood Salad)

seafood:

1 cup cleaned mussels
½ cup cleaned small clams
2 cups squid and cuttlefish
½ cup baby octopi (the size of a thumb nail)
1 cup lobster meat
6 large prawns
1 cup shrimp

court bouillon (celery, carrot, onion, parsley, lemon, garlic, salt, pepper, white wine)
lemon, garlic and salt to cook the squid and cuttlefish
heart of romaine lettuce
1 small firm bunch celery, or 1 celery heart

sauce:

¾ cup of olive oil and wine vinegar mixed, 2 parts oil to 1 part vinegar
1 tbsp. minced filets of anchovy
¼ tsp. French mustard
¼ tsp. English mustard

2 pinches powdered hot red pepper
a few drops of Worcestershire sauce
1 clove garlic, minced as fine as possible
a squeeze of fresh lemon
salt and pepper

118

If you start with mussels and clams still in their shells, scrub well, put in frying pans over high heat (with a drop of oil if you like, or a small amount of water with the clams) and cook until the shells open. Remove from the pan, then from the shells, strain a bit of the pan liquor over them, and let them repose a while in order that any remaining sand can settle out. Clean the squid and cuttlefish, remove ink sacks, bones, and skin if necessary, cut into pieces, put to boil for about a half hour or until tender. Add a few slices of lemon, a clove of garlic cut in two, and some salt to the boiling water. Clean the baby octopi and boil with lemon, garlic, and salt until tender. Poach the lobster, prawns, and shrimp in a court bouillon composed of cut up celery, carrot, onion, parsley, a few lemon slices, garlic, salt and pepper, water, and white wine. Cook until the shells turn a good pink color. Drain, remove the meat from the shells, cut into good size dice. [It may be that your fish market will have done all the preparatory labor for you, and that you can buy your clams, shrimp, and squid all ready to use.]

Mix together in a large bowl all of the shellfish and squid family, first being sure that everything is cut to about the same size. Wash the heart of a romaine lettuce, about six or eight small leaves in all, and break these into several pieces (about two inch size). Cut a washed heart of celery, or several firm stalks, into small pieces. Add the lettuce and celery to the seafood. Mix together all of the ingredients for the sauce, stir well, and turn over the salad. Mix a few minutes, then refrigerate until time to serve. Serves six.

[NOTE: Ernesto also uses sea dates—datteri di mare—shellfish that resemble mussels; sea truffles—tartufi di mare—that are closer to a clam with a ribbed shell; and scampi, shrimp, *and* prawns. Substitutions can be made according to what is available in your locality, since it is the mixture of textures and flavors that gives this salad interest.]

℥ FRITTATA ALLA BURINA (RURALE)
(Omelette, Country-Style)

2 zucchine
2 small (baby) artichokes, or the hearts and bottoms of 4 large artichokes
4 mushrooms
1 onion

olive oil
butter
6 eggs
salt and pepper
6 tbsp. tomato sauce

Cut the zucchine, artichokes, mushrooms, and onion into small pieces or slices. Fry them gently in olive oil and butter in a skillet that can go into the oven. When they are almost cooked, pour over them the six eggs, well beaten and seasoned with salt and pepper, and continue cooking until the eggs are partly firm. Spoon over the eggs six tablespoons of tomato sauce, and bake in a 350° oven for about ten minutes. Can be served hot or cold. Serves six. To increase or decrease, figure one egg per portion, and a proportionate amount of vegetables and other ingredients. You can also vary the vegetables, depending on what is available. Peppers and eggplant are good additions.

℥ RIGATONI ALL'AMMIRAGLIA
(Rigatoni with Seafood)

2 cups boiled squid
1 cup boiled clams
1 cup boiled mussels
6 scampi or prawns, or an equivalent weight of shrimp
½ lb. mushrooms
lemon, garlic, salt to cook the squid
court bouillon to cook the scampi

½ cup olive oil
2 cloves garlic, minced
1 small onion, minced
salt
1½ cups stewed tomatoes
1 cup dry white wine
hot red pepper (dry)
1 lb. rigatoni
chopped fresh parsley

120

Prepare the squid, clams, mussels, and scampi as described above (Insalata di Frutti di Mare). Reserve the clam liquor and court bouillon, and cut all the meat into pieces. Clean and slice the mushrooms. In a half cup of hot olive oil sauté the minced onion and garlic until it begins to take on a golden color. Add the sliced mushrooms and cook until lightly browned. Sprinkle with a little salt. Add stewed tomatoes and white wine and simmer until slightly reduced. Add the seafood, adjust salt to taste, and sprinkle in a few pinches of dried hot red pepper or fresh ground black pepper. Simmer about five minutes. If sauce becomes too thick, add some of the reserved cooking bouillon. Boil one pound of rigatoni in briskly racing salted water until just tender. Drain, turn into a hot serving bowl, and pour one-half of the seafood sauce over them. Mix well. Pour the rest of the sauce over the top, and serve immediately with a garnish of fresh chopped parsley. Serves six.

ℜ *TRATTORIA SILVANO PARIS* ℜ

THE secret of Paris, one of the most popular of Rome's trattorias, seems to be family continuity. Dario Paris founded the place in 1890, and turned it over to his son Giacomo after thirty years. The present proprietor, Giacomo's son Silvano, began his reign in 1958, and will continue, as he laughingly puts it, "we hope until 2000." The cook is Silvano's lovely wife Clara, who at first spent some time in the kitchen with the former chef—Silvano's mother.

The setting is best described as "folcloristico," a reflection of the spirit and tradition of Trastevere. This is the area of the wandering minstrel, the Roman folk singer, and the furtive little man with briefcase full of black market cigarettes. Those who dine here in summer will find their tables in the Piazza San

Calisto, just across from the Palazzo of the same name, a seventeenth century construction that was originally a cardinal's seat,
for many years a Benedictine monastery, and later the office of
the Congregation of Rites (familiar to readers of Morris West's
The Devil's Advocate, whose hero sat under its coffered ceilings
pondering the voluminous files of candidates for canonization).

At Paris, the specialties are about equally divided between land-
and seafood. A portion of mixed seafood salad, antipasto di mare,
will sharpen your appetite at the beginning of the meal. Its oil
and vinegar dressing is brightly accented with capers. Among the
pasta dishes there are several specialties to take note of: the rigatoni alla norcina, made with pure pork sausage (a norcino is a
pork butcher); homemade cannelloni from an old family recipe;
thin spaghetti sauced with assorted shellfish, spaghettini all'ammiraglia; and an excellent dish of rice cooked fisherman's style,
risotto alla pescatore.

Among the veal dishes, the tordi matti (veal birds) and lombata di vitellino al cartoccio con funghi (a thick loin of veal chop
smothered in mushrooms and capers, and tucked away to bake
in a huge parchment envelope) are especially delicious. The ostrica, a veal sandwich enclosing mozzarella and prosciutto, is out
of the ordinary, and the recipe is among those that follow. There
is a fresh assortment of fish daily, and the house specializes in
grilling them tenderly over the coals. The delicate scampi are famous among Paris devotees, and here is Clara's recipe for making
them on the piastra or griddle.

SCAMPI GIGANTI ALLA PIASTRA
(Giant Scampi on the Griddle)

scampi	olive oil
salt and pepper	a griddle
chopped parsley	

Split the scampi down the middle, wash and de-vein (leaving them in the shells). Heat the griddle very hot and brush with oil. Season the scampi with salt and pepper and put to cook. When they are done, remove them to a serving platter, sprinkle with the chopped parsley, and splash them with olive oil. Serve at once.

OSTRICA DI VITELLO
(Veal "Oysters")

per portion:

2 slices of veal steak, ¼ lb. each	wooden toothpicks
1 slice prosciutto (San Daniele, if possible)	salt and pepper
	butter
1 slice mozzarella (di bufala, if possible)	olive oil
	about ¼ cup dry white wine
1 sage leaf	1 clove garlic
	sage leaves

The recipe calls for the "noce" of veal, the nut or kernel next to the bottom round, but you can use any tender steak cut from the leg. Each pair of slices should be of approximately the same size and shape. On one slice of a pair, put one slice of prosciutto (Paris uses the ham cured in San Daniele), one slice of mozzarella (at Paris it is made from buffalo milk), and a leaf of sage. Cover the ham and cheese with the other slice of veal, and secure the "sandwich" with wooden toothpicks. Spread a flame-proof earthenware casserole with butter and a little olive oil, and arrange the skewered meats in it. Set to cook slowly for about ten minutes, turning once during the cooking so as to brown both sides. As soon as the meat has taken on a good brown color, pour some dry white wine over it, add a well-minced clove of garlic, and a few leaves of sage. Cook until the sauce reduces and the garlic is cooked—several minutes longer. Remove the toothpicks, arrange the meat on a warm serving platter, and pour over it the juices and scrapings from the pan. It is best to add salt and pepper at the table after tasting, since the saltiness of the prosciutto may vary.

123

RIGATONI ALLA NORCINA
(Rigatoni, Pork Butcher's Style)

1 lb. rigatoni	1½ cups grated Parmesan
1 pork sausage (about ½ lb.)	cheese
¼ lb. butter	salt and pepper

Bring a large pot of salted water to a rapid boil, throw in the rigatoni, and boil vigorously for about fifteen minutes, or until just tender (al dente). Drain and put them, without water, into a large pan on the fire over low heat. Add immediately one pork sausage, ground or finely crumbled (and best, I think, precooked), the butter in chunks, and one cup of the grated cheese. Mix with a wooden spoon, and cook for seven or eight minutes, stirring frequently, until the butter, cheese, and sausage are well blended. Add salt and pepper to taste. Turn out onto a service platter and sprinkle the rest of the cheese over the top. Serves four.

ALFREDO ALLA SCROFA
ALFREDO ALL'AUGUSTEO
ALFREDO IN TRASTEVERE

"I suppose you'll be going to Europe pretty soon again, won't you?" he invited.

"I'd like awfully to run over to Rome for a few weeks."

"I suppose you see a lot of pictures and music and curios and everything there."

"No, what I really go for is: there's a little *trattoria* on the Via della Scrofa where you get the best *fettuccine* in the world."

—SINCLAIR LEWIS, *Babbitt* (1922)

124

Of the several Alfredo restaurants in Rome, two base their fame on exactly the same noodles, and in fact, on the very same Alfredo. However, they are not branches of the same organization, but in lively competition, and they are furthermore each quite good. It is possible for both to claim truthfully the same origin, recipes, and specialties, for they were both founded by Alfredo Di Lelio, and continue to base their famous dishes on his early recipes.

Alfredo alla Scrofa is the original restaurant, dating from 1914, but the Di Lelio family no longer runs it. Ubaldo Salvatori, the present owner, has worked there since 1940, several years before Alfredo retired. For an interval after the senior Di Lelio left the business, his son took over its direction, but the lure of leisure was only temporary, and Alfredo decided to come out of retirement. He opened a new and grander place, Alfredo all'Augusteo, in the nearby piazza of Augustus Caesar's tomb, and there, amid lowered lights, leaping flames, and musical fanfares, he began dispensing the same recipes, performing the same ceremonies, and perpetuating the same claims to distinction that had brought him his original success. His son Armando, rather than compete with father, soon joined him, and has been the sole director since 1959, when Alfredo died.

Although both establishments are somewhat flamboyant, my own nerves fare better at Alfredo in the Via della Scrofa. There are marble floors and crystal chandeliers, and an avalanche of pictures and autographs covering the walls, a collection that Alfredo Di Lelio started forty years ago. You may find yourself eating in photographic proximity to Gregory Peck, Fernandel, Audrey Hepburn, James Stewart, or Gary Cooper, but whether your ambrosial egg noodles are really being tossed with the genuine gold utensils presented to Alfredo in the Twenties by Douglas Fairbanks and Mary Pickford, is a question that no one will answer.

Alfredo in Trastevere, no relation to the other two, also makes a claim to having the lightest, the butteriest, the most majestic fettuccine in Rome. In fact, he goes even further. This Alfredo claims to be "the King of Spaghetti alla Carbonara *and* Fettuccine." But his restaurant really bases its reputation on a whole complex of Roman dishes, and on the lovely Trastevere square in which it is set. For more than forty years it has been under the direction of its original owner, Alfredo Innocenzi. Within the last few years the Innocenzi family has followed the restaurant trend to the outskirts of Rome by opening what the Italians call a "restaurant-dancing," the Quo Vadis (Via Appia Antica 38). Alfredo, Jr. watches over those premises, but makes no claims at all about fettuccine. The menu there, besides dishes of an international variety, lists specialties of meat, fish, and fowl from the spit and grill.

At Alfredo alla Scrofa *the* pasta specialty, of course, is fettuccine, ribbons of egg pasta tossed with amazing rapidity to mix in three huge lumps of butter and heaps of powdery cheese. For the next course, the specialties are petti di pollo alla cardinale, chicken breasts cooked with prosciutto, cheese, and a good dunking of wine; and golden, pan-fried turkey breasts, filetti di tacchino dorato. There are fine sautées of kidneys and mushrooms, or sweetbreads and mushrooms with slivers of prosciutto added. In warm weather there is cold veal with a tuna and caper topping, and always delicate sole prepared with white wine and mushrooms. The dessert specialty is omelette flambée, but there is also chocolate cake, St. Honoré, Sicilian cassata, and sometimes wild strawberries from Nemi, that cost as much as a main course, but are worth it! Your total bill will be moderate enough, unless you have dined on imported foie gras, caviar, or filet of beef cut to order, all available here too.

The Alfredo recipe for fettuccine remains a secret shared by the two rival houses, but every Roman has his idea about the way they are made. Some say that it is the addition of a bit of oil to the dough that keeps the noodles so moist and light. Others say, not at all; it is the fact that they are cooked in milk instead

126

of water. Another school attributes the creaminess of the sauce to the quality of the cheese. They insist that the secret is to use cheese that is *not* old and very dry, the kind most usually touted as superior, but one that is still moist and therefore melts easily. Everyone seems to agree that the serving platter must be hot and the butter soft. The recipe that follows was given me by a Milanese friend, who says it was long ago given to her by the noodle king himself. It certainly tastes authentic.

FETTUCCINE ALL'ALFREDO
(Egg Noodles in the Style of Alfredo)

about 1 lb. fettuccine

4 handfuls grated Parmesan cheese, plus more cheese to sprinkle on

¼ lb. butter

½ pt. whipping cream

To make the fettuccine, use recipe for egg pasta, page 238. When the dough is rolled out into thin sheets, sprinkle with a light dusting of flour, then roll them up like jelly rolls. Cut through each roll at ¼ to ⅜ inch intervals, pick up each cut section by the middle and shake, and the long streamers will uncurl like confetti. Lay them out flat on towels, to dry for at least a half hour before cooking. Boil in plenty of salted water for only two or three minutes, as homemade pasta cooks very quickly. They tend to come to the surface when they are done. Immediately add ½ cup of cold water to stop them from cooking further, and remove with a large perforated spoon, or drain quickly in a colander. Place on a preheated platter on top of a large scoop of the following butter mixture:

Some time before cooking the pasta, melt the butter, add the cheese, and the cream slightly whipped, and beat together. Place one large scoop of this mixture on the hot serving platter when the fettuccine are ready, and the rest in large lumps on top of the fettuccine. Toss as quickly as possible, adding large sprinkles of cheese as you mix. Serves four.

[NOTE: if you use packaged fettuccine, they will increase in size somewhat more than home-made noodles, so adjust the quantity accordingly.]

CAMINETTO is in the "American" quarter, Parioli, but it is certainly a favorite Italian eating place, very much "di moda" these days. The food is good, the prices moderate, and the menu imaginative. Italo Santucci, the host, says that to describe his specialties would take at least a month, but that the real secret of his success is the lightness of his cooking. He uses the best oils and butters, and in just the proper proportions. But then again, he confesses, "you must possess eighty percent good luck, and only twenty percent ability; this is the real formula for one hundred percent success."

The setting is pleasantly wood paneled, there is a glass enclosed porch in front, and the wide sidewalk turns into a good-sized terrace for warm weather dining. The spirit is lively and the waiters manage to serve large numbers at one sitting with a good deal of efficiency.

Among that month-long list of specialties, these few stand out in my memory: fieno alla postarola, a haystack of mixed white and green fettuccine dressed with a sauce of peas, ham, mushrooms, tomatoes, butter, and grated Parmesan cheese; tortellini Caminetto, ringed ravioli-like pasta filled with a delicate chicken and veal mixture, and covered with a sauce of butter, mushrooms, and cheese; and nido di rondine, a swallow's nest of lightly browned, fried potato sticks filled with little croquettes of chicken in the shape of swallow's eggs, and sauced, in a complete departure from the avian theme, with tomatoes, mushrooms, and peas. Caminetto does up a pheasant in orange sauce, and features wild boar in its season. There are always on the menu a good list of meats from the spit or grill, notably Roman suckling lamb, Tuscan chickens and T-bones, venison (roe deer), and game birds.

Here are Signor Santucci's instructions for several of Caminetto's dishes:

128

VITELLA CAMINETTO
(Veal Scallops with Sautéed Vegetables, Caminetto Style)

1 lb. veal	2 ripe tomatoes, peeled and
butter	chopped
olive oil	salt and pepper
1 clove garlic [optional]	½ lb. sliced, sautéed
½ cup sauterne, or any fruity	mushrooms
white wine	1 lb. fresh peas, boiled
	parsley

The veal must be pounded, then sliced into very thin scallops. Brown the meat in a mixture of butter and olive oil until it is golden. Add one clove of garlic, minced, and continue cooking a few minutes. Pour over the meat one half cup of sauterne or other fruity white wine [at Caminetto they use the amber Frascati] and simmer until the sauce is somewhat reduced. Add the chopped tomatoes, and salt and pepper to taste. Continue simmering until the tomatoes are reduced to a purée. Add the mushrooms that have been sliced thin and sautéed, and the boiled fresh peas (cooked in well-salted water until just tender and rinsed in cold water to keep the color). Mix all together, simmer a minute or two to blend the flavors, and serve with a sprinkle of fresh parsley over the top. Serves four.

CIPOLLE AL FORNO
(Roast Onions)

1 large onion for each portion	salt and pepper
olive oil	

Put the onions to boil for five minutes. Drain, cool, and peel. Cut each in half horizontally and cut the rounded ends level so that the onions stand firm. Put enough oil to cover the bottom in a low baking dish. Put the onions in the dish, cut side up, pour more oil over them—a good slosh on each one—sprinkle with salt and pepper, and bake at 450° to 475° for forty-five minutes or an hour, or until they are nicely browned.

♩ FIENO ALLA POSTAROLA
(Egg Noodle Haystack)

1 lb. fettuccine, cut very narrow, half green, half white	2 tbsp. sliced mushrooms sautéed with garlic
2 cups tomato sauce	salt and pepper
2 slices prosciutto, in julienne	butter
2 tbsp. cooked peas	grated Parmesan cheese

Boil the fettuccine in abundant salted water. They are very quick cooking, so take care not to overcook. Drain, mix with a lump of soft butter, arrange in mounds on individual plates, then pour the sauce over them, finishing with a generous grating of Parmesan cheese.

SAUCE: Simmer together the tomato sauce, prosciutto, peas, and mushrooms; add salt and pepper to taste. Serves four.

♩ COSTOLETTE DI POLLO O VITELLO AL CARTOCCIO
(Chicken or Veal Baked in Parchment)

1 small chicken; or 4 slices veal, ¼ lb. each	4 tsp. capers
bread crumbs	4 slices prosciutto
olive oil	½ lb. mushrooms, sliced and sautéed in butter and garlic
salt and pepper	1 cup tomato sauce
4 pieces of parchment paper, butcher paper, or tinfoil, 18" by 24", cut into broad heart shapes	

Quarter and bone one small chicken, or have the butcher prepare it for you. Dip each quarter in bread crumbs, then brown in a skillet in olive oil. Season with salt and pepper. Oil one surface of four pieces of butcher paper or tinfoil. Put one piece of chicken in the center of one side of each paper heart. On top of each add one teaspoon of capers, one slice of prosciutto cut into julienne, one fourth of the sautéed mushrooms, and one fourth of the tomato sauce. Fold the paper so that the free side covers the chicken, and pleat or twist the edges together. Bake a chicken that weighed two to two and a half pounds in a moderately hot oven for about thirty minutes; increase cooking time for a larger chicken. Serves four. Cutlets of veal, one per portion, weighing about one quarter pound, can be substituted for the chicken. They will need to bake a bit longer than the small chicken, unless they are cut particularly thin.

TRATTORIA GALEASSI

GALEASSI is one of Rome's well established restaurants, having been on the spot since it opened as a tavern in 1909. It is also one of Rome's best situated, occupying one handsome corner of the old Piazza of Santa Maria in Trastevere. "Inside the old church," the waiter will tell you, "just to the right of the choir, you can look on the very spot where a fountain of oil flowed for a whole day when Christ was born, running off down into the Tiber." The church of Santa Maria in Trastevere was the first one dedicated to the Virgin Mary, and probably the first official Christian building in the city. Its date and founder remain uncertain, but it was noticeably on the spot by early in the fourth century. It has since been altered twice, but still contains some fine early columns, pavements, and art work, most notably the twelfth century mosaics which cover the upper façade. In the summer you can sit out in the square in front of Galeassi's and gaze on them while you dine.

Signor Umberto Galeassi, the son of the original owner, provides his guests with two spacious and comfortable rooms, besides the awning-covered summer terrace, and there is generally pleasant music supplied by strolling musicians. The large menu includes many of the specialties of the Roman cuisine. Signor

131

Galeassi recommends especially the spaghetti alla carbonara—bacon and eggs mixed with spaghetti, which is of course the way a Roman *would* prefer his bacon and eggs!—the cannelloni, and the spaghetti alla Galeassi: pasta with tomato sauce, mussels, and tuna. More delicate are the fettuccine mantecate, egg noodles richly pomaded with heavy cream, butter, and cheese; or the superb rice and shrimp dish, risotto con gamberi. The Galeassi pollo alla diavola is crusty and tender, the oxtail stew simmered in the classic manner. For those who like variety, there is the tegamino capriccioso, a mixed skillet of gently braised sweetbreads, liver, brain, and whatever strikes the fancy of the chef that day. The ossibuchi at Galeassi are smothered in mushrooms, and Signor Umberto has given me the recipe for them.

OSSIBUCHI CON FUNGHI
(Veal Shins with Mushrooms)

4 ossibuchi	lemon peel
butter	1 clove garlic
flour	1 anchovy filet
salt and pepper	broth
½ glass dry white wine	½ lb. mushrooms, sautéed
parsley	

The ossobuco is cut from the veal shin, and retains the round bone and its marrow (the prize of the dish). Each ossobuco should be a disc of about three inches diameter, and two fingers thickness (enough for one portion). Select a pan with high sides, one in which the ossibuchi will fit comfortably next to each other. Melt about four tablespoons of butter, or enough to cover the pan generously. Flour the ossibuchi lightly, and put them to brown over a medium flame. Sprinkle the top side with salt and pepper and cook until the bottom is well browned. Turn, and season again. Continue revolving until all the edges are browned. Bathe the ossibuchi with a half glass of dry white wine, and continue cooking until the meat soaks up as much as possible, and the sauce is well reduced. Add a little water, cover the pot, and cook over very low heat until tender—a good hour or more for American veal—taking care that the meat remains firm enough so as not to fall away from the bone. About ten minutes before serving, add to the pot a "piccolo trito"—a fine mince made of one tuft of parsley, a piece of lemon peel, one half clove of garlic, and one anchovy filet. Keep the pot simmering, turning the ossibuchi very gently so they can take on the flavor of the trito. After a few minutes, turn them out onto a warmed platter, scrape the bottom of the pot with a wooden spoon, deglazing the scrapings with several spoons of broth (or water). Add several lumps of butter, stirring constantly with the wooden spoon, until the gravy is smooth. Add the sautéed mushrooms, cook only long enough to heat through, and pour the sauce and mushroom mixture over the meat.

MUSHROOMS: Clean, slice, and sauté in butter with the other half of the garlic, finely minced. When brown, salt lightly. Serves four.

CAMPANA

THE Campana di Campomarzo "was in the little lane of the Campana between the Scrofa and the Piazza Nicosia, a street from which the inn has taken its name and where the civic number 18 has remained to our times. . . . [It is] recorded in the 1518 *Taexae Viarum*, and is named also in the census of 1526: Pietro de la Campana. In 1622 one Giacomo directed it; [there are] other records in the years 1782, 1786 and 1790." [10] In 1854, Campana was a stagecoach stop, and according to a contract still on

10. Translated from Umberto Gnoli, *Alberghi ed osterie di Roma nella rinascenza,* Spoleto, C. Moneta, 1935, p. 57.

the premises, Giovanni Sabatucci, its owner, agreed to provide six gentlemen traveling from Rome to various points in the Marches with "a coach conducted by a good coachman, for eight scudi a person, a good meal in the evening, decent rooms with good beds, clean linens, light, fire, and whatever else is necessary."

Today there are no longer coaches or lodgings, but the premises retain their modest character, and the emphasis is still on hospitality and good cooking. The present proprietor, Salvatore Iacobini, is the son of the Abruzzi family that has managed the restaurant for over one hundred and thirty years. Signor Iacobini tells me, and it is quite evident when you dine there, that he conducts the business with "passion and tenacity." He has several patrons of more than forty years' standing.

The menu at Campana is large and always includes a fine sampling of Roman and seasonal dishes. The cooking is excellent, and such standard ingredients as prosciutto and olive oil are of a noticeably high quality (the ham is a good mountain prosciutto, and the oil is from Sabina). The pasta specialty is tonnarelli alla chitarra, a dish from the Abruzzi with a sauce that Signor Iacobini has himself devised. The rounded, spaghetti-like noodles made of a rich egg dough are cut to shape on a wire-strung instrument that resembles a guitar and gives them their name. The sauce is a very delicate mixture of sweetbreads, porcini (wild mushrooms), mountain ham, and a pink touch of tomato tossed lightly around the tonnarelli. In the summer the assortment of cold meats is especially well-flavored, and the green sauce that accompanies them sharp and refreshing. When they are in season, Signor Iacobini recommends tiny Roman sweet peas cooked with prosciutto, the classic artichoke fried in deep oil or steamed Roman style, the roasted baby lamb (abbacchio), and baby kid (capretto). He also makes an excellent red mullet cooked in a paper case.

134

Here are a number of classic Campana recipes:

ZUCCHINE RIPIENE
(Stuffed Italian Squash)

8 medium zucchine (about 2 lbs.)

filling:

½ lb. ground beef

1 egg

3 tbsp. grated Parmesan cheese

white part of ½ roll, soaked in
milk, then squeezed out

chopped parsley

1 clove garlic, minced

salt and pepper

fresh grated nutmeg

sauce:

olive oil

1 onion, chopped

2 or 3 tbsp. dry white wine

salt and pepper

2 cups tomato sauce

Wash the zucchine and scoop out the flesh, leaving just enough to keep the shell firm. [This is such a popular dish that there is a special zucchine corer in Italy, much like an elongated apple corer.] Mix together the ingredients for the filling, and stuff the hollowed zucchine. Put some olive oil and the chopped onion in a low casserole or baking dish, and cook over the flame until the onion becomes golden. Add two or three spoons of dry white wine, the tomato sauce, and salt and pepper. Cook for a minute or two, then add the zucchine side by side. Put in a 300° oven and cook for about twenty minutes. Turn the zucchine over, then continue cooking until they are nicely tender, around forty minutes altogether. If you prefer, the zucchine can cook over a low flame instead of in the oven. Let them cool well before serving, as the flavors are lost if the dish is served hot; Italians often eat their stuffed zucchine as a cold appetizer.

135

FUNGHI TRIFOLATI
(Sautéed Mushrooms)

1 lb. mushrooms (Campana uses porcini, boletus edulis, when they are available)
¼ cup olive oil
1 large clove garlic, minced
salt and pepper

for fancier version, in addition:
2 tbsp. butter
2 filets anchovy
chopped parsley
½ lemon

Wash and trim the mushrooms, then cut into thin slices. Put these to cook with the olive oil and minced garlic over a brisk flame. When the mushrooms are nearly done, add the salt and pepper, and continue cooking until golden and tender. This is the simple form of funghi trifolati, and it can also be made using butter, or half butter and half oil. For a fancier version, at this point mash the butter and anchovy filets together, add to the mushrooms, cook gently until the butter melts, and serve with a dusting of parsley and a few drops of fresh lemon juice squeezed over the top. Serves two.

GNOCCHI DI PATATE
(Potato "Dumplings")

2 lbs. potatoes
¾ cup flour
optional: 2 beaten eggs and additional flour
salt

butter
grated Parmesan cheese
sauce according to taste: butter and cheese, tomato sauce, meat sauce, pesto, etc.

Boil and mash the potatoes. They should be as dry as possible. Mix with the flour and salt. Roll by hand on a floured surface to form long "frankfurters." Cut these into one-and-a-half inch lengths. Press the edge of the finger into each one to form a little dimple. These indentations serve to catch the sauce. Put to boil gently in salted water, a few at a time. Scoop out with a perforated spoon when they rise to the top, and keep warm in a buttered baking dish. Serve with lots of butter and grated Parmesan cheese, or any preferred sauce. For a richer version, add two beaten eggs and a little extra flour to the potato-flour mixture. Serves four.

GNOCCHI DI SEMOLINO
(Semolina "Dumplings")

1 quart milk
1 cup cream of wheat (or
  semolina)
2 tbsp. butter, plus butter for
  dotting

½ cup Parmesan cheese, plus
  cheese for sprinkling
4 beaten eggs
nutmeg
salt

Bring the milk to a boil and slowly add the cream of wheat, stirring continuously to keep it smooth. Cook over low heat until very thick, stirring to keep it from forming lumps or sticking to the pot. It is done when it is firm enough to stand away from the side of the pot when you stir. Remove from the heat, add the butter, cheese, beaten eggs (stir these in carefully a little at a time), a generous grating of nutmeg, and salt to taste. Mix well, then spread about half an inch thick over a buttered cookie sheet (or on a marble slab, if you have one). Refrigerate several hours, or until very firm. Cut into rounds about one and a half inches in diameter, and arrange these in a slightly overlapping pattern in a well-buttered baking dish. Sprinkle generously with grated cheese, and dot abundantly with more butter. Bake in a hot oven until golden. Serves six (but sometimes only four!).

GNOCCHI VERDI, I
(Spinach "Dumplings")

2 lbs. potatoes
¾ cup cooked spinach
2 beaten eggs
¼ cup flour
2 tbsp. Parmesan cheese

salt
nutmeg
butter and Parmesan cheese or
  sauce of your choice

Prepare the same as above, making the dough from the mashed potatoes, the cooked, chopped spinach pressed as dry as possible, and two beaten eggs. When well mixed, add a heaping quarter-cup of flour (and more if still too moist), two tablespoons of grated Parmesan cheese, salt, and a bit of grated nutmeg. When cooked, serve with butter and cheese, or sauce if you prefer. Serves four.

137

In the North, green gnocchi are made with ricotta and spinach, and are more commonly called ravioli verdi, although one Rome restaurant lists them as bouchées, and a Milanese friend tells me that they are familiarly called strangolapreti, "priest-chokers."

GNOCCHI VERDI, II, OR STRANGOLAPRETI
(Spinach and Cheese "Dumplings")

about 2 cups cooked, chopped spinach pressed as dry as possible (2 lbs. trimmed fresh spinach, or 3 boxes chopped frozen spinach make about 2 cups cooked)	2 lbs. creamy ricotta cheese 4 to 6 heaping tbsp. grated Parmesan cheese salt 3 egg yolks 3 to 4 tbsp. white flour

sauce:

Parmesan cheese and ¼ lb. melted butter

Mix the spinach and ricotta together. Add the Parmesan cheese and salt to taste. Add the egg yolks and flour, mixing all together well. The mixture should be fairly sticky. Flour your hands well, and put a small mound of flour on a board. Roll enough mixture in your palms to make a small roll about one-and-a-half to two inches long and about three-quarters to an inch thick. Roll in the mound of flour to form into an egg shape (about pigeon-egg size). Put each finished dumpling on a floured tray. Bring a large pot of salted water to a boil, but keep the water just barely bubbling or the gnocchi will fall apart. Drop them in one at a time as quickly as possible. A large pot will hold about half of the gnocchi at once, but if in doubt, cook the gnocchi in three batches. They will quickly float to the surface when cooked, and should be scooped out immediately with a slotted spoon, and placed on a warm platter. When all the gnocchi are done, cover them with a good dusting of grated Parmesan cheese and pour the melted butter over them. If you do this as the Milanese do, the butter should be nicely browned. Another sauce that goes well is melted butter, a few tablespoons of heavy cream, and enough grated cheese to thicken it.

138

It is common practice to add grated nutmeg or fresh chopped basil to the ricotta mixture, but these gnocchi are so delectable without additions you should try the unadorned recipe first. Serves six.

FRITTO MISTO ALLA ROMANA
(Mixed Fry, Roman Style)

This dish contains a variety of meats and vegetables fried golden brown. All of the following ingredients find their way into Roman mixed fries: veal scallops, brains, sweetbreads, calf's liver, artichokes, zucchine, little asparagus, cauliflower, potato croquettes, little balls of ricotta cheese, and even fried béchamel sauce (though the last three items are more frequently served at home than in a restaurant). Here are general instructions:

preparation:

VEAL SCALLOPS: Slice in very thin, small pieces. Dip in beaten salted egg, then bread crumbs or flour.

BRAINS AND SWEETBREADS: Blanche and trim brains as in NOTE, p. 273, and sweetbreads as on p. 154. Dip first in flour, then in beaten salted egg.

CALF'S LIVER: Slice in very thin scallops, dip in flour, then in beaten salted egg. Liver should be among the last ingredients put to fry, since it gets tough with prolonged cooking.

ARTICHOKES: Roman artichokes, or baby artichokes in the United States, can be sliced thin, floured, then dipped in seasoned egg. If you use large globe artichokes, break off the stem, cut off and discard the top to about an inch and a half above the base, pull off or cut off the leaves, and trim the bottom, rubbing it with a cut of lemon. Put to boil for about a half hour. Scoop out the choke from the cooled artichoke with the end of a spoon handle. Cut the artichoke bottoms into slices, dip in flour and seasoned egg. These will take less time to cook than the raw slices.

139

ZUCCHINE: Cut in strips, make a cut lengthwise in each one, and sprinkle with salt. Let stand for one-half hour to drain. Dip in flour only.

ASPARAGUS: The Romans use very small asparagus. They should be parboiled in salted water until just tender, drained, cooled, then rolled in breadcrumbs.

CAULIFLOWER: Divide into flowerets, boil in salted water until just barely tender. (If it is not still firm it will fall apart when fried.) Dip in a light batter of flour mixed with a little cold water.

POTATO CROQUETTES: Boil four small to medium potatoes. Mash with a small amount of butter over the lowest possible flame (they must be quite dry). Add one beaten egg, one-half cup of grated Parmesan cheese, a bit of minced parsley, salt and pepper, and a grating of nutmeg. Form in the palms of the hands into little balls. Dip these in flour, beaten egg, then bread crumbs.

FRITTELLINE DI RICOTTA: Mix about half a pound of ricotta with one egg, two tablespoons of flour, one tablespoon of sugar, and a little grated lemon peel. Form into balls, roll in flour, beaten egg, then breadcrumbs.

CROCCHETTE DI LATTE: Make a *very* thick béchamel sauce. Cool. Add one egg and mix well. When it is cool enough to handle, form into little balls, dip them in flour, beaten egg, and bread crumbs.

GARNISHES: Cut French bread into cubes, rub with garlic. Cut mozzarella cheese into cubes, dip in flour, beaten egg, breadcrumbs.

FRYING: Select a combination of four or six of the above ingredients and prepare them as indicated. Fry in deep, hot fat. The veal, raw artichokes, and cauliflower cook the longest, the béchamel croquettes, bread cubes, and mozzarella the fastest. Turn once to color evenly. Drain on absorbent paper and serve without delay.

For fifty years Comparone has been a favorite restaurant with the Romans, and its menu is crammed accordingly with many of their prized dishes. The trattoria is in the Piazza in Piscinula just off the Tiber, near the Ponte Garibaldi and the island, and dominated by the imposing Palazzo Mattei. In the summer a large deck, often umbrella-shaded, serves as dining room. The simple interior has been handsomely arranged, the walls lined with barrel staves, and the lamps constructed from barrel hoops. There are a number of wine bottles perched about, and garlands of drying red peppers.

Antonio Graziosi and his brother Severino have been the proprietors for about five years, although before that they put in the requisite training as Trastevere waiters. The chef, Giuseppe Di Iorio, has cooked nowhere but in Trastevere, the last twenty years at Comparone.

Among the specialties are bucatini alla amatriciana cooked *very* firm and chewy, the way the old Romans love their pasta best. The tomato sauce for these bucatini (a kind of long macaroni) is on the robust side, strongly accented with smoky bacon, hot red pepper, and the sharpness of pecorino cheese. Giuseppe has given me this recipe, along with several other specialties of the house. I have thoroughly enjoyed the cannelloni here, the spaghetti and clams, and the rice gilded with mushrooms and butter. Another specialty is the cuscinetto, veal filled with ham, cheese, and sage, and gently simmered in its own brown gravy. Tripe cooked Roman style, served speckled with mint and cheese, stewed ox-tails strongly flavored with celery, and braised veal rolls with ham are prepared expertly in the classic manner.

In spite of all these riches, my favorite dishes here are the two "casseroles," one of mixed meats, the other of assorted seafood.

141

The tegamino di frattaglie alla romana is a low-sided pan or baking casserole containing sweetbreads, lamb brains, chicken livers, and ham, all bathed in butter and white wine, and decorated with fresh peas and mushrooms. The tegamino alla pescatora is a fisherman's stew, rich with chunks of seafood, rings of squid, curls of shrimp, and mussels and clams in their shells.

Giuseppe's repertoire includes fresh broad beans simmered with pork rind, chicken and peppers, Roman suckling lamb cooked hunter's style, grilled chops of kid, salt cod (baccalà) poached in a spicy tomato sauce, excellent squab and quail, and a whole roster of stuffed vegetables: tomatoes, zucchine, peppers, and eggplant. The salad here has the favorite Roman wild herbs tossed among the cultivated greens whenever they are in season.

Here are a number of Giuseppe's recipes:

BUCATINI ALLA AMATRICIANA
(Macaroni with Tomato and Bacon Sauce)

¼ lb. smoked bacon, diced	2 cups stewed tomatoes (or 1
olive oil	lb. fresh, chopped)
dry red pepper (hot)	salt if necessary
white wine (between ¼ and	1 lb. bucatini
½ cup)	¾ cup pecorino cheese
	(or Parmesan)

Cook the bacon in a little olive oil, but do not allow it to get crisp. Add a dash of red pepper, about three good splashes of dry white wine, and the stewed or fresh tomatoes. Simmer the sauce for about eight minutes (or longer if you use fresh tomatoes) until it is slightly thickened and well blended. Add salt if necessary. Cook the bucatini in salted boiling water until they are not quite al dente (just before). Drain them well, mix with the sauce, add the cheese. Stir together and heat over a low flame for about three or four minutes. Serves four.

142

PICCIONCINO GLASSATO CON FUNGHI
(Glazed Squab with Mushrooms)

1 squab	1 piece of carrot
1 slice prosciutto	1 piece of celery
one or two sage leaves	1 piece of onion
1 clove garlic	dry white wine and/or cognac
salt and pepper	¼ lb. sliced, sautéed mush-
olive oil	rooms

[Optional: raisins or small browned potato balls can substitute for the mushrooms, or be added along with them.]

Stuff the cleaned squab with the prosciutto cut in coarse pieces, the sage leaves, and a clove of garlic. Season well with salt and pepper, and set to brown gently ["piano piano," as Giuseppe puts it] in a flame-proof earthenware pot with a bit of olive oil. When it is nicely golden all around, add the carrot, celery, and onion cut into pieces, and continue browning until they are soft and a good color. Splash with a little dry white wine and/or a small amount of cognac. Remove the squab to a separate platter, and cook the sauce over medium heat until it reduces a bit. Pass it through a strainer. Put the squab and sauce back on the heat with the mushrooms, raisins, or potatoes, and cook only long enough to heat through. One squab per portion.

QUAGLIE ALLA GIUSEPPE
(Quail in the Style of Giuseppe)

2 quail	1 or 2 tufts of fresh chervil (or
olive oil	a bit of it dried)
1 clove garlic	½ shot glass of rum
salt and pepper	lump of butter
2 or 3 sage leaves	

Split the quail down the back and spread flat. Heat some olive oil in a pan, add the garlic, minced, and the quail, breast side down. Cook over high heat until well browned, turning once. (This should take only a few minutes.) Add salt and pepper, the sage leaves, the

143

chervil, minced, and the rum. Cook for ten minutes or less, depending on the size of the birds, then remove the quail to a hot platter. Add a lump of butter to the sauce, and when it melts, pass the sauce through a sieve. Pour over the quail and serve immediately. Two quail per portion. [If quail are not available, you can substitute squab, but the cooking will take considerably longer, and one bird will suffice per portion.]

TEGAMINO ALLA PESCATORA
(Casserole of Seafood, Fisherman's Style)

per portion:

1 or 2 cloves of garlic, minced	⅛ lb. mussels in the shell
olive oil	⅛ lb. clams in the shell
1 slice of dentex	½ glass dry white wine
1 slice of ombrina	2 or 3 tbsp. tomato sauce or
⅛ lb. squid (or one small	stewed tomatoes
squid)	salt and pepper
⅛ lb. raw shrimp	chopped parsley

Put the minced garlic to color in the olive oil in a low casserole. When it is golden, add the fish in large chunks, and the squid cleaned and cut in small rings or strips. Pour the wine over the fish, add the tomato sauce, and a light sprinkling of salt and pepper. Bake in a hot oven about twelve to fifteen minutes. Add the shrimp, shelled and de-veined, and the mussels and clams in their shells, thoroughly scrubbed. Return to the oven until the shrimp cook rosy and the clams and mussels open. Sprinkle with parsley and serve immediately.
[In place of dentex or ombrina you can use pompano, croaker, seabass, halibut, rock cod, or any similar fish.]

TEGAMINO DI FRATTAGLIE
(Casserole of Mixed Variety Meats)

per portion:

¼ lb. sweetbreads
1 small lamb's brain (or half of a larger one)
one or two chicken livers
butter
olive oil

1 slice of prosciutto in julienne
dry white wine
salt and pepper
2 tbsp. cooked peas
2 tbsp. sliced, sautéed mushrooms

Soak the brains in cold water with a little vinegar added. Clean and trim the membranes. Wash and trim the sweetbreads and chicken livers. Cut all into large chunks. Take a small shallow baking dish and spread it well with butter and olive oil. Put the chunks of meat in the casserole and mix in the strips of ham. Sprinkle with about a shot glass of white wine, and dust with salt and pepper. Put to bake in a hot oven until plump and just tender. Sprinkle the peas and mushrooms over the top, return to the oven just long enough to heat through. Serves one.

AUGUSTEA

THIS restaurant, just off the Piazza Augusto Imperatore, is well located for sightseers. The piazza contains the cypress-bordered mausoleum of Augustus, a tomb that became a fortress during the Middle Ages, and still later a theatre and concert hall. Not far off is another early monument, the Ara Pacis Augustae, a symbol of the establishment of peace in the Roman Empire (circa 9 B.C.).

145

Ludovico Angelieri and Domenico Fidanza have directed this excellent place since 1952. It was a little pizza restaurant called Capri when they took it over, and during the years since they have changed everything but the old pizza oven that still blazes away in the kitchen. The restaurant is now a large, cosmopolitan establishment; animated clients, often fresh from the opera or theatre and still in their ball gowns and "smokings," frequent the glass-walled salon. There are some particularly interesting lighting fixtures along one wall, reminiscent of the sparkle of opera candelabra. They were made by the distinguished Venetian (Murano) firm of Venini, and are replicas, in miniature, of the spectacular crystal chandelier that Italy displayed at the Brussels World Fair.

Ludovico tells me that Augustea is one of the few restaurants that will never be recommended by taxi drivers or hotel portieri, since the management prefers to fill its tables without relying on the common practice of kicking back. Their system seems to work, for the place is generally teeming. Ludovico and Domenico are old restaurant hands, having each established careers at various Roman dining spots before they decided to pool their talents in a place of their own. Ludovico tells me that he has now spent more than forty years in restaurant work. There are, besides the bosses, a corps of efficient waiters, and six chefs in the bustling kitchen. Judging from the meals I've had at Augustea, every one of them has talent.

Augustea's menu is large and abundantly dotted with delicacies such as Malossol caviar, crostini topped with salmon, and the best hams and salamis that Italy offers. There are fine platters of involtini, chicken livers, and ossibuchi, and a fancy ground filet with butter and lemon. The real specialty is scaloppine: lightly floured veal scallops, browned in oil, then sauced with butter, white wine, a sprinkle of cooked Roman peas, and sliced mushrooms. [For one: 3 slices veal, beaten thin, 2 tbsp. oil, 1 tbsp. butter, ½ glass white wine, 2 tbsp. each, cooked peas and mush-

146

rooms.] There is a large variety of fresh fish daily, and the kitchen specializes in skillful seafood cookery. Before starting on their dinners, most Roman guests ask the waiter to bring them some focaccia, which is pizza baked without any filling. It is also called pan'arabo (Arab bread), because it resembles Middle Eastern flat breads baked without yeast. At the end of the meal, Ludovico and Domenico often offer their guests sambuca con la mosca, an anise-flavored liqueur afloat with coffee beans.

Here is Augustea's recipe for the pasta specialty, tortellini:

filling:

3 tbsp. butter	2 or 3 slices of lean
about 1 lb. total of the follow-	prosciutto
ing meats, in approximately	⅛ lb. brains
these proportions:	½ cup Parmesan cheese
¼ lb. pork	2 egg yolks
¼ lb. veal	salt and pepper
⅛ lb. turkey breasts	nutmeg
⅛ lb. chicken breasts	

pasta:

4 cups flour	2 half egg shells of water
3 eggs	

sauce:

¼ lb. butter	½ lb. fresh peas (weight in
½ cup Parmesan cheese	the pod), boiled
a little broth or cream	salt and pepper
½ lb. mushrooms sliced and	
sautéed in olive oil	

FILLING: Melt the butter in a large skillet. Add the pork, veal, turkey, and chicken, all cut into large pieces, and cook until nicely browned. Add the prosciutto and brains (soaked first in cold water with a little vinegar, then trimmed and cut into large chunks). When the brains are cooked, pass the whole mixture through a meat

147

grinder one or two times. Add the grated cheese, egg yolks, salt and pepper, and small nutmeg grated. Mix together well and put aside.

Pasta: Using 4 cups flour, 3 eggs, and about 2 half egg shells of water, proceed according to the recipe on page 164. Divide the dough into two parts and roll out into sheets. Place the meat mixture by the half-teaspoonful at intervals of about two inches. With a biscuit cutter or the rim of a small glass, cut out each mound of filling on a pasta disc. Fold each disc exactly in half over its filling so that you have a half-moon-shaped envelope. Pinch the edges together to seal in the stuffing. Pull each end toward the other, twisting and elongating the pasta so as to make a "ring." Pinch the ends together to complete the ring.

Preparation: Set the tortellini to dry for at least one-half hour. Put to boil in just bubbling, salted water (otherwise they will tear apart), cooking in several batches so that they aren't crowded. If you have chicken broth on hand, it will add to the flavor if you use it instead of water for the boiling. The tortellini should be cooked but still firm in about 18 to 20 minutes. Remove them with a slotted spoon, and add to the pot with the sauce.

Sauce: Melt the butter in a large casserole or pot and add the cooked tortellini immediately as soon as they are tender. Put over a lively flame and, stirring gently all the while, sprinkle in the grated Parmesan cheese. It must be of the sweet, fat, "soft" type in order to melt into a creamy sauce. Add more butter, a bit of the cooking broth, or a little cream if the sauce is too dry. Continue cooking and stirring gently for about 2 or 3 minutes or until the ingredients form a kind of "béchamel" sauce. At the last moment add the sautéed mushrooms, and the boiled peas, and season to taste with salt and pepper.

This recipe makes enough tortellini for eight people, more or less.

ROMOLO

Perhaps the best known of all Roman trattorias is Romolo at the Porta Settimiana in Trastevere. It is in the heart of old Rome, snuggled at the foot of the Janiculum slopes, and just at the border between the popular quarter and the patrician villas of the sixteenth century: the Palazzo Corsini, the Farnesina, and the Farnese Palace, close across the Tiber. It is most famous of all as the quondam abode of Margherita Luti, better known as La Fornarina, who was Raphael's most celebrated model and mistress. According to Romolo, Raphael was at work those days applying frescoes to the walls of the Farnesina for the banker Agostino Chigi. Whenever he felt the need for a break, he would join his friend Sebastiano del Piombo for a glass of wine at the nearby osteria—now the Trattoria Romolo. One day when he was thus occupied, Michelangelo made his way over from St. Peter's to see what Raphael was up to. When he entered the palace he found no one in evidence, but all of the tools of the interrupted work lay about. He ascended a ladder and drew the head of an angel into the painting. Then he was off. Raphael recognized the drawing immediately when he returned from the osteria, and left it just as the master had penned it, a black and white sketch in the middle of the fresco. It became known as "Michelangelo's calling card." Romolo says that the story is not legend, but based on the testimony of an old document.

Ever since the days of the old masters, artists have continued to congregate on the spot. Today there is a permanent exposition of modern paintings, including works by Mafai, Vesprignani, Sironi, Purificato, Giorgio de' Chirico, Afro, Scarpitta, and others of equal caliber. Even the menu jackets—surely among the most handsome in Rome—are bold drawings by such contemporary

149

artists as Mino Maccari and Sante Monachesi. The Roman poet Trilussa was a faithful client during his lifetime, and a plaque commemorates his presence at Romolo.

The menu is as attractive inside as out, and features the dishes most loved by the Trasteverini, with a few sophisticated additions like lobster, and good rich desserts. To begin with there is always a mixed antipasto, butter and anchovies (an old favorite), or small stuffed onions, which make a fine appetizer. Among the pastes are very good fettuccine or tortellini mantecate: egg noodles or little stuffed pasta rings, mixed with butter, cheese, slivers of prosciutto, fresh peas, and sliced mushrooms. The old-timers love Romolo's spaghetti alla amatriciana, a fine mix of smoked bacon, tomatoes, hot pepper, and pecorino cheese; but the favorite of all is spaghetti alla boscaiola, very firmly cooked spaghetti dressed with a sauce of tomatoes flavored with dried porcini mushrooms and tuna fish.

Romolo offers such classics as Roman-style chicken cooked with wine, peppers, and tomatoes; stewed oxtail; saltimbocca; broiled Tuscan chicken alla diavola; and such distinctive but rarer Roman restaurant dishes as fresh fava beans simmered in a sauce of onion, bacon, and tomato; fried mozzarella stuffed with ham and a hint of anchovy; or little eels from the Tiber stewed in tomato gravy with fresh peas (although now I understand that this old-time favorite must often be made with eels that never swam the Tiber). For those who want to order it—or, impartially, for those who want to avoid it—this dish is called ciriole con piselli. A more universally appealing specialty is a dish of golden pork chops, costarelle con la panuntella. Romolo grills them with the addition of olive oil and garlic to the skillet, and serves them nicely browned and seasoned with salt and pepper, with thick slices of bread dipped in the cooking fat. This dish takes well to a sprinkling of such herbs as rosemary, oregano, and fennel. To go along with it, Romolo recommends broccoli sautéed in oil with garlic slivers, salt, and freshly ground black pepper. (Cut the broccoli lengthwise to pieces of equal thickness so that they finish at the same time; cook covered; serve with a wedge of lemon.)

At Easter time one of the favorite Roman dishes is kid, and Romolo prepares it, as well as suckling lamb, in this enticing manner: he browns the chunks of kid or lamb in a skillet with olive oil, garlic, lemon peel, salt, and pepper (red is preferable to black); sprinkles them with enough dry white wine to make a sauce; and continues cooking the meat, covered, until it is tender, adding a bit of broth if the gravy needs thinning. When the meat is ready, he thickens the gravy by the addition of beaten egg yolks, two yolks for a recipe of two pounds of meat, and cooks it gently for a few minutes. [The best way to incorporate the eggs is by mixing a little of the pan juices into the beaten yolks first, then adding that mixture to the pan over the very lowest heat, and stirring continuously. Too much heat and the eggs will "curdle."] This dish is called capretto (or abbacchio) brodettato.

Here are the other recipes that Romolo has given me for several of the classic dishes on his menu:

BOCCONCINI
(Veal Tidbits)

2 lbs. veal in 2-inch chunks	½ cup Chianti or other dry
¼ cup olive oil	red wine
1 clove garlic	2 cups stewed tomato sauce
salt and pepper	

Brown the meat lightly in olive oil, then add the garlic, salt, and pepper, and simmer a few minutes longer. Add the red wine and the tomato sauce, and simmer over low heat for about an hour. If the sauce begins to get too thick, dilute with a bit of wine or broth, and cover. Serves four.

151

TRIPPA ALLA ROMANA
(Tripe, Roman Style)

1 lb. tripe
1 carrot
1 onion
1 stalk celery
salt

1 to 1½ cups sugo d'umido
  (see below)
grated Parmesan cheese
fresh mint

sugo d'umido:

beef or veal roast
lard
olive oil
butter
1 clove garlic
celery, carrot, onion, all
  chopped

parsley
marjoram
½ glass dry white wine
1 cup tomato purée or sauce
salt and pepper

Soak the tripe in several changes of cold water. Cut it into finger-sized strips, and put these to boil with a carrot, an onion, a stalk of celery, and some salt. Cook the tripe until tender but not mushy, which may take several hours (it varies with the tripe). Drain off the cooking broth and replace with sugo d'umido, about one quarter cup per portion. Simmer very gently for half an hour. Turn onto a warm platter, sprinkle generously with grated Parmesan cheese and a handful of chopped fresh mint. Serves four.

Sugo d'umido: Lard a good roast of beef or veal, then brown it in oil and butter. Add some celery, a carrot and an onion, a good dash of marjoram, and a chopped clove of garlic. Cook until the vegetables are golden, then add a little chopped parsley, a half glass of dry white wine, and about two cups of tomato sauce or purée. Add salt and pepper to taste. Simmer gently, covered, until the meat is tender, a minimum of two hours. The gravy is the sugo d'umido. The pot roast can be used for another meal.

152

ALTERNATIVE METHOD: Cook the vegetables in oil and butter until they are golden. Add tomato purée, white wine, and leftover meat gravy (about one cup). Simmer until the sauce is reduced to about two cups. Or brown small cubes of meat in place of a whole roast, then proceed as above.

For non-tripe lovers, the following egg "tripe" can be substituted for the cooked tripe, then dressed with the sugo d'umido, cheese, and mint. They need simmer only about five minutes instead of a half hour in the sauce.

"TRIPPA" DI UOVA
(Egg "Tripe")

8 beaten eggs
1 small bunch parsley, chopped
2 heaping tbsp. grated Parmesan cheese

salt
1 tbsp. olive oil
oil or butter for frying

Mix all ingredients with the beaten eggs. Heat oil or butter in an omelette pan until hot. Pour in one ladle of the egg mixture, tilt the pan to spread it quickly and evenly, and cook until the underside is brown. Flip onto a plate, then reverse it in the pan to cook the other side. Reserve the finished "pancakes" and continue until all the batter is used up. When they are cool, roll them up all together (stack one on top of the other, then roll up), like a jelly roll. Cut through the roll every half inch or so, and the result will be long strips of egg "tripe." To use in the above recipe, put a little of the sauce in a pan, add the "tripe," then ladle the rest of the sauce over them, heat through, and garnish as above. (Plain tomato sauce can also be substituted.) Serves four.

153

ANIMELLE AL PROSCIUTTO
(Sweetbreads with Ham)

1 lb. sweetbreads
very little salt, and pepper
2 tbsp. butter

2 slices prosciutto (about ⅛ lb.)
white wine or Marsala
parsley

Soak the sweetbreads in cold water for several hours. Drain, put in a pot with fresh cold water, bring to a boil. Remove from the stove and put the pot under a slowly running cold water tap until the sweetbreads are cool. Trim them, remove the fibers and membranes, and cut into large pieces. Melt two tablespoons of butter in a skillet and add the sweetbreads. Brown over a high flame, add salt very lightly, and a grating of fresh pepper. Cut the prosciutto into small pieces, add to the browned sweetbreads, continue cooking over lowered heat until the ham is heated through. Add one quarter cup of white wine or Marsala, cook until the sauce reduces, and serve immediately with a sprinkle of chopped parsley over the top. Serves four.

PASTARELLARO

IN 1848, when Pastarellaro began cooking operations in Trastevere, there were only "cantine" in the quarter for the sale of wine from the Roman hills. It is known that the proprietor of Pastarellaro, one Gigetto il Gobbo (Gigetto the Hunch-back), early began to offer his customers a pasta dish of rigatoni that was unique in all of Trastevere, and which has been called generally ever since "rigatoni del pastarellaro." But beyond that there is a generous amount of confusion about the restaurant's early days. In those times, a pastarellaro was a pasta maker who dispensed his dishes on a sort of short-order basis, and this is no doubt the origin of the restaurant's name, and of the prevalent idea that pasta was born in this locale. It is hard to tell which came first, the rigatoni or the pastarellaro, but it is certain that they were both extraordinarily good. By the time that Alexander III, the Tsar of the Russians, came to Rome with his court, Pastarellaro was so well established that the Tsar refused to take his meals anywhere else. Somewhat later, things were still in a laudable state, at least according to this excerpt from a 1911 letter addressed to the musician Maestro Forzano by Puccini: "A Roma si sta bene e si mangia divinamente specie al Pastarellaro—Capolavoro." "In Rome one fares well and eats divinely especially at Pastarellaro—a masterpiece."

The present owner, Severino Graziosi (of the Trattoria Comparone family), is proud of this tradition and still serves those good rigatoni. He took over the restaurant from his uncle, who bought the place after serving as a waiter there for thirty years. Besides the pasta specialty, Severino recommends the classic scaloppine, the saltimbocca alla romana, the casserole of mixed fish and shellfish, and the crema caramella. There is also porchetta, a dish that most restaurants do not list, and the whole range of Roman favorites, including mixed fries of fish or of variety meats and vegetables, lamb cooked in a spicy hunter's sauce, beans and pork rind, and a mixed field salad that is called here capricciosa di stoppia—stoppia being a field of stubble, where some of the best wild herbs spring up. There is, besides the usual chicken alla diavola, squab grilled in the same manner, and a handsome medallion of beef covered with béarnaise sauce. The ice cream bowl at Pastarellaro is described as a coppa sfiziosa, which is Neapolitan dialect, Severino tells me, for a cup that pleases.

Here are recipes for the original Trastevere rigatoni, and Pastarellaro's dessert specialty:

RIGATONI DEL PASTARELLARO

1 lb. rigatoni
¼ lb. soft butter
½ cup grated Parmesan
cheese
1 cup fresh, boiled peas

½ lb. mushrooms, sliced and
sautéed with garlic, salt, and
butter
1 cooked Italian sausage, cut
in small pieces

Boil the rigatoni in abundant salted water until just tender. Drain well and return to the cooking pot with the butter. Mix well until the butter melts, then add the cheese and stir in over low heat. Add the other ingredients, and cook only long enough to heat through. Serve with additional cheese to the side. Serves four.

[At Pastarellaro it is the custom to serve the steaming rigatoni in a rimmed oval platter, from which the host, being served last, eats his portion.]

CREMA CARAMELLA
(Caramel Glazed Custard)

custard:

2 whole eggs
4 yolks
½ cup sugar

2 cups milk
vanilla

caramel:

about ½ cup sugar

water

CUSTARD: Beat together the whole eggs, yolks, and sugar in a large bowl. Heat the milk but do not boil; add a bit of vanilla. Add the milk, beating continuously with a wire whisk or wooden spoon, a very little at a time. When all the milk is added, put the custard through a fine strainer. Pour it into a quart mold or six individual molds, prepared in the following way:

CARAMEL: Melt the sugar in a low saucepan with just enough water to make it sticky—about two or three tablespoons. Cook until

156

it takes on a good caramel color, but take care not to let it burn, as this will give it a bitter taste. The cooking should take only a few minutes. As it cooks, stir once or twice. Pour into the mold and tip back and forth until the caramel coats all of the inside surfaces.

BAKING: Put the caramelized mold filled with the custard mixture in a larger pan with about two inches of very hot water, and bake for about forty-five minutes in a moderate oven, 350°. The temperature should maintain the water just below the boiling point. If it starts to boil, add a spoon of cold water and lower the heat a bit. When a knife inserted in the center comes out clean, the custard is cooked. Refrigerate until ready to use. Loosen the custard around the edges with a knife, and reverse quickly on an upside down plate turned over the top of the mold. The Italians often prefer to unmold the dessert without chilling, so that the caramel has a runnier consistency. Serves six.

RE DEGLI AMICI

GIOVANNI GIANFELICI, who founded Re Degli Amici in 1927, tells me that his place is a little like the Colosseum in the way it attracts visitors to Rome by the droves. I would venture a guess that its central location, close by the Piazza di Spagna, has a great deal to do with it. It is a favorite rendezvous for many Romans, too, in particular journalists and painters. The custom at Re Degli Amici (which means King of Friends) is to exchange dinners for paintings, and the walls are hung accordingly with canvases and drawings by the local art colony's less prosperous, if no less well-fed, members. Although the paintings are the restaurant's main source of decoration, they are all for sale.

The culinary specialties include spaghetti alla carbonara, the pasta, egg, and bacon dish that Romans love so well, and cannelloni al Re Degli Amici, a rich, stuffed pasta pancake that Roman visitors never get their fill of. The scampi here are an excellent choice to follow, although Giovanni is equally proud of the golden turkey breasts, the medallion of beef, and the classic Roman mixed fry. The house specializes in macedonia of fruit, and it's a fine way to end the meal. Re Degli Amici is one of the few places in Rome where you can order pesto, the Genoese blend of fresh basil, cheese, oil, and garlic. It is absolutely habit-forming, poured generously over a tangle of noodles, and for those who can obtain (or grow) fresh sweet basil, here is the recipe:

PESTO

4 large cloves of garlic	4 tbsp. grated Parmesan cheese
2 shoots of *fresh* basil leaves	a fistful of pine nuts (optional)
1 sprig parsley (optional)	olive oil

Pesto is made in Italy by crushing the ingredients with a mortar and pestle (hence the name). A blender is a convenient substitute, although the texture may be changed slightly. Crush the garlic and the other ingredients in mortar or blender, adding enough olive oil to form a thick sauce. Use as a topping for cooked spaghetti, trenette, potato gnocchi, or other pasta of your choice. Two or three tablespoons are an excellent addition to thick vegetable soup, and faithful to Genoese tradition.

2. Ristoranti di Moda

THESE restaurants are currently "di moda" with Roman society: some because of the sophistication of their decor or setting; others because of the refinement of their cuisine.

159

RANIERI's history begins in the early 1800's with the birth in Naples of one Giuseppe Ranieri, an ancestor of the present owner. Giuseppe pursued cooking as a career, a choice for which he was so well suited that he eventually became chef to Queen Victoria of England. At this time in Mexico the Emperor Maximilian was striving most unhappily with the troubled administration of his government. The English queen, in a grand gesture of consolation, sent Ranieri to the Mexican court. When the Mexican revolution erupted and the Emperor was arrested, his Empress Charlotte appointed Ranieri her private cook, a move to allay her fear of being poisoned. With Ranieri in tow, she set off for Rome to plead with the Pope to save her husband's life. She was unsuccessful, and the Emperor was executed. This misfortune lost poor Charlotte her sanity, and Ranieri, consequently, his employer. He decided to stay in Rome, and in 1865 he bought the present establishment from a French restaurateur who had founded it in 1843. Ranieri's excellence in the kitchen quickly established a reputation that has attracted scores of admiring gastronomes ever since. It was a popular haunt of high officers and foreign residents during the French occupation, and ever since 1870 it has been a rendezvous for distinguished visitors to Rome. Its guest book contains the signatures of members of the royal families of Italy, Spain, Austria, Germany, Sweden, Greece, Russia, and England.

Though the restaurant is small, it is well arranged: pleasantly intimate though never crowded, a setting of dark wood, brocade, and faded velvet, as genteel and dignified as in the old days. The service is quiet and efficient, there are some fine wines on the list, and the menu is of a consistently high quality. Although the prices are moderately high, they are reasonable for what you receive.

Ranieri's maître d'hôtel, Signor Morandi, recommends three specialties among the pasta, and I would unhesitatingly add a fourth, the splendid lasagne verdi al forno. Signor Morandi is proud of the cannelloni alla casalinga—and they are, of course, superb—the ravioli alla fornarina, and the crêpes alla Ranieri. You may want to try the crêpes, since not many Italian restaurants include pancakes, filled or otherwise, on their menus, and these are especially light and cheesy.

There are several fine dishes to follow, four of which are house specialties: spiedino di vitella alla piemontese, mignonette di vitella alla Regina Vittoria, costoletta di pollo alla Ranieri, and our favorite—and perhaps also once a favorite of the unfortunate Emperor—pollo allo Massimiliano. Here is Ranieri's recipe:

POLLO ALLA MASSIMILIANO
(Chicken Maximilian)

per portion:

½ young chicken	fresh laurel leaves
olive oil	¼ cup brandy
salt and pepper	

Put half of a young chicken in a pan, season it liberally with olive oil, salt, and pepper, and weigh it down in a manner that makes it lie flat in the pan (a container filled with hot water, or a heavy kitchen tool such as a cleaver, placed on a lid slightly smaller than the pan, will do the trick). Brown it well first on one side and then the other, and cook until it is tender—about ½ hour—adding two or three fresh laurel leaves a few minutes before serving. When ready to serve, pour ¼ cup of warm brandy over each portion, ignite, and bring to the table flaming.

[NOTE: fresh laurel is essential, so do not substitute dried. It is preferable, should there be no bay tree in your vicinity, to use another flavor altogether: a branch of rosemary or a spike of fresh sage leaves, for example.]

THE excellent Al Pompiere has existed for over a century, situated until 1963 in the Piazza Mattei, next to the charming Landini Turtle Fountain, the Fontana delle Tartarughe. In the mid-sixteenth century, this quarter housed the old ghetto, where in those less happy days the city's Jews were segregated. In 1963 Pompiere moved to more patrician surroundings in the same neighborhood, the grand palace of the Cenci family. This structure, built over the ruins of the first century B.C. Theatre of Cornelius Balbus, dominated the scene early in the sixteenth century. Now handsomely brought up to date, it retains much of its original grandeur, and in fact, a few of the original ceiling frescoes. The inglorious Cenci clan is the subject of Shelley's tragedy, "The Cenci," which perpetuates the story of its infamies. Although his plot is based on the popular version of Cenci disreputability, historians show that the romantic tale is not altogether accurate. There is no evidence to support the story that Francesco, wicked as he may have been, made incestuous advances to his daughter Beatrice, but it certainly made a better play. In any case, Beatrice, along with one of her brothers and her stepmother, was put to death in 1599 for the murder of her father, though historians disagree as to how valid was the proof. Early in the seventeenth century, the palace, along with the rest of their estates, passed to the Borghese family by an edict of Pope Paul V (who was, incidentally, a Borghese).

Al Pompiere means "at the fireman's." Because one of the early proprietors was also a fire-fighter, the name originated and stuck —and according to its present owner, "so it will always be."

The menu is substantial, the cooking consistently excellent. You can dine here exceedingly well on such fare as tortellini, agnolotti, and fettuccine, but the pappardelle and cannelloni are even more remarkable. The pappardelle, wide feather-light egg noodles, are sauced with tomatoes, giblets, and drifts of cheese. The same dough, plumped out with a veal and béchamel stuffing, goes into the cannelloni. In a city of cannelloni specialists it would seem impossible to state that any one restaurant served this dish much better than another, but Al Pompiere is the champions' champion. This restaurant specializes besides in rice or spaghetti alla pescatora, a good way to sample all of the fruits of the sea. But in this same category I find it hard to pass up the fresh mussels in their broth of tomatoes and garlic. The fish prepared in parchment cases, especially the mullet (triglia al cartoccio), are firm and juicy and delicately perfumed with mushrooms and capers.

During the hunting season, the restaurant makes a specialty of several game dishes: wild boar in a spicy wine sauce, hare with polenta, thrush with garlic crusts, quail crisped in the classic style of the devil and served with rice, baby pheasants delicately simmered in red wine, and a hearty hunter's-style venison stew. All year round there are such dishes as cuscinetto al madera, little pillows of veal stuffed with cheese and ham and sauced with butter and Madeira, the classic saltimbocca, ossobuco, coda alla vaccinara, and thick, tender filets of beef.

Signor Manteferri, the host, has most obligingly given me recipes for several of his specialties.

COZZE ALLA MARINARA
(Mussels Mariner Style)

olive oil	4–6 skinned fresh tomatoes
4 cloves garlic, chopped fine	2 lbs. fresh mussels
4 filets of anchovy,	black pepper
chopped fine	parsley

In a large frying pan put a little olive oil, and the chopped garlic and anchovies. Cook until gently browned. Add the pulp of the fresh tomatoes, and cook until soft. Scrub the fresh mussels well, and add to the mixture in the pan. Continue cooking until all the shells open. Grind some fresh black pepper over them and sprinkle with a little fresh parsley. Serve at once in shallow-rimmed dishes. Serves four. [If mussels are not available, a good but somewhat different result can be obtained by substituting small fresh clams.]

CANNELLONI

filling:

1 lb. chuck beef or round steak (in one piece)
olive oil
salt and pepper

½ glass dry white wine
fresh nutmeg
3 ounces grated Parmesan cheese

béchamel sauce:

1½ quarts milk
6 ounces butter
¾ cup flour

1 tsp. salt
fresh nutmeg

pasta:

4 cups pastry flour, sifted
2 tsp. salt

3 eggs
½ cup water

sauce:

1 cup stewed tomato sauce [simmered with diced giblets or veal, if possible, or combined with a spoon or two of Bolognese sauce]

grated Parmesan cheese

Place the solid piece of chuck or round steak in hot olive oil in a frying pan and cook until it is well browned on all sides. Add salt and pepper to taste. When the meat is well browned, pour the white wine over it. Reserving the liquid in the pan, grind the meat as fine as possible, and add a liberal grating of fresh nutmeg [at least ¼ teaspoon], 3 ounces of grated Parmesan cheese, and the pan liquor, with all of the brown scrapings. Mix well together, and set aside.

164

Make a béchamel sauce. Signor Manteferri suggests that for best results you make it in this manner: after melting the butter in a large saucepan, add the flour a little at a time, stirring constantly to prevent sticking and lumping. Add the milk, already warmed separately, to the roux, stirring all the while. Add salt and a grating of fresh nutmeg, and continue cooking for several minutes until all is well blended and somewhat thickened. Add one half the cream sauce to the meat mixture and set the other half aside.

Prepare pasta for twelve squares, 6 x 6 inches. [In some American cities you can buy fresh pasta in sheets, to cut to any desired size in your own kitchen.] On a wide counter or table top, put 4 cups of pastry flour sifted with 2 tsp. salt. Make a well in the center, break into it three eggs, and mix them together with your fingers. Little by little mix in the flour that surrounds them, keeping a light touch and using a somewhat tossing motion. Add slowly not more than ½ cup of water, the less the better, but enough to make a workable dough. Knead for ten minutes on a lightly floured surface. The dough should be elastic and smooth to the touch. Roll out into sheets ⅛ inch thick, cut into 6 x 6 squares, and dry for ½ hour spread on towels or a tablecloth. [The Italian cook has a rolling pin three feet long and can roll out the amount of pasta called for in this recipe in two halves. It is a phenomenal sight, the easy back and forth motion, swift hands sliding in and out over the dough that has wrapped itself in a continuous overlapping sheet around the rolling pin, enlarging, growing slimmer, but never sticking. Every now and then, with a clean flapping sound, the round sheet flies off the pin onto the table, its direction to be reversed, or a test to be made of its thickness. Even if you have a three foot matterello, I suggest you cut your dough into several smaller sections and roll these out in standard American fashion. A pasta machine does an excellent job of rolling, and, if you are serious about obtaining good home-made pasta, it is a valuable addition to your kitchen. One part of it rolls the dough—three times, each turn at a narrower setting— and another part cuts the rolled dough into a variety of sizes and shapes. Italian cooks, even those who have grown up with a rolling pin in their hands and can turn out a batch of noodles with little more effort than we put into mixing the dough, approve of these machines.] When you boil the squares, be sure to use a large

165

vessel, plenty of salted water at a racing boil, and cook no more than three or four at a time; otherwise they will have a tendency to adhere one to the other, or double over on themselves. It is also important not to overcook them, two or three minutes should be sufficient, lest they split when you fill and roll them. As you remove them from the boiling water, plunge them immediately in a bowl of cold water for an instant, and then spread them on towels to dry. [Italians simply use the marble slab counters or tables in their kitchens, and if you are fortunate to have this kind of equipment, spread them straight away here.]

When the squares are dry, divide the meat-béchamel mixture among them, spooning it in the center of each square. Butter liberally four 8-inch Pyrex baking dishes. Roll up the stuffed sheets of pasta, and place three in each baking dish, side by side. Cover with the remaining béchamel sauce, pour over each dish about ¼ cup of stewed tomato sauce [with a little meat and giblet sauce mixed in, if possible], sprinkle generously with grated Parmesan cheese, and bake in a 375° oven until the cheese colors and the cannelloni sizzle. Serve at once. Makes four portions.

TRIGLIA AL CARTOCCIO
(Mullet Baked in Parchment)

per portion:

1 red mullet of about ½ lb.	parsley
½ clove of garlic	a square of parchment paper,
2 tbsp. chopped raw	oiled paper, or tinfoil
mushrooms	butter
1 heaping tsp. capers	oil

Chop together the garlic, mushrooms, capers, and parsley. Cut the mullet along its belly as deep as possible. Stuff with the mushroom-caper filling. Butter one side of the paper or tinfoil (thickly), place the fish in the center, sprinkle with olive oil, and close tightly in the paper. Bake in a shallow casserole in a medium-low oven for about thirty minutes, or until the fish is just cooked through.

RISOTTO (OR SPAGHETTI) ALLA PESCATORA
(Rice or Spaghetti Fisherman's Style)

½ lb. or 1 cup squid (as small as possible)
½ lb. or 1 cup cuttlefish (as small as possible)
2 lbs. mussels (with shells), or 1 cup shelled mussels
1 lb. tiny clams (with shells), or ½ cup shelled clams

1 lb. shrimp (½ lb. shelled)
½ to ¾ cup olive oil
2 cloves garlic, minced
6 filets anchovy
1 heaping tbsp. chopped parsley
salt
1 lb. rice (or spaghetti)

Prepare the squid and cuttlefish by opening just enough to remove the bones and ink sacks. For larger varieties it is also necessary to remove the skin, and to pound the meat to tenderize it. Cut into small pieces. If you cut crosswise through the whole body (scissors are useful here) you will get rings of meat. Set aside. Wash and scrub the mussels and clams in several changes of water. Put in separate frying pans [with about half a cup of water for the clams] and heat over a high flame until all the shells open. Remove the mussels and clams from their shells and put in bowls. Pour over them some of the cooking liquid mixed with water, and let stand for a few minutes. This should remove any last vestiges of sand and carry it to the bottom. Scoop out the clams and mussels, carefully avoiding the sand in the bottom. The cooking liquor can be used as part of the liquid for cooking the rice or spaghetti, but must be first strained through cheesecloth. Shell and de-vein the shrimp.

Heat the olive oil and minced garlic in a large heavy pan. When the garlic begins to color, add the anchovies, chopped fine, and the minced parsley. Cook gently for about five minutes, then add the squid and cuttlefish and simmer for fifteen to twenty minutes (longer if they are still tough). Add the mussels, clams, and shrimp and simmer over a slow flame for a few minutes or until the shrimp turn pink and are cooked through. Pour over 1 pound of hot cooked rice (or spaghetti), and mix together before serving. Six portions.

CAPRIOLO ALLA CACCIATORA
(Venison, Hunter's Style)

2 lbs. venison cut in chunks   salt and pepper
olive oil

sauce:

3 anchovies, chopped   ½ cup wine vinegar
2 cloves of garlic, minced   1 tbsp. butter mixed with
  rosemary   1 tbsp. flour
½ cup dry red wine

Cook the venison pieces in hot oil in a heavy skillet. Sprinkle with salt and pepper, and continue cooking until the meat is nicely browned. Meanwhile, cook the anchovies and garlic in a little oil until they just begin to color. Add a good sprinkling of rosemary (better fresh than dried), and the wine and vinegar. After a few minutes of cooking, add the butter-flour mixture, stirring continuously with a wire whip. Continue cooking and stirring until the mixture is smooth and thickened. Add the well-browned venison. Deglaze the pan with a little red wine and add to the stew. Simmer gently for about 1 hour or until the meat is tender. Serves six to eight.

[If there are no hunters in the family, lamb is a good substitute for the venison.]

PASSETTO

PASSETTO is not far from the Piazza Navona, a prime tourist attraction, but its tables are mostly filled with Romans, who widely regard it as one of the city's best restaurants. The decor is comfortably old-fashioned, and hasn't changed much over the years except for a bit of annual retouching. The restaurant serves out-

168

doors in the warm months on a large front terrace, with a buffet arranged so invitingly that it is guaranteed to awaken the most languid of summer appetites.

Passetto alertly fills its market baskets with the earliest fruits and vegetables of the season. They have the first asparagus, peas, and wild mushrooms; melons, figs, and berries are on the menu as soon as they grow sweet enough. This is one of the few restaurants that offers grapefruit, a citrus that many Italians have never even heard of. It is served as an antipasto, along with such distinguished company as smoked salmon, scampi cocktails, the veritable foie gras from Strasbourg, and Malossol caviar. The chef produces a fine liver pâté of his own, and the tray of mixed appetizers is varied and piquant. There are many soups and pastes to choose from, including potato gnocchi with fresh tomato sauce, ravioli, fettuccine, and Neapolitan pizza; the specialties are cannelloni and spaghetti alla amatriciana. For seafood lovers, the clams steamed open in a garlicky broth, or the mussels baked under a golden crust of bread crumbs, are as fine a beginning to a meal as I can imagine.

The menu is crammed with classics of the whole Italian cuisine: Milanese ossibuchi, baked lamb from the Abruzzi, filleted turkey breasts cooked in the rich style of Bologna, a Piedmont fondue sprinkled with white truffles, chicken and zucchine fried the way they make them in Tuscany. There are the choicest of veal loins roasted with mushrooms, sweetbreads delicately simmered in a sauce of Madeira and peas, and kidneys sautéed in a brisk brown mushroom gravy. When quail are in season, they are served up with golden toasts, and the roast beef at Passetto is cooked rare in the English fashion. They are particularly proud of their loin veal chop baked in a parchment case, and the excellent mixed platter of boiled meats. There are always fresh fish daily, including lobster whenever it gets caught. If truffle salad is on the menu, it is a rare treat: slices of fresh white truffles,

169

celery, and Swiss cheese, with a good dressing. Sometimes it is made with raw mushrooms. For cheese lovers, there is a good assortment, and Passetto always has ices, cassate, and cakes for serious dessert eaters.

Signor Guerrini, one of the restaurant's three able directors, has kindly given me Passetto's recipes for baked mussels, and mixed boiled meats.

COZZE GRATINATE
(Baked Mussels)

Scrub the mussels thoroughly and put them in a pan over a hot flame. Remove as soon as they open, and discard the empty half of each shell. Put the mussels in a baking dish and sprinkle generously with bread crumbs, minced parsley, and olive oil. Bake in a very hot oven until they become crusty and golden. (If mussels are not available, substitute clams.)

BOLLITO MISTO
(Mixed Boiled Meats)

To make their bollito misto, Passetto uses five or six meats, as below. For the home kitchen any two meats and the sausage will be enough.

1 lb. beef, lean and fat mixed (chuck, or similar cut)	a piece of calf's head
1 lb. veal loin	2 large onions
1 tongue, about 2½ lbs.	2 large branches celery
2½ to 3 lb. chicken	2 large carrots
1 lb. of cotechino (pork sausage)	parsley

Put the beef, veal, and tongue to boil in a large pot of water seasoned with rock salt. Add one onion, one branch of celery, one carrot, and one tuft of parsley. Put the chicken and calf's head with the remaining vegetables in another pot of salted water. Cook the pork

170

sausage, **wrapped in cheesecloth**, in a third kettle. Skim any foam that forms as the meats boil. The cooking time depends entirely on the size and quality of the meats. In general, the calf's head and sausage need about an hour to an hour and a half; the veal, beef, and tongue between two and three hours; the chicken an hour (unless it is a boiling hen, in which case it will take as long as the meats). If one piece of meat finishes before the others, remove it to a separate platter. When all the meats are cooked, strain the cooking broths together, discarding the liquid from the cotechino. To make a good consommé, clarify the mixed broth with egg whites, as described below. Serve the meats, either warm or cold, with green sauce, mustard, and other such spicy accompaniments, the recipes for a variety of which are found on pages 237–8.

To CLARIFY THE BROTH: Remove all fat from the broth, and let it cool. Beat lightly a little water, a little cooled broth, and the whites of three or four eggs together in a bowl. Add the remaining broth slowly to the egg mixture. Pour back into the pot and put to heat on the stove, stirring quietly, but thoroughly and continuously, with a wire whisk (the object is to spread the egg whites constantly through all of the broth). When the egg whites have turned opaque and white, and the liquid comes just to the point of boiling, set the heat as low as possible, and continue to cook without stirring for at least ten minutes. The egg whites rise to the top, carrying all of the sediment, and the liquid below becomes clear. The whole operation, including the stirring, must be performed with gentleness, for agitation will defeat the process. Place a damp kitchen towel over a large bowl, and tenderly ladle the broth and egg-white mixture into it. Gather up each side of the towel and twist, one end toward you, the other away from you. In this way you will wring out the liquid through the towel into the bowl. Adjust seasoning, and reheat when ready to serve.

171

"Trentuno," which is how the Italians pronounce "31," caters to a chic and highly cosmopolitan clientele. At the lunch hour one finds government chiefs, ministers, deputies, and prosperous businessmen; in the evening Roman aristocracy, foreign visitors, cinema directors, producers, and actors. The decor is sophisticated and new—Trentuno has only been operating for four years —and the menu is full of delicacies and imaginative dishes. All of this sparkle is thanks to Carlo Muzi, whose experience in international restaurant circles reads like a United Nations brochure. Although he is only forty-eight, and spent four years in a concentration camp during the war, he has managed to turn up at the 1939 World's Fair in New York as a director of the Italian Pavilion, and on other occasions at the Ambassador and at the 123 Club in the same city (for a total of four years in the United States). He has worked at various posts in Salsomaggiore, Milan, Naples, Venice (for the 1938 exposition), San Remo, and Capri (where he managed the sumptuous Canzone del Mare). He has put in working time in Egypt and Greece, and his French experience embraces Chamonix, Deauville, Aix-les-Bains, various other *plages* and watering spots, and, of course, Paris.

It comes as no surprise, then, that the menu lists a sprinkling of international favorites beginning with caviar and foie gras among the excellent Italian dishes. The latter include such pastes as "elephant's teeth" cooked with assorted shellfish, and penne "all'Arrabbiata," pasta plumes with a "furious" red sauce. The capellini, delicately thin egg noodles, and the rigatoni, both in excellent sauces, are among the specialties for which Carlo has given me recipes.

Trentuno's chef makes a number of first-rate filet of sole dishes, scampi, lobster, and a whole range of omelettes. From the grill you can order everything from minute steaks and chateaubriand to chicken and kidneys. There are pepper steaks, entrecôte with marchand de vin sauce, boneless chicken, and veal in a multitude of disguises. One of the most unusual of Vicario's entrées is chicken cooked in vinegar. The recipe will be found below, along with that for scaloppina Carlaccia, a dish that has little resemblance to other preparations of similar name. This veal scallop nestles inside a delicate pancake spread with a rice and mushroom soubise, sauced with Marsala, butter, and rich meat gravy. There is, finally, a whole range of gooey desserts as well as crêpes and ice creams, just in case all you ate beforehand was an omelette with fines herbes.

Here are Carlo's recipes:

POLLO ALL'ACETO
(Chicken in Vinegar)

1 chicken, about 2 lbs.	salt and pepper
flour	1 glass red wine vinegar
olive oil	½ cup rich meat gravy or
clove of garlic	demi glace
rosemary	1 lump butter
2 boned anchovies	

Cut the chicken into eight pieces, discarding the back, and reserving the giblets for another purpose. Wash, pat dry, and flour evenly [the easiest way is to shake the chicken with some flour in a paper bag]. Heat some olive oil in an iron skillet. Add the garlic cut in two, the rosemary, and the anchovies mashed to a fine paste. When the garlic is golden, remove it. Put in the floured chicken pieces, salt lightly, and sprinkle with pepper. Cook in the flavored oil until well browned all around, which should take about thirty minutes. Remove the chicken to a separate platter, turn up the flame, and add the vinegar to the cooking oil in the pan. Boil the gravy over a brisk flame until the acidity is completely eliminated. The test is to fan the hand over the pan toward you; when the sharp vinegar smell is gone, the sauce is ready. Add the meat gravy or demi glace, lower the flame, and simmer a minute or two. Swirl

173

a lump of butter, which should be soft, into the gravy, and add the chicken pieces. Simmer in the sauce for about ten minutes before serving. Serves two or three.

LA SCALOPPINA CARLACCIA
(Veal-Stuffed Pancakes)

1 large pancake for each portion (see recipe below)	sage leaves
	salt and pepper
1 to 2 tbsp. soubise for each portion (see recipe below)	wooden toothpicks
	flour
1 veal scallop of a little under ¼ lb. for each portion	Marsala
	meat gravy or demi glace
butter	

Make the pancakes rather large, one for each portion. Spread the soubise like a paste over each pancake. The scallops should be cut from the "noce" or filet—our closest equivalent being the round cut. Melt some butter in a low-sided pan, and brown the veal scallops with a half leaf of sage for each, and a sprinkling of salt and pepper. When they are nicely colored, remove from the pan and place one on each soubise-spread pancake. Reserve the pan with butter for later use. Roll the pancake so that it completely encloses the veal. Fasten with toothpicks. Dip in flour, then sauté in a second pan in butter until brown. Put them in the sage-flavored butter in the first cooking pan, add a little more butter, and a splash of Marsala. Heat for a minute, then add a little meat gravy or demi glace, and cook until the sauce is very thick. Put the filled pancakes on a serving platter and pour the sauce over them.

crêpes, or crespelle (pancakes)

½ cup flour	1 tbsp. oil
4 eggs	butter or other shortening for cooking the pancakes
1 cup milk	
salt	

Beat the eggs, milk, salt, and oil together with the flour. Grease a medium frying pan with butter or other shortening. When it is hot, ladle in one large spoon of batter, or enough to coat the bottom

174

of the pan thinly and evenly. Swirl or tilt the pan to spread the batter quickly. Cook until bubbles form and the underside is lightly browned. Reverse onto a plate and then slide back in the pan to cook the other side. Athletic cooks may prefer to toss the pancakes to reverse them; the only trick here, as in golf, is to keep your eye on the ball. You should measure the amount of batter each time, so that the pancakes are uniform. Spread them side by side on a counter or table. Makes twelve large pancakes.

soubise:

¼ cup raw rice
1 large onion, minced fine
1 large lump butter (3 or 4 tbsp.)

¼ lb. mushrooms, minced fine
salt

Boil the rice for about five minutes in salted water; drain. Melt the butter in a low skillet. Add the onions and mushrooms, and stir well into the butter. Add the rice, mix all together, cover, and cook over a very low flame for three quarters of an hour, or until the mixture is very soft. Add salt to taste.

CAPELLINI MARIA LUISA

About 1 lb. fresh capellini for four persons (but it goes a long way)
butter for greasing the pan
1 cup heavy cream
4 slices of prosciutto, cut in julienne

¼ lb. mushrooms, sliced and sautéed in butter with a little garlic and salt
4 heaping tbsp. fresh boiled peas
butter
grated Parmesan cheese

Cook the capellini in boiling salted water, and drain as soon as they are tender. Butter a porcelain, enamel, or earthenware baking dish and turn the capellini into it. Pour the cream over them, mix in the prosciutto in julienne, and the cooked peas and mushrooms. Dot generously with lumps of butter, and sprinkle with grated cheese. Put under the broiler or salamander until golden. Serves four amply.

RIGATONI MODA DEL VICARIO

1 lb. rigatoni	½ cup heavy cream
¼ lb. butter	salt
½ cup grated Parmesan cheese	1 slice of chicken, ground
2 egg yolks	

Boil the rigatoni about fifteen to eighteen minutes in racing, salted water. They must be still firm when cooked. Drain. Put in a large pot and stir with a mixture of the butter, cheese, eggs, cream, salt, and the ground chicken meat which has been passed through a sieve. Mix well, then cover, and cook over lowest possible heat until the noodles and sauce amalgamate. Turn out on a warm platter, and serve at once. Serves four.

GIGGI FAZI'S

HOSTARIA ROMANA

PRACTICALLY everyone in the Fazi family is a restaurateur, but Giggi says that the best cook of them all was his mother. He himself started in the family business at the age of six. He was employed to wash the dishes and glassware, since his family believed in learning things from the beginning. Now he directs one of the liveliest and most popular of Rome's restaurants, just a short walk from the glamor of the Via Veneto. He moved here in 1962 from nearby quarters in the Via Sallustiana that were called officially the Giardino d'Inverno. The atmosphere of his places is such, however, that they are always known, no matter what the name, simply as Giggi Fazi's. Now handsomely established in the Villa de li Patrizi, the restaurant remains as popular as ever. The filtered light and soft foliage of the garden, and the same good cooking, charm Romans and visitors alike.

The menu is thoroughly Roman, even to the dialect and humor with which it is written. In the words of Giggi, one begins with (among other appetizers) "porcheriole romane," an assortment of "Roman rubbish." Then there are tiny tubular pastes served in broth, and labeled unceremoniously "cazzetti d'angelo," a bawdy reference to the angels; however, Giggi cautions, if you ask the pasta maker for half a chilo, you'll never get to buy them by that name. The spaghetti carbonara with eggs, cheese, and bacon, an old Roman standby, are "terribly chic." The fish is always "pescato stammattina da Giggi a Fontan de Trevi," "fished this very morning out of Trevi Fountain." The game, on the other hand, was "nabbed by Giggi in the parks of the Villa Borghese." Out-of-season or early commodities Giggi labels frankly as "costing an eye." The cheeses include the "rind of an almost Swiss cheese," and a gorgonzola so vigorous that it "whistles." "Pappina casareccia" turns out not to be pap at all, but homemade ice cream.

Giggi has put together a small cook book that explains, with the help of some energetic drawings, many of the dishes on his menu. He offers "la gallina de mare": salted codfish simmered in a lively tomato gravy that is sprinkled with raisins and pine nuts; squid sauced with tomatoes and peas, all hinting of garlic, hot pepper, and white wine; a country style omelette with onions, tomatoes, and zucchine; and richly stewed tripe, Roman style. There are many bean dishes: ceci or kidney beans with pasta, dried broad beans with pork rind, fresh fava beans cooked with onions, bacon, and white wine, and lentils with pork sausage. Among the variations on veal, the messicani here are especially intriguing: rolls of meat stuffed with veal, egg, sausage, and cheese, browned in oil, and simmered until tender in milk, butter, and Marsala. They are traditionally served with mashed potatoes to catch all the good gravy. The artichokes here, often the

177

second bloom of the plant, the cimarolo, are cooked gently with wine and oil in a covered clay pot. When they are available, wild asparagus are on the menu, boiled just tender, and dressed with oil and a bit of fresh lemon juice. Giggi serves the tiny green field chicory cooked with oil, garlic, and just a dash of hot red pepper. He also offers spiky puntarelle, served fresh with a sauce of oil and vinegar, garlic, red pepper, and anchovies, and a garnish of hard-boiled egg wedges—clearly a salad for vigorous eaters.

Here are a number of fine recipes from Giggi Fazi:

ER BRASATO DE BOVE
(Braised Beef)

3 lb. roast of beef (bottom round, sirloin tip, or rump)	1 cup meat broth
salt and pepper	1 cup dried mushrooms (boletus edulis, if obtainable)
olive oil	
2 cups Barolo or heavy red wine	

for stuffing:

3 or 4 slices (a little less than ¼ lb.) prosciutto, including fat	1 stalk celery
	½ carrot
salt and pepper	2 or 3 cloves garlic

Cut small pockets all over the meat. Stuff with the well-minced mixture of prosciutto, salt and pepper, celery, carrot, and garlic. Reserve the rest. Season the larded meat well with salt and pepper, and put in an earthenware casserole first bathed with olive oil. Add the remaining "stuffing" to the pot, cover, and set to cook very slowly for three hours or so. Every now and again, sprinkle with red wine alternating with meat broth until all is added to the pot. While the meat is cooking, put the dried mushrooms to soak in a bowl of warm water (for at least an hour). Add them, drained, to the pot a half hour before the meat is finished cooking. Serves six

178

Palazzi (Camilluccia)

Giggi Fazi's Hostaria Romana

Tre Scalini

A sidewalk caffè on the Via Veneto

Trattoria Galeassi

Da Meo Patacca

Romolo

Da Pancrazio.

Da Giggetto

Ristorante-Pizzeria La Capricciosa

Casina Valadier

to eight. [I find the meat cooks more evenly if you turn it from time to time in the sauce.]

LA FAVA ROMANA
(Fava Beans Roman Style)

1 onion
2 slices bacon
olive oil
1 lb. (shelled) fresh fava beans
(or any fresh broad bean)

a few pieces of lettuce leaves,
chopped
½ cup white wine
salt and pepper

Mince a small onion and two slices of bacon as fine as possible. Put some oil in an earthenware cooking pot, and add the onion and bacon. When they begin to take on a little color, add the shelled fresh beans and lettuce leaves, and mix together. Cover and cook over a lively fire for about ten minutes. Mix the beans with a wooden spoon, add a half cup of dry white wine, stir, and continue to cook for about ten minutes or until the beans are tender. Serves four to six.

L'ORATA
(Red Snapper in Tomato Sauce)

1 lb. fish such as red snapper,
bream, grouper, sea-bass
¼ cup olive oil
1 clove garlic
1 piece dried hot red pepper

½ cup tomato pulp (cut-up
ripe tomatoes)
salt
¼ cup dry white wine
parsley

Clean the fish and rinse well with running water. In an iron skillet, put the olive oil, the fish, the garlic in slivers, the dried red pepper, the cut-up tomato, and a sprinkling of salt. Cover and cook gently for about fifteen minutes. Add the white wine, cover again, and continue cooking for about fifteen minutes longer, or until the fish is tender and cooked through. Serve it piping hot, "calla, calla," with a trimming of chopped fresh parsley over the top. Serves four.

LA PASTA E CECI
(Macaroni and Chick Peas)

1 lb. dry ceci beans (also called chick peas, garbanzo beans)
salt
½ cup olive oil
2 cloves garlic, minced
dry hot red pepper

rosemary
1 cup stewed tomatoes
½ lb. macaroni, cannolicchi, occhi di lupo, or similar small, tubular pasta

Soak the ceci beans overnight in cold water. Drain, and put to boil with at least two quarts of cold water, lightly salted. Keep just at a simmering boil, but do not allow to drop below the boiling point. If the water evaporates below half, add boiling water up to that level. While the beans are cooking, make a soffritto of the oil, garlic, and a little red pepper by cooking together gently. When the ceci are tender (probably about two hours, although the cooking time varies greatly with the bean), mix in the soffritto. Add a sprinkling of rosemary and the stewed tomatoes, stir well, and continue to cook over a low flame. After the flavors have mingled well, turn up the fire until the liquid bubbles, and immediately add the uncooked pasta. They should be just tender in about twelve minutes. Remove the pot from the stove, but wait for twenty minutes before serving. The flavor is much better if the dish is not too hot. Serves six to eight. [It is most important to cook the beans exactly as directed, or they may not become tender. It is also important that there be at least a quart of liquid for the pasta to cook in, and that any additions are of *boiling* water.]

PASTA E FACIOLI
(Macaroni and Beans)

This recipe is almost the same as the above recipe for macaroni and ceci beans, except that the soffritto which is added to the cooked beans is made of 1 chopped onion, ¼ chopped carrot, 2 or 3 branches of chopped celery, salt and pepper, and a slice or two of diced potato (not essential), all sautéed in olive oil. This should then simmer for about a half hour with the cooked beans before the pasta is added.

[NOTE: There is neither rosemary nor hot red pepper in this dish, but the dried beans, like the ceci, should first be soaked overnight.]

BRACIOLA DI MAIALE CON LI BROCCOLI STRASCINATI
(Pork Chop with Broccoli)

pork chop:

1 large pork chop (approximately ½ lb.) per portion	salt and pepper olive oil

broccoli:

1 bunch broccoli	1 piece dried hot red pepper
olive oil	salt
1 clove garlic	few drops white wine

CHOP: Place the pork chop on a plate, sprinkle with salt, pepper, and olive oil. Leave to marinate for at least an hour, better half a day, without refrigeration. When ready to cook, place on a grill over a good wood fire, and broil.

BROCCOLI: Wash and trim the broccoli, removing the tough portions of the stems. Boil in salted water until it is just beginning to be tender. Do not overcook, since it will undergo further cooking. While the broccoli is boiling, heat some olive oil in a heavy iron skillet. Add a clove of garlic in thin slices, a small piece of hot red pepper, and sauté a few minutes. Add the drained, parboiled broccoli. Salt well, and stir around so that the vegetable becomes infused with the flavored oil. Simmer for about ten minutes. Then add a few drops of white wine, cover, and cook over a slow fire for three or four minutes longer. Serve as an accompaniment to the grilled pork chops. One bunch of broccoli serves four.

ℒ *ANGELINO A TOR MARGANA* ℛ

SET in a corner of one of Rome's old quarters, this trattoria at first glance has the appearance of a small, intimate family restaurant. It is, however, very sophisticated in its operation, and attracts a worldly clientele. The Piazza Margana, little known to most Romans before Angelino called their attention to it, retains a good deal of its early character. An old tower, the Tor Margana, stands on the little square, a monument to the days when country hay wagons came through the adjoining gate and deposited their loads, when umbrellas sheltered a rural market filled with peasant wares set up against the wall, and when the road itself was no more than earth scattered with weeds. Angelino's menu jacket reproduces a painting of the nineteenth century scene.

Papa Angelino Biasciucci, after whom the restaurant is named, used to work in a very small osteria in the neighborhood. In 1931 he opened his own place in the Piazza Margana, catering at first to modest country merchants and the working class of the neighborhood. In those days, there were four tables out front, weather permitting. Son Armando, who as boss since 1950 has come to be known to everybody as "Angelino," once worked for the Trattoria Romolo. In fact, in 1956, he married Romolo's daughter. He is jovial and hospitable, and takes good care of his guests. The senior Mrs. Biasciucci and a sister-in-law do all of the cooking, turning out a cuisine that is typically Roman.

The trattoria is perhaps best known for its sponsorship of a widely respected prize in arts and letters, the Premio Tor Margana. The prize itself, a silver replica of the Tor Margana designed by Roberto Ruta, has been awarded every several months since February, 1958 (with some interruptions) to an outstanding architect, painter, sculptor, actor, writer, or other creative personality. The most unusual thing about it, aside from the fact

182

that very few restaurants concern themselves with bestowing official kudos on practicing artists, is that its jury is made up of extremely young men. No one of the judges is past his mid-forties, and most are in their thirties. The Tor Margana is especially distinguished as a prize, because it is awarded by rising young men to those whom they consider their greatest masters. Among the recipients so far have been the author G. B. Angioletti (the first of the prizewinners), the literary scholar Mario Praz, Anna Magnani, Salvatore Quasimodo (who has won some other prizes in his time), and Gian-Carlo Menotti. The award ceremony, covered by all the major newspapers and magazines, calls for a festive gathering at Angelino, and a good Roman dinner. On the occasion when the award went to Giacinto Spagnoletti for his edition of the Roman poet Gioachino Belli's letters, the menu for the evening was selected from an 1831 Belli poem describing a great dinner: it included "stufataccio, certi gnocchi da fàcce er peccataccio, peperoni, caciofiore, vino de tuttopasto, caffè e ciammelle" ("a humble stew, gnocchi good enough to sin for, peppers, cheese, wine, coffee and sweet cake").

The specialties at Angelino begin with tonnarelli, a pasta from the Abruzzi. The egg dough, cut on a stringed instrument and consequently called alla chitarra, is sauced with butter, grated Parmesan cheese, small Roman peas cooked first in butter, and sliced sautéed mushrooms—wild porcini, when they are available. The trick of the creaminess of the sauce, Angelino (Armando, that is) explained to me, is that the serving platter must be scalding hot, the butter in the smallest pieces on the bottom, the boiling pasta added immediately from the pot, and the whole tossed with the speed of light.

Angelino's pollo alla diavola is prepared slightly differently from the usual method, and the secret is one that Armando prefers to keep. However, he has most happily parted with Mamma's recipes for bocconcini and involtini of veal, and an excellent peperonata. The latter he serves with the bocconcini or with

183

pieces of chicken sautéed in the venerable Roman manner. The menu features such other Roman dishes as tripe, roast baby lamb, squid with tomatoes and peas, baked eggplant, and brains cooked in butter with mushrooms. There are besides, fat skewers of grilled scampi, chicken livers delicately perfumed with sage leaves, fresh fish cooked to your pleasure, roast squab in season, and such warm weather treats as cold veal with tuna-mayonnaise, and chicken salad all'americana. The desserts include assorted ices and fruits, and such riches as charlotte and Saint Honoré.

Here are the recipes for some Roman classics:

POMODORO PASSATO
(Stewed Tomato Sauce)

2 lbs. very ripe tomatoes (plum, or pear-shaped, if available)
olive oil
1 small onion
1 piece carrot

1 small piece celery
salt and pepper
one or two fresh basil leaves (optional)
pesto of 2 cloves garlic, 1 very small onion, 1 branch parsley

Wash the tomatoes, cut them in large pieces, and put in a stewing pot with a small amount of olive oil (but no water). Heat slowly until they begin to soften, stirring them with a wooden spoon. When they are soft, add the onion, carrot, and celery, cut into small dice, and season with salt and pepper. If fresh basil is available, a leaf or two is a good addition. Cook slowly for about an hour, or until all of the ingredients are reduced to a thick sauce. If too thick, add a little white wine or water. Pass through a sieve or food mill to obtain a purée. Make a pesto of the two garlic cloves, onion, and parsley by mincing first, then mashing with a pestle. It should be as fine as possible. Add this to the tomato sauce, and simmer about ten minutes before using. Two pounds of juicy ripe tomatoes yield about three cups of sauce. Romans sometimes serve their tomato purée with a garnish of fresh chopped mint.

PEPERONATA
(Stewed Peppers)

1 lb. sweet peppers, green or red

1 jigger glass olive oil

½ onion in small dice

1 to 1½ cups stewed tomato sauce (see recipe above)

salt and pepper

Clean the peppers and remove the stems and seeds. Cut into wide strips. Heat the olive oil, which should be enough to cover the bottom, in a skillet. Add the finely diced onion and fry gently until it is golden. Then add about one cup of tomato sauce and bring to bubbling. Add the strips of pepper, cover the pot, and cook over low heat for about forty-five minutes, or until the peppers are limp and tender. Add more tomato sauce as necessary, and correct the seasoning. Makes enough peppers to serve with the bocconcini for four. [Many cooks prefer to first spear the peppers on a fork and toast them over a flame until their skins can be removed; or to heat them in olive oil until the skins can be removed; then to proceed as above.]

BOCCONCINI DI VITELLO CON PEPERONI
(Stewed Veal Tidbits with Peppers)

1 lb. or more choice, lean veal, cut into chunks

1 jigger glass olive oil

salt and pepper

1 cup stewed tomato sauce (see recipe above)

1 jigger glass dry white wine

4 servings of peperoni (see recipe above)

Heat the olive oil in a heavy skillet. Season the veal pieces, and add to the pan. Cook until the pieces are browned nicely on all sides. Pour a cup of tomato sauce over them, stir continuously for a few minutes, then continue to simmer over low heat until the veal is tender. This will take at least fifteen minutes, but varies with the quality of the meat. When it is cooked, add the white wine, mix well, and cook just long enough to heat through. Serve with the peperonata to the side, or over the top. Serves four.

185

INVOLTINI DI VITELLO
(Veal Rolls)

Involtini are made in exactly the same way, except for their shape. The veal should be sliced into small, thin "steaks," flattened with a meat mallet, then rolled up. They can be stuffed with any one of, or a mixture of, such ingredients as cheese, ham, sautéed mushroom slivers, capers, sage leaves, or even a few slices of white truffles. Involtini are generally served with sautéed mushrooms or green peas.

3. Old-Style Trattorie

THESE restaurants are small and unpretentious, equivalent to the old Paris bistros, where the hearty cooking is simple but first-rate, and the cost very reasonable. The decor, like the cooking, remains largely undemonstrative, innocent of the flourishes of professionals. The atmosphere has the intimacy and warmth of a family enterprise. Two of these trattorie, located in the "ghetto," specialize in dishes characteristic of the Roman Jewish quarter.

187

৯ৎ MARIO AL LARGO PALLARO ৫

Quarsiasi persona
Dev'esse persuasa
Che qui se magna solo
Quello che passa casa
—MARIO

BY means of this Roman verse, Mario tells his customers that when they come to his restaurant they eat only what he chooses to serve them. And what he chooses to serve is always an abundant, well-prepared supper of several courses. For the dozen years that he has operated the restaurant, Mario has been following the same system with great success. The premises remain open until very late, sometimes four a.m. or after, so this is a place to remember for dinner after the theatre, or if a siege of hunger strikes after the witching hour.

Mario's restaurant, which goes by an odd assortment of names (among them Pallaro Mario, Giovanni Batista Fazi Trattoria, Ristorante Mario Fazi al Largo Pallaro, and, most commonly, the name above), consists of several modest, run-down rooms, and an outdoor summer area in the street. Not so modest is the usual dinner, which starts with a delicious omelette of zucchine and tomatoes (mostly served cold), or baked eggplant (always served hot); *and* croquettes of rice and cheese (supplì), as well as of chicken or another savory; *and* beans in oil (fagioli al fiasco); *and* sometimes, this depending largely on availability, golden fried zucchine flowers bursting with cheese and anchovies. Generally, after the hors d'oeuvres comes a large bowl of fettuccine, so splendid as to suggest that here indeed is the real King of Roman Fettuccine. The noodles are as light as air, but tossed with butter and cheese they have a very substantial flavor. Don't be alarmed should the waiter announce instead that this evening you are having lasagne. It's all the same thing, just cut wider. A diploma

188

inscribed in Latin hangs on the wall, testimony of a Roman eating society to the goodness of these noodles. After the pasta you receive a steaming entrée that changes with the day of the week, or the whim of the chef. Generally on Mondays there is a rich stew seasoned with celery (stufatino con sellero); on Tuesdays a substantial pot roast, stracotto (which literally means extra-cooked), and sometimes beans and macaroni; Wednesday is the day for breast of veal and Thursday for roast of veal with Roman peas. This being a faithful Roman trattoria, Thursday is also the day for gnocchi. On Fridays there is a dish of salt cod, baccalà, and on Saturday, still faithful to Roman eating habits, there is tripe. Sometimes gently sautéed veal or stewed chicken alternate with the other dishes. The entire meal, everything included, comes to a little over three dollars, high for such an unpretentious type of Roman eatery, but still quite a bargain by our standards.

Mario happily shared his recipes for baked eggplant (alla parmigiana and Roman style) and those remarkable zucchine flowerets. Here are the instructions he gave me:

MELANZANE ALLA PARMIGIANA
(Eggplant Baked with Cheese and Tomato Sauce)

2 medium eggplants
salt
flour
olive oil
butter

about 2 cups stewed tomato sauce
½ lb. disc of mozzarella cheese
grated Parmesan cheese

Peel and slice the eggplant into sections about one-half inch thick, in the manner of a pineapple. Salt well, and place in a colander with a weight pressing down on them for several hours, or until the liquid drains out. Dip them in flour and fry in abundant olive oil until they are nicely browned on both sides. Butter generously an earthenware casserole, and alternate one layer of eggplant, one layer of tomato sauce, one layer of mozzarella cheese in slices, and a sprinkling of grated Parmesan cheese. Repeat a second round, finishing with some lumps of butter and a good dusting of grated cheese. Bake in a prewarmed oven (around 375°–400°) for twenty minutes to half an hour, or until the dish is hot and bubbly. Feeds at least six. (Romans sometimes add slices of hard-boiled egg among the layers.)

MELANZANE ALLA ROMANA
(Eggplant Baked with Cheese and Meat Sauce)

Proceed as above, substituting a rich meat sauce (see p. 229) for tomato sauce.

FIORI DI ZUCCHINE RIPIENE
(Stuffed Zucchine Flowers)

12 zucchine flowers	1 small tin of anchovy filets,
1 small oval of mozzarella cheese	or approximately 1 filet per flower
	olive oil

pastella:

½ (generous) cup flour	salt
⅔ cup water	

Take out the stamens of the zucchine flowers, and trim the bottom ends with a knife, removing the stems and "sticky" pieces. Wash well, dry on a towel, and sprinkle with salt. Cut the mozzarella in pieces of a size to stuff the flowers. Sprinkle each piece with pepper, then stuff the flowers by opening the petals. Cut the anchovies into small pieces, and stuff into the mozzarella. The petals tend to close naturally, holding the stuffing in. Blend the flour, water, and salt quickly, and just enough to make a smooth paste. Dip each flower in the batter, and deep fry (or fry in deep oil in a skillet) until they are golden. Drain on absorbent paper, salt lightly, and serve at once.

[NOTE: You can vary the stuffing by using mozzarella alone, or by adding prosciutto instead of anchovies. Three or four flowers make a portion, when served as an hors d'oeuvre.]

190

THE charming trattoria Otello nestles in a quiet, hidden court-yard in the very center of downtown Rome, just a cobbled block, in fact, from the Piazza di Spagna. The lovely garden court was once the stable of the Princess Boncompagni, whose palazzo has stood in this spot for more than one hundred years. At the center of the courtyard a fountain luxuriates in a drapery of velvety fruits and satin vegetables, a skillful display of foodstuffs juxta-posed by some Matisse-like hand. If you order grapes, pears or figs, the waiter will pluck them out of the composition, dip them in the fountain, and serve them still glistening with droplets. Eggplants and mushrooms disappear into the kitchen as they are needed, and return some time later in a pungent cloud of steam. During the eighteenth-century Princess's occupancy today's foun-tain was the royal bathtub.

A pergola wound with grape vines shields the little courtyard from summer heat. Here, or into the fine old palazzo formerly frequented by nobility, politicians, (and horses), stream faithful clients, many famous in the arts, the movies, the theatre, or television. There are plenty of average Roman citizens, too, and many tourists, predominantly French, Swedish, and American. Signor Otello tells me that he has played host to the painter Novella Parigini, the sculptor Fazzini, and such movie notables as Belinda Lee, Simone Signoret and Yves Montand, Zsa Zsa Gabor, Henry Fonda, Audrey Hepburn and Mel Ferrer, Edmund and Alice Purdom, and a similar roster from the Italian movie industry.

Otello's cooking, robust rather than delicate, nevertheless man-ages to achieve a lightness that many a more pretentious estab-lishment could envy. Mushrooms are sprinkled about liberally on abbacchio, San Pietro, or turkey breasts. The menu also lists fine stews, sautées, and grills, especially good cannelloni and lasagne,

191

and a host of dishes based on eggplant or zucchine. The highly successful melanzana alla romana, together with a mixed salad, a carafe of Frascati, and a refreshing cup of iced fruits, makes a simple but memorable lunch.

The following recipes are typical of Otello's cookery.

MINESTRONE

fresh and dried vegetables (see below)	1 clove garlic
olive oil	parsley
salt and pepper	¼ tsp. sage
chicken or meat broth	1 cup small pasta or ½ cup rice
1 tbsp. tomato paste	Parmesan cheese
1 tbsp. butter	

A good minestrone depends on an abundant variety of vegetables, fresh and dried, each added according to the time needed for its cooking. According to the season, a rich soup such as Otello serves might contain such vegetables as carrots, celery, onions, potatoes, zucchine, peas, green beans, fava beans, a small head of cabbage (or half a large one), eggplant, spinach, and dried beans (white or pink, soaked overnight in cold water and drained).

Cut one onion, one carrot, and a branch or two of celery into small dice, and simmer them gently in two or three tablespoons of olive oil. Add salt and pepper to taste. When the vegetables begin to take on a little color, add some dried beans (soaked previously) and two cups of broth or water. Simmer for three-quarters of an hour. Cut up all the other vegetables except the cabbage, add them with one tablespoon of tomato paste, enough broth or water to cover, and bring to a boil. Add the cabbage, shredded in long noodle-like pieces, and continue to cook until it has wilted. The vegetables should be just covered with the broth, but the soup should remain thick. Simmer for another three-quarters of an hour. Add a tablespoon of butter blended with a crushed clove of garlic, a sprig of minced parsley, and about a quarter teaspoon of sage (or a few fresh leaves) and stir in well. When the butter has melted, add a cupful of small pasta such as elbows or shells, or one-half cup of

192

rice, and cook until they are just tender. Stir in one or more spoons of grated Parmesan cheese until the soup is rich and thick, and serve more cheese on the side. In summer Otello serves this soup cold. The Genoese add a few spoons of pesto instead of the butter and herbs called for here. Some cooks prefer to cook the cabbage or some of the beans separately until they are soft, and then pass them through a food mill, and add the purée to the soup.

MACEDONIA DI FRUTTA
(Fruit Compote)

There is really no exact recipe for this Italian improvement on the fruit cocktail. Its nature and flavor change with the fruits in season, but a good macedonia depends on three things: an adequate variety of mature fruit—and when dictated by seasonal lulls, canned or, in the United States, frozen fruits—cut into large chunks and sugared well; a serving temperature that is refreshingly cool; and the addition of maraschino liqueur. Some cooks substitute Marsala or white wine, but maraschino is the traditional and characteristic ingredient. In the summer Romans often eat macedonia with a scoop of ice cream on top.

CHECCO ER CARRETTIERE

FRANCESCO PORCELLI was the third generation of his family to peddle wine from a traveling cart. Over thirty years ago he decided to settle down to a more stationary existence. He gave up the cart and began selling his wine instead in a century-old tavern in the Via Benedetta in Trastevere. He called the place Checco er Carrettiere—Checco being the nickname for Francesco, and er Carrettiere being Roman dialect for cart driver. Before long he was serving food, along with the wine, and today he has a full-scale trattoria. The atmosphere is jolly, there is spirited music in the evenings, and Signor Porcelli is a friendly and attentive host. He is proud of his history, and tells me that he can actually trace his family tree back beyond the three generations of cart drivers to the year 1480.

Checco's food is very good, the menu full of favorite Roman dishes. Some of the ingredients for the night's cooking form a fine display from which you can select your dinner. There are always fish caught fresh that day, and vegetables from the Roman countryside that have just come from the market.

One of the specialties, a type of ravioli, has been known at Checco's for the last few years as "dischi volanti," or flying saucers. They are, under whatever name, an excellent way to start a dinner, and one of the recipes that Signor Porcelli has given me. Other specialties are spaghetti alla carrettiera, a variation on a Trastevere favorite that combines tuna fish, tomatoes, and mushrooms for its sauce; a fine oxtail and celery stew; Roman-style tripe served with fresh-chopped mint and gobs of grated cheese; and beans simmered with pork rind and ham bones and covered with a grating of sharp pecorino cheese. If the host suggests fish, it would be sound to take his advice, and if he should mention that there is capretto, don't pass it up. Checco prepares this suckling kid so that it is light, moist, and tender, with a skin that absolutely crackles.

CAPRETTO ARROSTO
(Roast Kid)

1 joint of capretto	salt and pepper
ham fat, salt pork, or very fat bacon	olive oil or melted butter
2 or 3 cloves of garlic	dry white wine
2 sprigs rosemary	fresh lemon wedges

Wipe the meat clean. Mince together the ham fat, garlic, and rosemary, and add salt and pepper. Cut slits all over the meat, and

194

stuff the fat and herbs into the pockets. Brush with olive oil or melted butter and put to roast in a moderately hot oven, about twenty minutes to the pound. When it is nearly done, pour a bit of white wine over it. Continue to roast until the skin is crisp. Serve with fresh lemon wedges.

[NOTE: Capretto is often available at Easter time in American cities with sizeable Italian populations. If you can't find suckling kid, substitute a leg of young spring lamb.]

DISCHI VOLANTI ALLA TRASTEVERINA
("Flying Saucers" Ravioli)

pasta dough (see recipe page 164)	¼ pound filet of beef
1 large lump of butter	white wine
½ clove garlic, minced	2 beaten eggs
¼ pound chicken	½ cup Parmesan cheese
¼ pound turkey	nutmeg
¼ pound veal	salt and pepper

Divide the prepared dough in two and roll out into sheets, one slightly larger than the other.

FILLING: Melt a large lump of butter in a skillet. Add the garlic, chicken, turkey, veal, and beef, and cook about fifteen minutes or until gently browned. Moisten with a few drops of dry white wine. Put through the food chopper two or three times; it must be very smooth. Add two beaten eggs, the grated Parmesan cheese, a fresh grating of nutmeg, and salt and pepper. If too dry, add another egg.

PREPARATION: Put about one teaspoon of filling every inch and a half over the smaller sheet of dough. There should be enough dough around each portion to amply cover a fifty-cent piece. Fit the second sheet loosely over the first, letting it fall between the mounds of filling. With a floured biscuit cutter or the rim of a juice glass, press out each mound or disc. Pinch the edges together. Boil in a large container of bubbling salted water until the flying saucers rise to the surface, and are tender to the taste. Lift them out with a perforated spoon and place in a preheated deep serving platter. Mix immediately with the following sauce.

195

sauce:

¼ lb. butter, and more as
   needed
1 clove garlic

1 lb. mushrooms
salt and pepper
½ cup grated Parmesan cheese

Melt the butter in a saucepan. Add the garlic, finely minced, and the mushrooms, sliced thin. Cook until golden, then add salt and pepper. Pour over the cooked discs, sprinkle on the grated cheese, and mix rapidly until the pasta is well coated with the sauce. Add a lump of butter and sprinkle additional cheese over the top. Makes about 150 discs and serves eight.

FAGIOLI CON LE COTICHE E LE OSSA DI PROSCIUTTO
(Beans with Pork Rind and Ham Bone)

4 good strips of ham rind or
   pork rind (with the fat)
1 large ham bone with some
   meat attached
2 lbs. fresh beans or
   1 lb. dried
olive oil
1 onion

1 stalk celery
1 carrot
dry white wine
2 cups stewed tomatoes
salt and pepper
grated pecorino or Parmesan
   cheese

Cut the bone in half, and put it together with the ham rind to soak in boiling water for a half hour. Drain, and put in fresh water to boil for about two and a half hours. Shell the beans and add them to a pot of boiling, salted water. If you use dried beans, they should be soaked overnight in cold water, drained, put in a pot with abundant cold water and salt, and brought to a boil. There should be enough water to boil for about two hours and still retain liquid in the pot. Cook the beans until tender (about two hours, but this varies with the kind). The Romans like to use a variety they call regina, but any broad bean will work well.

While the beans and ham bone are cooking, heat some olive oil in a large pot. Add to it the onion, celery, and carrot all cut into fine dice, and cook until they take on a golden color. Add three or

196

four splashes of dry white wine and continue cooking a few minutes more. Add the stewed tomatoes, salt and pepper. Drain the ham bones and rind and add to the pot. Add the beans and their cooking liquid (or enough to make a loose sauce, but not so much as to turn it into soup). Simmer all together for fifteen minutes or more. This dish should never be served hot off the stove. Remove from the heat about ten minutes before serving. Accompany with grated cheese. Serves four.

TRATTORIA IMPICCETTA
"GIARDINO DEI POETI"

IMPICCETTA, Garden of the Poets, is a typical old-quarter establishment in one of the noisy crowded streets between Viale Trastevere and Santa Maria in Trastevere. Its walls display a scattering of original 'cimeli'—memorabilia and objets d'art of bygone eras —as well as more recent Roman verse. The 'garden' is in reality an enclosed room at the rear of the simple restaurant, decorated to achieve an outdoor effect, bright and alive and skylighted. On its back wall there is verse in Roman dialect. Across the street there is a real outdoor area for summer dining.

The original name "Impiccetta" evolved from a nickname given its energetic proprietor, Alfredo Garotti, when he was a youth. It was a comment on his personality—outgoing, prankish, involved in everything going on around him. For fifty years or so the trattoria has been a gathering place for Roman poets, hence the second name, which honors them. Trilussa, Giulio Cesare Santini, and Ciaralli were once numbered among its affectionate literary clientele. But besides the poets, the king of Sweden, the brothers of the late Pope John, and the race driver Fangio have tasted its Roman cooking and enjoyed its unpretentious atmosphere.

197

The lusty verses in the trattoria extol foods and wines. Signor Garotti likes this couplet, printed beneath the picture of Trilussa, a handsome, graying gentleman, his wine glass to his lips:

> Dentro 'sta boccia trovi er bonumore,
> Che canta l'inni e t'imbandiera er core.
> —TRILUSSA

> (In this glass you find the good spirit
> That sings anthems and beflags your heart.)

The verse masterpiece, however, is certainly the Ballad of the Garden of the Poets:

LA CANZONE DEL GIARDINO DEI POETI

I

> Ricordete quann'entri à sto giardino
> che si l'ambiente è greve e un po' marano
> co' la Cucina bòno e cor bon Vino,
> c'è er core de Trastevere Romano! . . .
>   Beve fratello,
> arza er bicchiere e pensa nder guardallo,
> ch'è fosforo che metti ner cervello,
> quelli mille reflessi de cristallo!
>   Qui a 'sto locale,
>   te scordi er male,
>   nun ce so' affanni,
>   caleno l'anni!

II

> Forse tu me dirai che so' parole,
> ma er vino, fa passà qualunque male,
> e quel che manni in corpo è tutto sole,
> e nun c'è gnente che sia artificiale.
>   Beve e cammina
> e nun te ne curà si lampa e tona,

ner Monno vale er Vino e la Cucina;
ma puro un core de na pacioccona.
   Qui a 'sto locale,
   te scordi er male,
   nun ce so' pene,
   stai sempre bene!
   Guarda er bicchiere
pieno de vino e fonno come er mare:
affoghece qualunque dispiacere
mentre la poi pensà come te pare.

FINALE

   Qui a 'sto locale,
   te scordi er male . . .
   Viè' che t'aspetta
   l'oste Impiccetta,
   trovi er bon vino
   ce stai sereno:
   mò che ce semo
   magnamo e bevemo!
        —IMPICCETTA

A rough translation would be:

I

Remember when you enter this garden
That, if the atmosphere is a little rough and course,
With the good food and good wine
There is the heart of Roman Trastevere!
   Drink brother,
Lift your glass and while you're looking at it,
Think that it's phosphorus that you're giving
     your brain,*
Those thousand reflections of the crystal!

* Phosphorus is thought by the Italians to be a good brain food.

THE RESTAURANTS

Here in this place,
You forget all bad things,
There are no worries,
Your years are no concern!

II

Perhaps you'll say that these are just words,
But wine cures all your troubles,
And what you're taking into your body is all sun,
And there is nothing that is artificial.
  So drink and go on,
And don't be bothered by lightning and thunder,
In this world what really counts is wine and good food;
But don't leave out also the heart of a good woman.*
  Here in this place,
  You forget all your troubles,
  There are no sorrows,
  You always stay well!
  So look at the glass
Full of wine and as deep as the ocean:
Drown any sorrow
But at the same time you can think as you please.

FINALE

Here in this place,
You forget all your troubles ...
Come, the host Impiccetta is awaiting you,
You will find here good wine,
You will be merry:
And as long as we're here
Let's eat and let's drink!

*pacioccona, Roman dialect, is an untranslatable word that embodies in its meaning the good nature, femininity, and great beauty of a heavy woman, a difficult concept for us to appreciate.

200

The food here is hearty and appetizing, the menu large and varied and typically Roman, and the prices modest. The chef prepares two of his specialties daily—spaghetti all'Impiccetta and pollo alla diavola. Besides these, on Tuesdays there is stufatino cor sellero (stew with celery); Thursdays one finds gnocchi de patate (potato gnocchi); on Fridays there is all manner of fresh fish, but in particular zuppa de pesce, a fish stew made here, according to Impiccetta, "a modo mio"—in my own style; and on Saturdays a trio of specialità, consisting of Roman-style tripe, pajata cooked to your pleasure, and braised oxtail, coda alla vaccinara, in a robust sauce. Of all his specialties, Impiccetta is proudest of pollo alla diavola, which he praises, characteristically in verse, at the top of every menu:

> *Pollastro alla Diavola*
> *da Impiccetta?*
> *T'aggusta muccio*
> *come 'na maschietta!*

> *(Chicken alla Diavola*
> *at Impiccetta?*
> *You'll find it as tasty*
> *as a pretty young girl!)*

Impiccetta's spaghetti uses tuna, mushrooms, giblets and tomatoes. Here is the recipe he gave me:

SPAGHETTI ALL'IMPICCETTA

2 tbsp. olive oil
2 tbsp. minced fresh basil
1 tbsp. minced parsley
giblets of 2 or more chickens, diced
approximately 2 cups stewed plum tomatoes
1 lb. fresh, thinly sliced mushrooms
9 ounces (or 1½ tins) tuna fish
salt and pepper
2 lbs. pasta

Put the olive oil, fresh basil, parsley, and giblets to cook in a large casserole. Let it all simmer until the giblets are nicely browned. Then add some fresh tomato—Signor Garotti instructs, "as much as is needed" [or add two cups of stewed plum tomatoes]—the fresh mushrooms, and the tuna fish. Mix, and allow the mixture to cook until it is reduced to a good consistency, about an hour and a half over a low flame. Add salt and pepper "in the proper amount." These proportions make enough sauce for about two pounds, or six good portions, of pasta, which should be cooked in abundant briskly boiling water with a sprinkling of coarse salt.

A clove of minced garlic blends well with the basic flavors, and a little white wine does no harm, and if the sauce is getting too thick, a great deal of good. Cook the spaghetti al dente, drain and mix with a liberal pat of butter, and ladle the sauce on top. Do not serve with cheese if you want to do this all'italiana, for Italians rarely use cheese on a fish dish.

VINCENZO

VINCENZO CANALI, the proprietor of this small trattoria, is inordinately proud of his district, and is a spirited student of its history. He pointed out to me all of the neighborhood landmarks, as well as several places that are less well known. "That little church of San Benedetto in Piscinula is not in the guide books," he told me, "but it has one of the smallest belfries in the city, and was the first tower to stand as a watch post over the island." [He was referring to the Isola Tiberina, just a hundred meters or so distant.] He reflects with visible pleasure that his unassuming trattoria is located in the very center of the Trastevere quarter that once housed powerful, often tyrannical, barons. It is in the shadow of the Palazzo Tolomei, the last Roman refuge of that luckless Sienese family mentioned by Dante, and there are still some of the houses of the great Mattei family nearby, most notably the palazzo that faces the Via dei Funari and extends into the Piazza Mattei. Further along Vincenzo's street, the Via Lungaretta, is the Casa degli Anguillara, whose watch tower once kept guard over Trastevere. In the Middle Ages one of the pugnacious Anguillara refused to uncover his head before the Emperor, claiming he had a bad cold. A more conservative member of the same clan, Orso, left its portals on Easter Sunday, 1341, to perform the ceremonies on the Campidoglio which crowned Francesco Petrarca Poet Laureate. The partly reconstructed house, now known as the Casa di Dante, is a repository of Dante materials and a haven for scholars.

With the same pride in tradition, Vincenzo strives to keep his restaurant characteristic of the old quarter. Its decor is simple and unchanging, its atmosphere animated, and its menu filled with dishes which real Romans adore. The wines are the best from the Castelli, and, Vincenzo promises, "insure appropriate cordiality along with every meal." Although he feels that there is really no dish to set apart as a specialty "because every one of them is a masterpiece of the Roman cuisine," he conceded that his fish cookery *was* perhaps something extra noteworthy. He is proud of his zuppa di pesce, and has given me the recipe for it, as well as for the rice cooked with a mixture of seafood, fisherman's style. He produces excellent scampi delicately grilled or baked "al gratin" (another of the recipes he gave me), winey mussels in tomato and garlic broth, and fine spaghetti and clams.

This is one of the very few trattorias that still serves pagliata, a very special kind of tripe, and Vincenzo offers it cooked in a sauce for rigatoni, or bathed in oil and roasted on the grill. The abbacchio here is usually spiced with vinegar and anchovies, and stewed hunter's style. The mazzancolla, a large prawn especially dear to the Romans, is served up roasted pink and juicy. Vincenzo also bakes pizza of very fine quality, and makes his own agnolotti and cannelloni. The mixed fry from this kitchen contains golden brains and spinal "marrows," Roman artichokes, and, depending on the season, wild mushrooms or zucchine. Dessert lovers will be happy with the charlottes, trifles, and Saint Honoré that are almost always on the menu, and red wine drinkers will be pleased to find Chianti.

RISOTTO ALLA PESCATORA
(Rice with Seafood and Tomato Sauce, Fisherman's Style)

rice:

3 tbsp. butter
½ onion, minced

1 lb. raw (unwashed) rice
salt

sauce:

¾ cup olive oil
2 cloves garlic, minced
½ red pepper, minced
1 cup mussels and clams (cleaned and shelled)
1 cup shrimp (cleaned and shelled)

2 cups squid and cuttlefish (cleaned and cut into strips)
6 cups whole tomatoes (stewing type), peeled and cut in chunks

preparation:

¼ cup broth

fresh chopped parsley

RICE: Melt the butter in a skillet, add the minced onion, and sauté gently until the onion takes on a good color. Add the rice, and mix continuously until all the grains are well coated with the butter and onions. Cook, mixing frequently to keep it from sticking, until the rice is golden. Salt to taste, and add boiling water—just enough to cover the rice. Put the skillet in a hot oven (about 400°) and leave it, without mixing, until all of the water is absorbed. It should take between twenty and thirty minutes, and the rice should still be firm and slightly undercooked. Turn the rice out on a marble table top (or heatproof kitchen counter) and spread it to cool.

SAUCE: Put the oil to heat in a good sized saucepan, add the garlic and red pepper, and fry gently a few minutes. Add the seafood, and simmer for fifteen minutes. Then add the tomatoes (canned can be used), and a little of the broth left from preparing the clams (or the juice from the can, if you do not use fresh seafood). Simmer briskly for another fifteen minutes, cover, and reserve until ready to use. (It will have more flavor if it stands at least an hour.)

PREPARATION: Put the rice in a large casserole or skillet, add the sauce (leaving apart about one tablespoon per portion to spoon over the top), mix in the broth, and cook over a low flame until the rice is cooked through, and the sauce thickens. Heat the additional sauce and pour over the top, sprinkling with chopped fresh parsley. Serves six to eight. A more economical dish can be made by cutting the amount of seafood and tomato in half.

SCAMPI "AL GRATIN"
(Baked Scampi)

per portion:

6 or 7 large scampi (or jumbo prawns)	chopped parsley
	bread crumbs
olive oil	garlic
salt and pepper	

Split the scampi in half through the back, clean them, and put them shell side down in a flat baking dish. Splash them generously with olive oil, dust with salt and pepper, and trim with minced parsley over the top. Put in a hot oven to bake. Meanwhile mince garlic (amount according to your taste) and mix it with the bread crumbs, about a teaspoon per scampo. Sprinkle abundantly over the scampi, return to the oven, and cook until the bread crumbs brown. [A few dots of butter on the bread crumbs help them to brown nicely.]

205

ZUPPA DI PESCE
(Fish Soup)

Vincenzo uses scorpion fish (like our rock fish), ray, angler, grey mullet, moray, and sea polyps (very small octopi) in his fish stew. We cannot duplicate this precise blend of textures and flavors, but our selection should include six varieties that will provide as much contrast of meat and taste as possible.

3 lbs. assorted fish with heads and tails
2 cups olive oil
2 cloves garlic, minced
10 filets of salted anchovies, cut up
1 minced red pepper
salt to taste
4 quarts boiling water

2 lbs. stewing tomatoes, peeled and cut up (or 2 cups thick purée)
French bread
butter
garlic
olive oil
minced fresh parsley

Clean the fish, remove the heads and tails, and reserve. Cut the fish into good sized chunks and set aside. Prepare a broth by sautéing in the olive oil the garlic, the anchovies, the red pepper, and salt to taste. When all of the ingredients are soft and well blended —about ten minutes—add the boiling water, the stewing tomatoes or purée, and the heads and tails of the fish. Boil gently until the meat falls away from the heads. Strain the broth through a sieve. Poach the chunks of fish in the broth until they are just cooked (do not overcook or they will fall apart). Cut the French bread into ten or fifteen two-inch croutons or slices, rub with a bruised clove of garlic, spread with butter, and toast in the oven or fry in olive oil until crisp and golden. Place the toasts in deep soup bowls, spoon the broth and fish over them, and decorate with minced parsley. Serves five.

TAVERNA MARGUTTA

Via Margutta is as near as Rome comes to Montmartre or Greenwich Village, a narrow cobbled street bordered by modish shops, art galleries, and ateliers, and peopled by genuine artists, real and fancied Bohemians, and the usual fringe of untalented aspirants who trust to osmosis for their success. It is territory for browsing, for there is everything to see from the latest canvas of a contemporary master to the manufacture of antiques. At the very end of the street towards the Piazza di Spagna, stands the unadorned Taverna Margutta, a rendezvous for artists, students, and travelers from all over the world. Proprietor Colombo Graziani is known as the King of Margutta, "Il Re Marguttiano," and it is no wonder, for he is a genial, boisterous character. Always full of fun himself, he sees to it that his clients eat well, and are cheerfully diverted. Sometimes he joins the guitarist in a chorus or two to serenade a sweet young lady, he embraces departing friends with bearlike effusiveness, and showers warmth and affection generally on all comers.

The interior of the Taverna is pleasantly old-fashioned, furnished with white-draped tables, curve-backed chairs, and a collection of clients' original paintings that Papa Colombo has accumulated over the years. The substantial food is nicely cooked, and the à la carte menu is very inexpensive; when I was last there, the price-fixed menu (soup or pasta, entrée, vegetable, and fruit) was a veritable bargain, even with wine and service in addition. The dish that Colombo is most proud of is his homemade cannelloni filled with ricotta cheese and bathed with cream and tomato sauces. An old Roman favorite, saltimbocca, is one of the specialties: veal, ham, sage, butter, and white wine sautéed to a delicate gold. Colombo recommends his roast baby lamb, and the delightful piccata, veal cooked gently in butter with a few slices of lemon, and a touch of green parsley. The Taverna, says

207

the host, can "produce all of the Roman dishes that exist in the culinary art." Here are his recipes for several of them:

CANNELLONI ALLA COLOMBO

pasta made of egg dough, see
  page 108
1 lb. ricotta cheese
3 eggs, beaten
3 tbsp. grated Parmesan
  cheese

¼ to ½ nutmeg, according to
  taste
salt
3 cups tomato sauce
a little meat sauce (optional)

béchamel sauce:

¼ lb. butter
4 tbsp. flour

2 cups milk

Boil the pasta cut in squares of four by four inches, plunge in cold water, and set out to dry on a table or counter top. Mix together the ricotta, beaten eggs, cheese, freshly grated nutmeg, and salt to taste. Spoon a little of the filling on each dried square of pasta, and roll up. Put a little tomato sauce in the bottom of a baking dish, and lay the cannelloni in side by side. Pour the béchamel, tomato, and meat sauces over the rolls, and bake in a hot oven for about eight minutes or until they begin to brown. Serve with more grated cheese on the side. Serves six.

POMODORI AL RISO
(Tomatoes with Rice)

per portion:

1 large, *firm* tomato
salt
sugar
olive oil or butter
about ½ cup raw rice
1 clove garlic, minced

a few fresh leaves, or a sprinkle
  of dry, sweet basil
parsley, chopped
oregano
1 tbsp. grated Parmesan cheese
salt and pepper
2 tbsp. olive oil or butter

Remove the stem and stand the tomato stem side *down*. Cut off the top third straight across. With a teaspoon, scoop out the top and all of the pulp from the body of the tomato, and put it through a food mill or coarse strainer. Sprinkle the inside of each tomato shell with salt and a little sugar, and pour in a small quantity of olive oil or drop in a lump of butter. Mix the rice with about 2 tbsp. of the tomato purée, and add the minced garlic, the basil, parsley, oregano, one tablespoon of grated cheese, salt and pepper, 2 tbsp. olive oil or butter, and stir together well. Fill each tomato abundantly with the rice mixture, and top with the tomato lid. Place in a baking dish, and sprinkle with salt, dot with butter, and bake for an hour in a medium oven (375°). The rice should be al dente, still firm, when cooked. [I like to vary the seasoning sometimes with tarragon instead of basil.]

PISELLI AL PROSCIUTTO
(Peas with Ham)

3 lbs. fresh, young peas in the pod
2 tbsp. butter
¼ onion, finely minced
a little chicken broth

2 slices prosciutto cut in julienne
salt and pepper
1 shot glass white wine

Shell and wash the peas, and put to drain in a colander. Meanwhile melt the butter in a skillet, and sauté the onion in it gently. When the onion is limp and glazed, add the peas and just enough chicken broth (or water) to keep them moist while they cook at a brisk boil for about fifteen minutes (the Roman peas take only about ten, and so will very tender new peas when you can find them). Test to determine when they are barely cooked. Add the julienned slices of prosciutto, salt and pepper to taste, and a jigger of white wine. Cover and simmer for five minutes. An alternative is to use bacon in small dice, about three pieces, and cook it apart in a little water to keep it from frying; then add as for the prosciutto. Not everybody makes this recipe with the addition of wine, but it is a nice touch. Enough for six portions.

209

STUFATINO
(Beef Stew)

½ carrot
1 branch celery
1 small onion
¼ cup olive oil
1½ lbs. beef for stew (preferably rump roast, top or bottom round, or sirloin tip, though less distinguished cuts will serve)

½ cup dry white wine
2 cups chopped and skinned fresh tomatoes, or 2 cups canned tomatoes
salt and pepper
1 clove garlic (optional)
chopped parsley

Chop the carrot, celery, and onion into small pieces and set to cook in the olive oil. When they are blond and glazed, add the meat cut into chunks, and brown on all sides. Turn frequently so that the vegetables do not burn. When the meat has taken on an even color, add the white wine, cook for two or three minutes; then add the tomatoes, salt and pepper to taste, and if you are using it, the garlic, crushed. Reduce the sauce for a few minutes, then add enough water to cover the meat, and simmer very gently for about two hours. Garnish with fresh chopped parsley. Colombo serves his stufatino with fresh broad beans, boiled for about an hour, sprinkled over the top, or with new potatoes, boiled in their jackets, then skinned before serving. He also makes the recipe with veal instead of beef, cutting down on the amount of water added, and reducing the cooking time. Serves three or four.

DA GIGGETTO

THOUGH Da Giggetto itself couldn't be less assuming, it is set among mighty ruins. Perched on the threshold of the Portico of Octavia, the restaurant provides its guests with authentic Roman decor that dates back to the days of Augustus. The huge portico, once large enough to enclose two temples, retains only a few of its original three hundred columns. It was rebuilt several times before the Middle Ages, and then the imminent collapse of some of the supports led to large scale replacements. Beyond the columns and archways is the church of Sant'Angelo in Pescheria, where from the late sixteenth until the late nineteenth century Jews were herded to attend compulsory Christian services.

Summertime at Giggetto is most advantageous if you want to examine the Portico unhurriedly, for the restaurant's outdoor tables are set just next to it. Any time will do if you are interested in tasting some of the Roman specialties that Dino Trocchi, the chef, prepares. The trattoria has emphasized Roman cooking, in particular some of the Jewish dishes of the old ghetto which it borders, ever since it opened almost forty years ago as a small osteria. The same family has always owned it, the founders Luigi and Ines Ceccarelli having passed over the direction recently to their son Franco.

The two main attractions from the Jewish cuisine are artichokes cooked golden in deep, hot oil, and filleted salt codfish fried crisply brown. The menu is extensive, crammed with such dishes as rice croquettes (often with meat sauce); crostini under a buttery anchovy dressing; delicate egg noodles (tonnarelli) tossed with mushrooms, peas, and prosciutto, or with tuna, tomatoes, and dried mushrooms; dried beans and pork rind; and fresh fava beans with bacon. Fish soup is a house specialty, and so are a whole collection of little stews based on octopus, squid, or cuttlefish. Steaming heaps of mussels and clams cooked with wine, garlic, and tomatoes, are always good here.

From among a huge assortment of entrées, the stuffed squab (you can also have it broiled alla diavola, if you prefer) and the pork liver served with crunchy squares of toast, struck me as unusual. At the end of the meal there is celery or fennel, fresh and cool, to dip in little cups of seasoned oil (sedani or finocchi a pinzimonio). Most of the vegetables are bitter greens or broccoli

211

served with lemony dressing, although you can order them tossed in oil and garlic over the flame, if you prefer. There are usually eight or more cheeses to choose from, and such cool weather dainties as dried dates, figs, and shelled nuts. For sweets eaters, Dino always has a gooey dessert or two on hand. There are local wines by the flask, but most unusual for a trattoria of this type, a rather extensive collection of other Italian bottlings, primarily Tuscan.

The recipes that Dino has given me are for the Jewish dish of boned codfish, and two typically Roman ways of preparing cuttlefish.

FILETTI DI BACCALÀ SPINATI
(Boneless Codfish)

1 large piece of dried salt cod-fish, between 1 and 1½ lbs.	olive oil for frying lemon wedges

pastella:

2 cups flour	water
¼ tsp. baking powder	1 tbsp. olive oil

Soak the dried codfish in cold water overnight. Drain it well, remove the skin and bones (cut along the main column, separate and lift the flesh, lift out the bony skeleton in one piece). Cut the fish into pieces about twice finger length and about two inches wide. Combine the ingredients for the pastella, using just enough water to make a rather thick paste. Mix only well enough to combine the ingredients, avoiding a smooth blend that is too elastic. Dip the fish filets in the batter, and set to fry immediately in a skillet in abundant hot olive oil. Cook covered, over a lively flame, but turn to brown evenly. Serve as soon as they are nicely colored, with a garnish of lemon wedges. Serves six.

212

SEPPIOLINE AFFOGATI
(Stewed Cuttlefish)

1 lb. (before cleaning) cuttlefish or squid
4 tbsp. olive oil
1 clove garlic, minced

1 small piece hot red pepper
salt
½ glass dry white wine
chopped fresh parsley

Clean and skin the cuttlefish, removing ink sack and bone. If the seppioline are large, beat them with a heavy mallet to make them tender. Cut the meat into slices, and set to cook with the olive oil, garlic, and hot red pepper in a small earthenware pot. Cover and cook until the cuttlefish is just about tender (about half an hour), then salt to taste, and add the white wine. Simmer ten minutes longer, and serve with a frill of parsley over the top. Serves two or three.

SEPPIOLINE CON PISELLI
(Stewed Cuttlefish and Peas)

same as above, plus:

3 ripe tomatoes or about 1 cup
chopped

½ cup small fresh peas or
cooked peas

Proceed as for seppioline affogati (above). After the cuttlefish have simmered in the white wine, add the fresh tomatoes cut in chunks, and the peas if they are very small and will cook in ten minutes. Simmer until the peas are tender. Otherwise cook the tomatoes for ten minutes, then add the previously cooked peas, simmering just long enough to heat them through. Serves two or three. Without the addition of peas, this dish is called seppioline in umido.

"THE Lucullan and Classical Kingdom of Jewish Style Artichokes" is the way the owner describes Piperno, Rome's oldest continuing Jewish restaurant, known to armies of tourists for its specialty of fried artichokes. Pacifico Piperno started operations over a hundred years ago, and his grand nephew Mario is now the King of the Artichokes. The restaurant lies in the quarter that housed the old ghetto, where for three hundred years from the mid-sixteenth century the city's Jews were collected, confined, and deprived of many of their liberties. A Jewish synagogue, erected after Pope Pius IX relaxed the restrictions on the Jews, stands not far off by the banks of the Tiber. Nearby the restaurant, on the same hill, stands the Palazzo Cenci, seat of that ill-fated Renaissance family.

The restaurant's decor is uncomplicated, and its menu offers a cross-section of Roman cooking. Besides the magnificent artichokes, Piperno specializes in another Jewish delicacy, boneless fried codfish. The dried fish, baccalà, must soak overnight to twice its original size. Then it is skinned and boned, cut into sections, and dipped in Piperno's batter of flour, milk, oil, and water. After fifteen minutes of frying in a pan of olive oil, the fish comes forth light, crisp, and delectable.

Here are Piperno's recipes for Jewish style artichokes, and another local favorite, Roman style artichokes:

CARCIOFI ALLA GIUDIA
(Artichokes Jewish Style)

The Romans use two or three good-sized artichokes per portion, and, blessed with a uniquely tender vegetable, they can eat the entire blossom. Americans must obtain very small artichokes with immature chokes and tender leaves to prepare this recipe. Remove the outside leaves, and trim off the sharp points on the remaining

214

leaves (easiest with scissors). Leave an inch or two of stem, if the produce dealer hasn't already relieved you of it. Wash the artichokes, and soak in cold water with lemon juice to prevent discoloration. Drain, dry, and invert each artichoke on a wooden board or counter top. Tap it smartly down, in order to press open the leaves. Fill a large earthenware pot (traditionally used for this recipe, probably because it maintains a steady temperature and assures an even color) two-thirds full of olive oil, and heat medium hot. Lower the artichokes into the oil and fry them, turning from time to time so that they cook evenly, until they are a light brown. Remove to a drainer until ready to serve. Then fry them again in the hot oil, first upside down, pressing them hard against the bottom with a wooden spoon to open them out. (If you are using very small artichokes, this is not necessary.) Turn and fry quickly until they are crisp and golden. Salt lightly and serve immediately. [Both Elizabeth David in *Italian Food* (p. 252) and Ada Boni in *Il talismano della felicità* (p. 809) suggest that a few drops of cold water shaken from the hand over each nearly cooked artichoke assure a "crisp and crackling" result. Should you try this, I repeat Mrs. David's warning to stand clear—it avoids crisping and crackling *you*.]

CARCIOFI ALLA ROMANA
(Artichokes Roman Style)

The Romans stuff these steamed artichokes between the leaves, then consume the entire vegetable, leaves and all. We can best duplicate their recipe by trimming off the large outside leaves of a globe artichoke, cutting off the top, and cutting out the choke. Stuffing can be in the cavity, as well as here and there among the leaves, but we cannot consume all of the plant in any case. Use two large artichokes per portion. Trim off the hardest leaves and sharp points, remove the top and choke, and cut flat across the bottom. Rub with fresh lemon to keep from blackening. Use one clove of garlic and a few fresh mint leaves per artichoke. Chop together, add salt and pepper to the mince, and stuff the artichokes by forcing apart the leaves. Place the artichokes side by side in a casserole, and anoint with olive oil, about ¼ cup for each artichoke. Add a glass of water

215

or white wine to the pot, and season with salt and pepper. Cover and cook gently until the artichokes are tender, about forty-five minutes to an hour. Serve with a bit of the liquid poured over them. Romans often eat these cold. The small, immature blooms of the artichoke plant can be prepared this way successfully, and perhaps even more easily, since there is no need to remove the choke. They will cook in less time.

DA PALOZZO

IN GENZANO DI ROMA

GENZANO is one of the Alban Hill towns south and east of Rome, about a twenty mile drive from the capital. Its terraces descend to Lake Nemi, a crater that was once dedicated to Diana, but which more recently has derived its fame from such earthy delights as strawberries and flower festivals. In ancient times the celebrations were of a more barbaric nature. The position of the priest of Diana called for a fight to the death between the current office-holder and a challenger, and was the inspiration for Frazer's *The Golden Bough* (the ritual required that the challenger first break off a golden branch from a tree in Diana's grove). The site of this ceremony was the town of Nemi, about two miles from Genzano, where excavators have found ruins of Diana's temple.

Several hundred years ago, two Roman ships were discovered on the lake's bottom. These enormous craft, which were probably ancient pleasure ferries, were too difficult to reclaim until the 1930's. Then they were placed in a specially built lakeside museum, only to be completely destroyed along with the building during World War II, when German soldiers recklessly set fire to them. A new, vastly empty museum contains smaller scale models, and a few charred remains.

216

In June the town of Nemi holds its strawberry festival. The tiny wild berries from this area are the best of them all, and the tag "fragoline di Nemi" on a menu assures you of a veritable delicacy (at a commensurate price). Sometimes the pickings are sparse, and I understand that one recent festival, as gay and strawberry-filled as ever, displayed berries that had to be brought in, alas, from elsewhere.

June is also the month of the Genzano flower festival, one of the most remarkable in the country. On Corpus Christi, the entire main street is a solid carpet of fresh flower petals, laid out in intricate patterns and designs. The flower-laying teams start their work at four in the afternoon and finish by evening. Beforehand they have drawn chalk outlines the length of the Via Italo Berardi; and the most difficult faces have been entirely completed on plaques indoors, to be brought into place when the festival commences. But most of the work is done on the spot with millions of gorgeous petals, their freshness preserved in the cool caves of the Genzano hillside.

If you drive around the lake on a penetrating-hot summer day (less hot than a hot summer day in Rome), you skirt fields of flowers under cultivation, vineyards, chestnut woods, stands of wild blackberry, and hillsides overgrown with wild mint, strawberries, and vivid cyclamen. The beauty of the spot is not dramatic but tumble-down, derived from a sense of almost humdrum ease, from the pleasant buzz of insects, from the scent of bruised mint underfoot. An osteria, badly needing paint and general shoring up, offers slices of excellent home-made sausage, salami, or local cured ham stuffed between Gargantuan slabs of Genzano bread. There is wine of the region, fresh and gently bubbly, and a rough table under a vine-shaded pergola along the side of the lake.

The best place to eat in the Lake Nemi area—nothwithstanding the number of older, fancier establishments—is the Trattoria Da Palozzo. This simple restaurant was started in the spring of

217

1962 by Alfredo Ronconi, who is called Palozzo, and his mother-in-law, whose husband had once been a great restaurateur. Perched high above the lake, with a lovely summer porch overlooking it, Da Palozzo is as pleasant a place to spend a summer evening as I can imagine. The breezes never stop, and by the end of dinner the warmth of a sweater or jacket is essential. The indoor dining room is cheery and animated all year around. The kitchen is spacious but with the quality of a cozy country home. Several ladies are always enjoying themselves around the stove, chatting amiably, sprinkling a bit of salt with the fingers, tipping a wine bottle over a bubbling pot. There seems none of the rush or distraction that one associates with a busy restaurant kitchen; the orders are put together as if they were to go on the family table for supper.

Although there may well be one, I have never seen a menu at Palozzo. Everyone seems to order by discussion. The host suggests three or four dishes, and the pros and cons, preferences and dislikes of the guests are aired before the choice is made. There are several culinary attractions worth pointing out, the most distinguished being game of all descriptions. Palozzo is skilled at its preparation, and you may very well turn up some buckshot to prove that it's real. The delicate egg noodles with a meat sauce based on hare (pappardelle alla lepre) are splendid here, and when hare is not being hunted Bolognese sauce is a fine substitute. Incomparable little birds called beccafichi obligingly feed on figs, which enhance first their own pleasure, and subsequently that of the fortunate Palozzo diner who receives them flaming on a spit. Quail and all sorts of small game birds are grilled over carbon, while the four-legged beasts are disguised in velvet sauces redolent of wines and spices. When game is not available, the restaurant has wonderful ways with lamb, veal, and fowl. The zingarella, an excellent veal dish, is one of their specialties, and one of the recipes given me by the owner. If you like wild mushrooms, the porcini at Palozzo are sautéed with garlic and wild

218

mint. The bread, baked in Genzano, is the best kind of rough country loaf, so good of its type that it is widely sold in Rome. The secret of its special country character is that it is baked in ovens that burn chestnut logs. The natives cut it in healthy slabs, bathe it with a little water, season it with salt and pepper, spread it with pieces of fresh tomato and a dusting of fresh chopped basil, and put it in the oven until it is hot and aromatic. They call this passanella.

Wine in Genanzo has the fragrance and freshness characteristic of pressings from the Roman castelli. There is an unsophisticated but charming red, naturally effervescent, and light enough to drink in frighteningly large quantities. The white is, like Frascati, limpid, amber, and pleasantly fruity.

Here are three recipes from the very generous Signor Palozzo:

UCCELLINI SUL CARBONE
(Game-Birds Grilled over Charcoal)

quail, figpeckers, ortolans, or game-birds of your choice	salt and pepper
laurel leaves	brandy
olive oil	fennel seeds

Thread the cleaned birds on skewers, with laurel leaves between them. (The Italians leave the heads on, and eat everything, bones and all.) Anoint with olive oil and season with salt and pepper. Grill them over a good bed of charcoal, turning continuously so that they brown evenly. Baste with oil (or white wine) as they need it. When they are cooked, place the skewers on a heatproof serving platter, sprinkle with fennel seeds, and pour over them a bit of warmed brandy. Light immediately, and serve flaming.

[Although squab are much too big to be called a true substitute —no one would think of eating one bones, head, and all—they do take well to the flavor of fennel and brandy.]

219

LEPRE IN SALMÌ
(Hare in Wine Sauce)

1 hare (or domestic rabbit)
dry red wine
1 carrot
1 or 2 stalks celery with leaves
1 onion
1 sprig parsley
giblets and liver of the hare
1 fresh laurel leaf or 3 dried
a sprinkling of fresh thyme, oregano, sage, rosemary; or 1 heaping tsp. dried herbs, combined

2 or 3 cloves
salt and pepper
2 tbsp. lard
butter
½ tbsp. flour
½ cup stewed tomatoes
2 anchovy filets
1 jigger glass red wine vinegar
1 clove garlic, minced

Cut the hare into pieces and marinate at least overnight, but preferably longer, in red wine to cover, with the following additions: the carrot, celery, onion, and parsley, all diced; the giblets and liver, diced; the laurel, fresh or dried herbs, cloves, salt and pepper.

Melt the lard and a little butter in a heavy skillet. Brown the hare in the hot fat, first drying each piece with absorbent paper. Add the vegetables, herbs, and giblets from the marinade, a few at a time, draining them first in a slotted spoon (but save the marinade). If the meat and vegetables are too wet, they will not brown nicely. When the vegetables and hare have taken on a good color, sprinkle with about half a tablespoon of flour, blending it well with the fat. Cook a few minutes and then add the marinade, the stewed tomatoes, the anchovy filets, chopped, the red wine vinegar, and the minced garlic. Cook gently over low heat until the meat is tender, about an hour for domestic rabbit, longer for wild hare. If the sauce becomes too thick, dilute with a little broth or water. When ready to serve, remove the meat to a serving platter and keep it warm. Strain the sauce and pour it over the meat. The best accompaniment is polenta. A small domestic rabbit will serve three or four; a larger hare six to eight.

ZINGARELLA DI VITELLO
(Veal with Spicy Sauce)

Zingarella means little gypsy.

6 slices choice veal, ¼ lb. each, 3 to 4 inches across	butter
flour	6 tsp. tomato-meat sauce (or thick tomato sauce)
olive oil	¼ cup dry white wine

pesto:

8 pitted green olives	5-6 gherkins
2 filets of anchovy	1 tuft parsley
1 clove garlic	6 tbsp. olive oil
1 heaping tsp. capers	

Pound the veal thin and flat, flour the pieces lightly, and brown well in half olive oil, half butter. When nicely colored, pour the white wine over the meat and cook a few minutes. Spoon one teaspoon of tomato-meat sauce over the meat, turning the meat over several times in the oil-wine-tomato gravy until it takes on a nice rosy color. Add a generous spoonful of pesto (see below) for each portion to the pan gravy (*not* over the meat), and blend it in well. Then turn the meat back and forth in the gravy, until it is well infused with it. To serve, put the meat on a warm dinner plate and pour the gravy over it.

PESTO: Mince, then mash, all of the ingredients with the oil until the mixture is pastelike. If you have a blender, it will produce just the right consistency. The zingarella serves six.

4. *Elegant*

THESE luxury restaurants go beyond the kind of international sophistication which is characteristic of them all. Their settings have an elegance that is more than merely professional decor, their service is performed with the proper flourishes, their wine lists are extensive, their food distinguished. Their prices are high by Roman standards, and rightly so; yet it is still possible to dine in any of them very well indeed for much less than a comparable meal would cost in Paris or New York.

222

IN 1300 the Albergo dell'Orso was a humble inn where Dante Alighieri reportedly once lodged. Reconstructed on more fashionable lines early in the fifteenth century, the hostaria subsequently attracted such company as Rabelais, Montaigne, and Goethe. Its luster dimmed over the centuries, and by the beginning of this one it had fallen into sinister disrepute. In 1940 Antonio Prantera refurbished and reopened the three-story building, and the Inn of the Bear has been Rome's most elegant bar, restaurant, and night club ever since. Tucked at the end of a narrow street a flight below but just off the main river thoroughfare, this Medieval building with Renaissance overtones is really a reflection of Signor Prantera's exquisite taste. He has an unerring sense of color and light, and knows that pale linen, a pink glow of candlelight, and a mixed bouquet of field flowers will underscore such beauties of the past as the coffered ceilings, the fourteenth century staircase, and the hangings and fittings of the Renaissance. It is his genius that saves the newest construction, the Borgia Room, from the label of ostentation that gold cutlery, tall stemmed crystal, and regal blue linen might otherwise earn it. His musicians have talent. Among them their repertoire embraces arias, French music hall ballads, Neapolitan folk songs, and the best of Cole Porter. Their performance is unobtrusive and part of the background as it should be, but I often think this is more the pity!

The Blue Bar, once tucked away in an intimate corner off the grand entry hall, has been moved front and center to replace it. Although it is larger now and still luxuriously handsome, it is also the main passageway that leads to the Borgia Room, the upstairs dining room, and the swanky third floor Cabala nightclub. The intimacy is lost, but the passing parade is fascinating. Chiffons swirl past, silks and heavy brocades rustle by, precious stones drip

223

and flash, and minks chum with chinchillas. Occasionally dark-suited gentlemen stop at the bar and command a Carlos I, while their wives melt visibly with each strum of the guitar. The air is heavy with French scent, and a babble, half Texas–half principessa, competes with the pianist's spirited interpretations.

The Borgia Room offers an elaborate menu all its own, the most attentive waiters on the premises, and a violinist and pianist to provide background ensembles. The regular dining room, on the second floor, is slightly less luxurious, but there is enough of the really grand manner there to please most sybarites. There is, further, a price-fixed menu of substantial range that makes it possible to eat elaborately at half of what such a meal might cost in a comparable American restaurant. Of course, all of the delicacies, like caviar and vegetables out of season, and the beverages, alcoholic and otherwise, are à la carte. A small orchestra entertains diners in the connecting salons of this upstairs dining room, and there is dancing for the nimble-footed.

As to the food, there is a large selection from the Italian cuisine, with specialties from all parts of the country, and several international dishes of renown. Do not be misled into thinking that you will dine only on rich or "showy" dishes. If you like, there are the simplest broths and omelettes, and humble spaghetti alla carbonara right alongside the creamiest cannelloni. There is a handsome selection of antipasti from a rolling cart to start things off, and a beguiling stand of fancy patisseries to end with. In between there are entrées in flames and in parchment cases, in elaborate or simple sauces and even straight off the grill. If you are in the mood for seafood, bouquet de poisson Tony combines filet of sole, clams, mussels, and shrimp in a cream and Scotch whisky sauce. You can have ham in Madeira, sweetbreads in Marsala, or chicken in champagne. Beef and veal come in many guises, from the tournedos Rossini with pâté de foie gras, truffles, and a dark winey gravy, to golden breaded bolognese cutlets enclosing prosciutto and bubbling cheese.

224

There are always early vegetables, and I recall eating my first matchstick-thin, wild asparagus at Signor Prantera's tables. Besides all of the fancy baked goods for dessert, there are flaming omelettes, mousses, ice cream delights, crêpes, bursting-ripe fruits, and a good tray of cheeses. The Hostaria dell'Orso, as you might expect, has an outstanding wine cellar, as good as any in the city—if not the best.

Tony Prantera, a very warm and cordial host, is enthusiastic about sharing recipes, and gave me these:

FILETTI DI SOGLIOLE "ORSO"
(Filets of Sole, Orso Style)

per portion:

1 sole weighing about 1 lb.	butter for frying
2 large prawns	1 ripe stewing tomato
2 mushroom caps	1 lump butter
flour	2 tbsp. meat juice or gravy
salt and pepper	chopped fresh parsley
1 or 2 yolks of egg	

Fillet the sole (or buy 4 small filets per portion). Shell and de-vein the prawns. Rub the mushroom caps clean with a damp sponge. Dip all in flour, then in beaten egg yolk, and set to fry in a skillet with melted butter. When everything is nicely browned on all sides, arrange the fish with the prawns and mushroom caps over it on a silver serving platter. Sprinkle with salt and pepper, and pour on a sauce made by cooking together the fresh tomato (pear type, if possible) peeled and chopped, a bit of meat gravy, and a good lump of butter, until it is reduced to a creamy consistency.

FRITTURA DI MARE
(Seafood Fry)

At the Hostaria dell'Orso, the seafood fry contains filets of sole, shrimp, scampi (prawns can be used), and rings of squid. You can substitute other fish or shellfish, but they should always be boned, and the shellfish peeled and de-veined. To prepare the squid, clean and remove the ink sack and bone, by cutting off the ends and working the innards out. The body, still intact, can then be cut through (with scissors) to form one-inch-wide rings. Each diner should have samplings of each fish; two small filets of sole, a half dozen small shrimp, three or four scampi, and a half dozen rings of squid is the suggested portion.

PREPARATION: Dip all of the fish and shellfish first in milk, then in flour. Heat abundant olive oil in a deep pot (deep frying pots with their own drainer baskets are perfect). Put the fish and shell-fish to fry, adding the rings of squid last since they will not endure excessive frying. When all the pieces have a good crisp coat, drain them in the frying strainer or on absorbent paper. Sprinkle well with salt and serve immediately on a silver platter decorated with a lace paper doily, lemon wedges, and tufts of parsley.

ROGNONCINO FLAMBÉ
(Flamed Veal Kidney)

1 young veal kidney	salt and pepper
olive oil	2 jigger glasses of cognac or
butter	calvados

Cut the kidney in half lengthwise. Cut out the tubular vessels and tough membranes with sharp scissors. [Though the Hostaria dell'Orso recipe does not follow this procedure, you can first soak the kidney in cold water for an hour or so.] Slice the kidney in small pieces. Heat a little oil in a skillet, add the kidney slices, and barely fry them in the oil as quickly as possible. Turn them into a colander or strainer to drain for five minutes to remove any disagreeable odor. Melt some butter in another skillet, and return the kidney slices to fry until they are nicely browned and tender. Remove to the table (if you have chafing dish equipment, this is a good recipe for it), add salt and pepper, swirl in a lump of butter, and pour over the kidney two shot glasses of warmed brandy or calvados. If you have a flame underneath the skillet, warming is not necessary. Ignite and serve immediately as the flame dies down. One small kidney will serve two.

UOVA ALLA FIORENTINA
(Eggs Florentine)

2 lbs. fresh spinach

salt

1 or 2 poached eggs per portion

grated Parmesan cheese for topping

béchamel sauce:

2 tbsp. butter

2 tbsp. flour

1½ cups milk, warmed

salt

mornay sauce:

above béchamel, plus:

1 cup grated Parmesan or Swiss cheese, or 1 cup half Parmesan and half Swiss

Wash the spinach carefully, and discard tough stems. With just the washing water that clings to it, put the spinach to boil in a heavy pot or skillet, covered, turning once or twice. In a few minutes it will be completely cooked. Strain through a fine food mill, or blend in an electric machine. Melt the butter, add the flour little by little, stirring continuously, then add the warmed milk gradually, blending in evenly with a wire whisk. Cook, stirring all the while, for several minutes until the sauce has thickened and the flour has cooked through. Salt to taste. Add one tablespoon of the béchamel to the spinach and more salt according to taste. Mix well together and turn into a large boat-shaped porcelain casserole, or divide among four individual oval baking dishes. Poach one or two eggs for each portion and arrange on the spinach beds. Heat the remaining béchamel with one cup of grated cheese, added little by little, until the cheese has melted and the sauce has thickened. Pour the mornay sauce over the eggs and spinach, sprinkle with more grated cheese, and slip under the broiler (or salamander) until the top is browned. A few spoons of the mornay mixed with a tablespoon of whipped cream spread over the top before the final sprinkling of cheese will insure a fine golden color. Serves four. [A little nutmeg grated into the spinach is a pleasant addition, and a dash of hot red pepper picks up the mornay sauce nicely.]

227

LASAGNE PASTICCIATE
(Lasagne Casserole)

pasta verde:

4 scant cups flour, or about
1 lb.
3 large eggs
½ lb. spinach, boiled and
puréed
1 tsp. salt
water as needed, drop by drop
butter

béchamel sauce (about 3 cups
or double the preceding
recipe)
Bolognese sauce (see recipe
below)
2 cups grated Parmesan cheese
1 small oval of mozzarella
cheese

PASTA VERDE: pour the flour in a mound on the table top, and make a well in the center. Break the eggs in the middle, add the spinach (boiled and puréed as in preceding recipe for uova alla fiorentina), and salt. Mix together with the fingers, adding flour from the edges little by little, and water by the drop as needed, until it is all worked together. Pat into a ball. Flour lightly and knead for at least ten minutes, or until it is very smooth and elastic. Roll out in two or four parts until it is as thin as possible. The Italians wrap the tissue-thin dough around their long rolling pins and work it ever thinner by pushing inward and outward over the pin as it rolls. If you have a pasta machine, this is a good time to use it. Cut the finished dough in squares roughly three by three inches. Set these to cook in boiling salted water a few at a time (they are very quick cooking). Drain, plunge into a bowl of cold water, and set out to dry on towels.

Butter a large fireproof clay casserole, and spread with a little béchamel and Bolognese sauces. Lay down a covering of pasta squares, slightly overlapping. Over the first pasta layer spread another covering of béchamel and of meat sauce, and sprinkle with about one-half cup of Parmesan cheese. Add another pasta layer, repeat the sauces and cheese, and add the third and last layer of lasagne. Top with the mozzarella cheese in slices, the rest of the Parmesan, and cover over with Bolognese sauce. Bake in a 375° oven for twenty-five to thirty minutes, then stick under the broiler or pass in the salamander to brown the top well. Serves six to eight.

228

SALSA BOLOGNESE
(Bolognese Sauce)

soffritto:

1 carrot, chopped
1 onion, chopped
4 cloves garlic, chopped
1 branch celery, chopped

olive oil
fresh basil (optional), chopped
parsley, chopped

sauce:

1 lb. beef and veal, ground together
1 or 2 pieces chicken without bones, cut in chunks
chicken giblets and liver, diced
1 pair sweetbreads, braised, cut in pieces

1 cup dry white wine
2 cups solid pack tomatoes
1 tbsp. tomato paste
salt and pepper
whole nutmeg

SOFFRITTO: Sauté the carrot, onion, garlic, and celery in olive oil until glossy. Add a little fresh basil and parsley. SAUCE: After a few minutes, add to the soffritto the ground meat, chicken, giblets, liver, and sweetbreads, and brown over a brisk flame. Pour white wine over the browned meats and vegetables, and add the solid pack tomatoes, tomato paste, salt, pepper, a good grating of whole nutmeg (half of a small nutmeg is not too much), and some juice from the braised sweetbreads. Simmer gently for at least two hours. The sauce should be on the thick side. If too runny, reduce by turning up the flame for a few minutes.

To braise the sweetbreads (which is not absolutely necessary, but adds a fine flavor to the sauce), soak them first in cold water. Blanch in boiling water for a few minutes. Drain in cold water, and trim all the membranes and extraneous matter. Sauté a small onion and a piece of carrot, both minced, in butter; add a clove of garlic, the sweetbreads and their trimmings, about one cup of warm beef bouillon, salt, pepper, a little thyme, a bay leaf, and some parsley. Cover and simmer in a hot oven (450°) for twenty minutes. Strain and reserve the cooking liquor for the Bolognese sauce. [Sweetbreads prepared in this way are ready to use in many other dishes, sauced, creamed, and as filling for vol-au-vents, for example.]

229

PALAZZI
(CAMILLUCCIA)

Palazzi is about fifteen or twenty minutes drive from the center of Rome. High on Monte Mario, with a splendid view over all the city, this icy blue-white villa seems remote from the noise and rush below it. A fascinating—if somewhat chilling—period piece, this modernistic retreat was built by Mussolini for his mistress, Claretta Petacci. Architecturally it is a product of the 30's: sleek, faceless, rounded-where-it-should-be-square, and heavy on the dramatics. A long driveway leads up to the parking plaza, where an attendant relieves you of your car. Much is left unchanged from the original set-up. The present reception room, once the living room, looks like the lobby of a small deluxe hotel, its furnishings impersonal, its grand piano polished but silent, a trout pond in the center of the floor. The ground floor study is a compact version of the living room. The adjacent small bar is the most pleasant and intimate setting in the villa. An enormous ramp sweeps to the second floor, bounded on one side by a continuous glass enclosure which encases myriads of exotic birds that frolic and flutter from branch to driftwood branch. The former reception room makes a splendid front dining room, but it is not nearly as spectacular as the summer terrace, which descends a few wide steps from the villa and encircles a lighted swimming pool, with an outdoor bar off to one end. An excellent dance orchestra plays from a platform over the pool. The upper levels, formerly a second-floor kitchen and dining-room, with the bedrooms above, now contain decks, terraces, offices, and assorted dining accommodations for private parties. Clara's bedroom, rumored to have a mirrored ceiling, is off-bounds to visitors. The whole layout is plush and theatrical, and if one had no knowledge

230

of its former occupants, it would be hard to believe that anyone had ever called this home.

The Petacci family owns the property still, but they act only in the capacity of landlords. The actual director is Signor Palazzi, an experienced restaurateur originally from Milan. His first restaurant in the Rome area was at the Ciampino airport, and he has more recently opened another at the new Fiumicino airport. The Monte Mario establishment was opened more than ten years ago. Mario, the capable maître d'hôtel, has been with the establishment since its opening day.

The menu is international with strong Italian underlinings, the cooking is delicate and expert, and the prices high but not outrageous. There are various antipasti, including the whole range of delicacies from smoked salmon and imported caviars to prosciutti from San Daniele del Friuli and foie gras from Strasbourg. The best choice among a good variety of soups, risottos, and pastes is certainly the house specialty, crespelle alla Sorrentina. These delicate egg pancakes are first stuffed with cream sauce combining cheese and eggs, then baked in small pieces with puréed tomato poured over them. If you prefer your eggs in other forms, the menu here is one of the few that offers an elaborate variety.

There are other light entrées: vol-au-vents, creamed mushrooms, Welsh rarebit, and such Italian favorites as fried mozzarella sandwiches, or crostini under a cover of melted provatura and anchovies. You can find all kinds of steak, chop, and lobster dishes here, besides a large variety of the more usual Italian fare. The dessert list includes soufflés and crêpes Suzette, along with the zabaglione and macedonia al liquore.

Mario has given me recipes for several dishes from the menu:

231

CERVELLA AL BURRO NERO
(Brains in Brown Butter)

1 small calf's brain	flour
lemon or vinegar	3 tbsp. butter
one small carrot	1 tsp. capers
one small onion	vinegar (best, red wine
salt	vinegar)

Soak the brain in cold water with a bit of lemon juice or vinegar for an hour or so, drain it, trim off the membrane. Put it to boil in a half quart of water with about 2 tbsp. of vinegar, one carrot and one onion, both sliced, and a dash of salt. When the water comes to a boil, turn down the flame and simmer for about ten minutes. Put the pot under slowly running cold water, until the brain is cool. Cut it into several pieces, pat dry with a paper towel, and dip lightly in flour. Put about 1 tbsp. of butter to melt in a small frying pan. When it is hot, add the brain and brown gently, turning so the pieces cook evenly. Sprinkle with salt and pepper while the brain cooks. Remove it to a warm plate, add another tablespoon or two of butter and continue cooking the sauce until it takes on a deep golden-brown color. Add a spoonful of capers and several drops of wine vinegar, and reduce the sauce for a few minutes. Pour over the brain and serve immediately. Serves one or two. [The average calf's brain used in Italy is well under half a pound, probably smaller than you will find in the United States. The other ingredients of this recipe should be slightly increased if you start with a larger brain.]

CERVELLA DORATE
(Golden Fried Brains)

Prepare 1 small calf's brain as above; soak, trim, boil, slice, and dip in flour, but in this case season with salt and pepper just before flouring. Heat one kettle of oil very hot, fry the slices of brain until golden, remove and drain on absorbent paper. Sprinkle with chopped parsley and garnish with lemon wedges.

CERVELLA DORATE ALLA MILANESE
(Golden Fried Brains Milanese Style)

Proceed as above. After flouring, dip in beaten egg, then in bread-crumbs. Fry as above. Garnish with lemon and chopped parsley.

[For any of the above recipes, you can substitute lamb's brain.]

Here is the Camilluccia version of a classic Roman dish:

POLLO ALLA ROMANA
(Chicken Roman Style)

1 small chicken
olive oil
1 clove garlic

salt and pepper
2 mature fresh tomatoes
½ lb. sweet green peppers

Heat the oil and cook the garlic, minced, until it is just golden. Add salt and pepper, the tomatoes, blanched, skinned, and cut into quarters, and the sweet peppers, seeded and cut in strips. When they are about half done, add the chicken cut in quarters (or eight pieces, if you prefer). Cover and cook very gently for about half an hour. Remove the skins from the peppers with two forks, cover and continue to cook over the lowest heat for thirty minutes longer, or until very tender. Serves two.

PERE BELLA ELENA
(Baked Pears with Ice Cream and Chocolate Sauce)

for each portion:

1 baked pear (recipe below)
1 scoop vanilla ice cream
(recipe below)

½ cup chocolate sauce (recipe below)
dab of whipped cream

Put two halves of a baked pear on a serving dish, top with a scoop of vanilla ice cream (the homemade type will be rather soft) and garnish with a splash of chocolate sauce and a glob of whipped cream.

233

PERE COTTE (Baked Pears): Peel one pear per portion, halve, scoop out the stem and seeds, and place in a baking dish, cut side up. Pour about a half cup of dry white wine per portion over the pears, and add a little for good measure. Sprinkle each pear with a heaping tablespoon of sugar. Bake in a moderately hot oven about thirty minutes, or until tender when tested with a toothpick. Cool before serving. [If you plan to serve simple baked pears, a dish found frequently on Italian menus, leave the pears whole after peeling them, and increase the baking time to at least 45 minutes. A little lemon rind grated over them before they bake is a pleasant addition. Serve with their syrup. This is also the classic baking method for apples (mele cotte). They should first be cored, but not peeled, and must be baked in the wine and sugar for about an hour.]

For those who want to make the ice cream at home, here is a recipe for six portions:

GELATO DI VANIGLIA
(Vanilla Ice Cream)

2 cups rich milk	4 large egg yolks
½ cup sugar, plus 2 tbsp.	1 tsp. vanilla

Heat the milk, preferably in the top of a double boiler, until it is very hot but not boiling. Mix in the sugar. Beat the egg yolks in a pyrex bowl. Pour a very little of the hot milk into the eggs, beating continuously, and when it is well mixed in, pour the egg mixture into the rest of the hot milk, always stirring. Continue cooking and stirring but do not allow the eggs to reach the boiling point. When the mixture is thickened and very creamy (it should coat an upright spoon without running off), stir in one teaspoon of vanilla. If you have a freezer (crank-type), pack with crushed ice and rock salt, fill the mold with the custard, and turn 4-5 minutes until the ice cream is ready (this will differ according to your machine, so best to follow your customary procedure). If you are using the freezer or freezing section of your refrigerator, turn temperature to very low. Put custard in the trays or in a mold, cover tightly with foil or lid,

234

and freeze for three or four hours. To be certain of a smooth-textured ice cream, it is a wise precaution to stir the mixture in the trays as often as every forty-five minutes.

SALSA CIOCCOLATA (Chocolate Sauce): Put 6 squares of cooking chocolate and one half cup of cold water together over low heat, stirring continuously. Add sugar to taste if chocolate is unsweetened. Remove as soon as the chocolate is melted.

SEMIFREDDO AL CAFFÈ
(Coffee Mousse)

1 pint whipping cream   6 tbsp. sugar (or more to taste)
½ cup powdered coffee

Whip the cream stiff, fold in the powdered coffee and sugar, and put in freezer trays or a bombe-shaped mold (as they do at Palazzi). Put in the freezer, turned very low, for three hours. At Palazzi they unmold the semifreddo and serve it in slices. Serves six. [Chocolate sauce (recipe above) is an excellent addition spooned over the coffee mousse.]

CAPRICCIO

GINO MUZY first opened the restaurant in 1946 in the Via Lombardia, with a normal complement of twelve tables, and another dozen in a little summer garden. During several years of service on Italian liners and in Rome hotels, he had made the acquaintance of numerous diners-out, who found his restaurant so much to their liking that it was an immediate success. The guest list

235

now numbers celebrities from all about, including kings, queens, and lesser royalty, "even some," says Signor Muzy, "without a throne." By 1956, Capriccio moved to larger, handsomer quarters in the Via Liguria, near the United States Embassy and the Via Veneto.

Signor Muzy remodeled a part of the Palazzo of Prince Raimondo Orsini, leaving intact several existing salons below the restaurant. He converted the eighteenth century rooms on the second floor into spacious and sophisticated dining salons and bar, and constructed a particularly charming summer terrace, the most distinguishing feature of which is a magnolia tree that branches through it on its way up to the fourth (or by our way of counting, fifth) floor of the palace. The trunk of this giant emerges through a gallery of modern art on the street level below, strangely at home among the twists and hammerings of abstract metal sculptures and canvases boldly sloshed with the colors of a modern palette. The only whimsical thing about the restaurant is its name, which Signor Muzy found by chance in a magazine ad for a perfume. A few years ago he added a night club downstairs, open in the winter season.

The cooking is expert, and the menu very large, crammed with expensive international delicacies along with moderately priced classics from the Italian kitchen—including many regional specialties. The antipasto cart is fine for sampling, but for those with more decided palates there is lobster cocktail, caviar, and pâté of goose liver. The cannelloni are exceptionally delicate (and among the recipes that Signor Muzy has given me); and there are such surprises as pilaff, Neapolitan pizza, and vol-au-vent. The chef can turn out with facility all of the usual Italian refinements on a scallop of veal, omelettes, several variations on sole, lobster, and scampi, good chicken livers perfumed with sage, a mixed grill, and even hamburger steak. And there are desserts gooey enough to tempt the stanchest fruit eaters, most notably a rummy charlotte Capriccio, puréed chestnuts and whipped cream, and Sicilian cassata.

236

BOLLITI MISTI
(Mixed Boiled Meats)

"If you want to make a good bollito misto," says Signor Muzy, "you will need a good cut of boiling beef, veal, tongue, chicken, cotechino, and a calf's head." The essence of the dish is its variety of flavors, but even in small quantities this is more of an assortment than the average family will want to prepare at one cooking. However, it is an excellent choice for a buffet or company dinner, with the added dividend that it can be finished well in advance. The classic recipe for boiling the meats and preparing the broth will be found on page 170. The broth makes up the first course, with pasta or other garnishes, if you choose; the meats can be served hot or cold, depending on the season. The Italians traditionally serve tangy green sauce as the accompaniment, although some prefer oil and salt, but I think this dish is even more interesting, especially for a buffet, when accompanied by several sauces. Horse-radish mixed with sour cream is always good with boiled meats, and a strong mustard should certainly be on the table. Here are the recipes for the green sauce and a salsa piccante.

SALSA VERDE
(Green Sauce)

parsley (one fistful)
1 tbsp. capers
2 or 3 filets of anchovy
2 or 3 gherkins
1 clove garlic
1 tbsp. minced onion or 1 chopped scallion

1 small boiled potato, peeled (or the equivalent amount of stale bread—white part only—soaked in water, then squeezed dry)
½ cup olive oil
1 tbsp. vinegar
salt and pepper

Put all of the ingredients except the oil, vinegar, salt, and pepper into a blender, or cut them into the finest possible dice. When mixed together, add the olive oil very slowly, starting with a few drops and blending continuously, until the sauce is about the consistency of mayonnaise (done by hand, it will be somewhat more liquid). Add the vinegar, stir in well, then add salt and pepper to taste. Refrigerate several hours before using. Yield: one cup of sauce.

SALSA PICCANTE
(Spicy Sauce)

⅔ cup olive oil
⅓ cup vinegar
2 to 3 tbsp. tomato purée
1 hard-boiled egg, chopped fine
1 tsp. capers

1 small clove garlic, minced fine
1 heaping tsp. finely minced onion, or 1 chopped scallion
sprig of parsley, minced
salt and pepper

Mix oil and vinegar, add other ingredients, mix well. Yield: about 1½ cups sauce.

CANNELLONI CAPRICCIO

pasta:

2 whole eggs
2 scant cups flour

salt
¼ cup water

filling:

olive oil
1 3-oz. piece of veal
a little less than 3 oz. prosciutto

salt and pepper
nutmeg
2 whole eggs
2 tbsp. Parmesan cheese

béchamel:

⅛ lb. butter
3 tbsp. flour

1 ample pint milk

salsa bolognese:

olive oil
1 carrot
1 onion
1 stalk celery
1 lb. ground beef
¼ lb. pork in small pieces
¼ lb. veal in small pieces
¼ lb. prosciutto [or Canadian bacon]

chicken giblets (the more the better)
sweetbreads
diced turkey or chicken
1 calf's brain [optional]
¼ lb. chicken livers
½ cup dry white wine
2-3 tbsp. tomato paste
nutmeg
salt and pepper

238

garnish:

butter   Parmesan cheese

PASTA: Sift the flour onto a table or into a large bowl, make a well in the center, break the eggs into the well, and add the salt. Mix the egg into the flour little by little with the fingers and hands, adding the water gradually as it is needed. When the ingredients are mixed together well, gather them into a ball and knead on a lightly floured table or board until the dough becomes elastic—ten or fifteen minutes of hard working. Divide the dough into two or three sections, and roll each of these into thin sheets. Cut the sheets into squares of about 5 inches and let them dry about thirty minutes on a towel before boiling. Use a large pot and plenty of racing, salted water. Boil three or four squares at a time, and remove after two or three minutes (if they overcook, they will split when you fill them; they should be tender but still firm). Plunge each cooked square into a bowl of cold water, then spread on towels or marble to drain.

FILLING: Sauté in olive oil the veal and prosciutto. Season well with salt and pepper and fresh grated nutmeg. Continue cooking until nicely browned. Put through the meat grinder, then add two beaten eggs and two tbsp. grated Parmesan cheese. Mix well, and roll into little sausages. Put one on each square of cooked pasta, and roll up.

BÉCHAMEL: Melt the butter in a saucepan, stir in the flour little by little, then add the milk, warmed, a little at a time. Stir continuously over low heat until smooth and thickened.

SALSA BOLOGNESE: Sauté in a large skillet in olive oil the carrot, onion, and celery, all minced, until limp and glossy. Add the ground beef, and the pork, veal, prosciutto, giblets, trimmed sweetbreads, and turkey or chicken, all cut into dice. If you add the calf's brain, it should be soaked first for an hour in cold water with a dash of vinegar, then trimmed, and cut into large pieces. When the meats have simmered together about half an hour, and have taken on a good color, add the chicken livers cut into large pieces, white wine, 2 or 3 tablespoons of Italian tomato paste (or more of American, if you wish; Italian brands are strong), fresh grated nutmeg, salt and pepper to taste. Continue simmering at least an hour longer.

239

If the sauce becomes too thick—it should be on the thick side—thin with white wine or stock. Makes six large servings for topping pasta. [You can refrigerate what you do not use for the cannelloni, serve it later in the week over spaghetti, fettuccine, or any other pasta.]

PREPARATION: Butter a low casserole liberally, spoon in a little béchamel sauce, then a little Bolognese sauce. Put in the cannelloni side by side. Pour over them the rest of the béchamel and several spoons of Bolognese sauce and sprinkle generously with grated Parmesan cheese. Bake in a 375° oven about fifteen minutes or until brown and bubbly. Serves four or more.

GEORGE'S

SEVERAL years ago Giorgio "George" Coray decided to leave his position as chief barman at the Hotel Excelsior, to launch a bar and restaurant of his own. He only went as far as the Via Marche, the little street which runs behind the hotel, and there he established what he charmingly called "George American Bar." Vernon Jarratt bought the place from him in 1956. Jarratt had been an officer in the British Army stationed in Italy during the war years of 1939–45, long enough to convince him to settle down there. For the first few years after the war he was film attaché at the British Embassy, but he gave up the diplomatic side for the real thing, and stayed in the film business until a year after he took over George's. There, in a garden that could grace any movie set, he moves among his guests behind a pair of erect waxed moustaches, dispensing bits of diplomacy here and there, and looking very much like a less zany Salvador Dali.

240

The Jarratt imagination has turned the century-old villa into one of Rome's most charming restaurants, especially for outdoor dining. A delicate pastel setting with erect columns, soft foliage, an urn here and there, the terrace seems designed for a dining company of nymphs, and in fact, it was once the "ninfeo" of the villa. Betty Shaw-Lawrence has captured the spirit of elegant repose in a painting for George's menu. The Jarratt humor is evident in a mural in the bar, a spoof of the non-stop cocktail drinker, who stands on his mark before a long row of filled glasses, poised for the starting gun of the bartender. Jarratt and his Italian-born wife Enrica once affected the same postures and had themselves photographed at the bar for their annual Christmas greeting.

Vernon Jarratt has traveled the gourmet route extensively in Italy and abroad; his menu is highly international, and includes some Italian regional dishes not commonly prepared in Rome restaurants. The diner who wants something British will find roast beef, smoked trout, and Elizabethan syllabub. There are American planked steaks for beef lovers, gazpacho and paella for those who are fond of Spanish cooking. The chilled gazpacho is a pleasant way to start a summer meal, and is served by Jarratt as an unadorned soup with the cut-up raw vegetables to be added from the side. If you like Eastern dishes, there is Anatolian kebab and Iranian caviar. Francophiles will find poulet à l'estragon, crêpes Suzette, vichyssoise, and kidneys flamed in calvados. The menu is enlivened further by such items as turtle soup, Swiss eggs, chippenham cheese, Welsh rabbit, Scotch woodcock, and iced Singapore soup, a version of vichyssoise with the playful addition of a dash of curry and a sprinkle of croutons over the top. In duck season there is the traditional bird with orange sauce. George makes two excellent filets of sole: one poached in champagne, the other delicately fried in oil to a crisp golden brown, then stuffed with beurre maître d'hôtel (butter, parsley,

241

lemon juice) and six fat scampi. The Italian part of the menu is ample enough, ranging from stracciatella, pesto, and cannelloni, to scampi and ossibuchi.

George's wine list is one of the most extensive in the city, and includes some little known Italian wines, and a large company of French vintages, "on which," Jarratt relates with some pride, "connoisseurs have often been good enough to compliment us." The bar is well stocked, and you can find dry martinis, mint juleps, black velvets, the various Pimm's cups, pink gin, Irish coffee, and fertile turtles—the George version of bullshot, which substitutes turtle soup for consommé.

George's has also taken over the Grand Hotel Villa Fiorio in Grottaferrata, about twelve miles from the heart of Rome. I haven't been there, but Jarratt tells me that the food is deliberately a little simpler than at George's, "rather on the lines of a goodish French auberge." I do notice from the brochure he showed me that there is a very large swimming pool and a hillside full of trees.

As for recipes, Jarratt has been most generous, and from among the many international dishes that he has given me, I have chosen these two Italian-style delicacies: the rigatoni in an ambrosial egg and cream sauce, and the grilled veal steak finished crisply with slices of fried artichokes, which he calls by its French name, paillard.

RIGATONI GEORGE'S

1 pound rigatoni (or a little more)
½ lb. prosciutto
1 cup heavy cream
4 egg yolks

5 ounces butter
grated Parmesan cheese
nutmeg
salt

Cook the rigatoni in abundant boiling water until they are al dente, which should take about fifteen minutes. Meanwhile in a pan large enough to hold the cooked rigatoni, melt half of the butter. Cook the ham, cut into julienne, very lightly in the butter. Beat the egg yolks and cream in a separate bowl, just enough to blend them well. Add a little freshly grated nutmeg. As soon as the rigatoni are tender, drain them thoroughly in a colander, add them to the pan with the butter and ham, pour the cream-egg yolk mixture over them, and add the other half of the butter. Let the rigatoni simmer in this sauce for a few seconds, stirring constantly, and taking care not to damage the rigatoni. The art of this dish consists in not letting the egg begin to cook—the sauce must remain quite creamy. The Parmesan cheese should be added to each portion after the rigatoni have been served. Serves four to six.

PAILLARD GEORGE'S
(Veal Steaks with Artichokes)

6 veal steaks (ask the butcher to cut them for paillards)
salt and pepper
olive oil
6 baby artichokes
oil for deep frying

Season the veal steaks, anoint lightly with olive oil, and grill them. While they are on the grill, cut six young and very small artichokes into paper thin slices, and fry until crisp in deep oil. Drain on absorbent paper and salt lightly. To serve, put the cooked steaks on a warmed platter and cover with the cooked artichokes. Serves six.

[NOTE: This dish is particularly good in Rome because of the very special Roman artichoke. If you cannot obtain baby artichokes that are tender enough to prepare in the same way, sauté halved frozen artichoke hearts in hot oil. Unfortunately they are too soft to fry crisply, but the flavor will be good. It is also probable that for grilling, small beef steaks or filets would be superior to veal steaks in the United States.]

THE gardens on the historic Pincio Hill provide an appropriately aristocratic setting for one of Rome's most elegant and expensive restaurants, the Casina Valadier. In the beginning years of the nineteenth century, during the French occupation of Rome, Joseph Valadier, a Roman architect of French descent, received a commission to transform the ancient hillside orchard of the Agostiniani into a public garden. There he built as well an exquisite small palace to house Napoleon François Bonaparte, the son of Napoleon and Maria Louisa of Austria, who was called from his birth the King of Rome. It was not by any means the first royal domain on this site. In antiquity Lucullus feasted Cicero, Pompey, and other notables at mighty and splendid banquets in his villa on this hill. Somewhat later, the villa came into the possession of the lascivious Messalina, the Emperor Claudius' fifth wife, who, having decided that she wanted it, had the owner disposed of and promptly took title. In the fourth century the Pinci family owned the property, and it is after them that the present gardens are named. A slow walk up the shady approach bordered with a profusion of purple, pink, and blue cineraria does not suggest that this was once the scene of such notable excesses.

In 1922 the Valadier villa was changed into a restaurant by Alfredo Banfi, who was wise enough to retain the original spirit of the place: the classic architecture of Valadier remains little changed. Outside, a gently curving double staircase leads to a portico; beyond, through a small hall, is the quietly elegant dining room. A porch circles two sides of the building, and in good weather it affords the pleasure of a lunch or dinner al fresco, and a romantic, spire-studded panorama of the whole city, broken only by occasional flocks of starlings cavorting erratically as they go about their skywriting. The ground level contains a caffè where strollers touched by summer lassitude can linger over an ice or

244

aranciata and cast a lazy eye over rooftops baking in the oven of the August afternoon.

Though the menu, as one would expect, lists many dishes not available in more modest restaurants, I was especially pleased to find that even the simple dishes that Valadier offers come from its kitchen done to perfection: the chicken livers and sage, brown and aromatic, juicy scampi, a bowl of rich broth, these all mark the virtuosity of the chef. It is difficult to decide: should it be cannelloni—they look delicious as the waiter whisks them by —or something from the antipasto tray, pickled and spiced? Or perhaps those shrimp and rice, pink and steamy? The cold buffet of cooked meats is appealing served from a traveling cart. There are many elaborate dolci, including the excellent semifreddo Valadier, a frozen "zabaglione" with a tangy sauce. The Valadier recipe is somewhat complicated, combining a thick sugar and grated orange peel syrup first with egg yolks, then egg whites, then whipped cream, blended with tedious care at a slow tempo, and then frozen to be served many hours later with a liqueur sauce. With humble apologies to the Valadier gelatiere, I suggest a recipe for an excellent and very similar dessert, whose gourmet qualities obtain from a much simpler procedure:

SEMIFREDDO SEMI-VALADIER

zabaglione: for each portion:

1 egg yolk   ½ egg-shell Marsala
1 tbsp. sugar

semifreddo:

½ pint heavy cream for every six portions

245

sauce: for each portion:

½ tbsp. orange marmalade   ½ cup orange liqueur (Aurum, Cointreau, Triple Sec, or Grand Marnier)

ZABAGLIONE: Combine egg yolks, sugar, and Marsala in the top of a double boiler. For larger quantities, combine ingredients in a mixing bowl first and cook small portions separately in the double boiler, lest when they expand they overflow. Beat strenuously over just barely hot water (if the water is too hot, the zabaglione will overcook in spots) until it is of creamy consistency, thick, and at least three times its original size. [Up to this point, you have the classic zabaglione, and it can be served immediately in glasses or bowls.] If you are making large quantities, remove the cooked mixture to a cool bowl and continue beating until it has cooled completely. Continue until the original ingredients are used up, beating each new batch carefully into the mix in the bowl.

SEMIFREDDO: Whip the heavy cream until moderately stiff, and fold into the cooled zabaglione. Pour into a cake pan or ice tray and freeze a minimum of three hours before using.

SAUCE: Over low heat combine orange marmalade and orange liqueur. Simmer briefly and cool before serving over the semifreddo. [If you prefer to add the orange marmalade to the frozen mixture, fold it in as the last ingredient before freezing, and substitute a sugar syrup of equal parts sugar and water in the sauce. Other variations include the use of Marsala or mandorcrema (almond-flavored Marsala) blended with a little white wine. I have used an excellent ginger-flavored orange marmalade from my local market, which has the advantage of a fine reddish color. You can make this same frozen dessert without adding whipping cream—still good, but less velvety.

246

RISOTTO ALLA CERTOSINA
(Rice with Scampi or Prawns)

¾ lb. scampi [you can substitute prawns]
butter and olive oil for cooking
½ cup dry white wine
½ lb. sliced fresh mushrooms

2 cups stewed plum tomatoes
salt and pepper
3 cups dry rice, plus water or
   chicken broth for cooking

Peel and de-vein the scampi. Cook them in a little butter and olive oil, preferably in a copper skillet, until they turn pink. Bathe them with the dry white wine and add the mushrooms. Cook all together for about three minutes. Add two cups of stewed tomatoes and season with salt and pepper. Let the mixture bubble for about two minutes more and then transfer it to a double boiler. Cook the rice. [½ cup dry rice per portion. If you have chicken broth on hand use it as the cooking liquid; it will improve the flavor of the dish.] When the rice is ready, add the sauce and scampi. Note: I find the flavor of garlic excellent with scampi, and so I add a finely minced, small clove while they cook. Another procedure for cooking the scampi is to start with a soffritto, a sauté of onion, carrot, and celery, in fine dice, cooked golden and limp in the oil-butter mixture. Add the scampi and continue as above. Serves six.

5. Seafood

ROMANS have a healthy appetite for creatures from the sea, so most restaurants offer some seafood dishes. The three restaurants that follow make fish cookery their particular specialty, although they also provide dishes for the carnivorous.

AL MONUMENTO

IN OSTIA ANTICA

BEFORE Christ was born there was a Roman colony, Ostia, where the Tiber empties into the sea. It was the capital's bustling port, and at the peak of its civilization it housed 80,000 Romans. It declined after several centuries, thanks to politics and malaria in about equal proportions, and, forgotten by time, its ruins sank into the shifting sands. It is once again a remarkable city, but the people who now roam the streets are archaeologists and travelers. Exploring the excavations is one of the most rewarding trips you can make from Rome, an easy fifteen miles away. You can wander through the remains of ancient streets, ferret out the remnants of shops and temples, private homes and apartment houses, taverns and restaurants, warehouses and public baths. Painted adornments and mosaics are not as bawdy as those in Pompeii, and as a consequence the pack of self-appointed "special" guides, souvenir vendors, and generally unsavory characters associated with the city in the South are mercifully missing here. In the summer months there is a brilliant drama season in the ruins of the ancient theater, with shadowy half-lit umbrella pines and a real starry sky as the backdrop.

The whole area surrounding the mouth of the Tiber was until this century a great salt marsh. Known as the Stagno di Ostia, the swamplands were dreaded for their malaria, and were worthless as land for cultivation. Late in the nineteenth century a band of six hundred immigrants from Ravenna, Lugo, and Forlì reached this inhospitable terrain in their search for a new area to farm. There was no visible sign of habitation except for an old hunting lodge overlooking the ruins of a sixteenth century

249

castle. The migrating Romagnoli took it over, lit up the fires in the chimney, and set about reclaiming the swamps, and growing grain. A midwife among them, Grandma Maria, had her old family rolling pin along, and shortly she was turning out, with the newly milled flour, large sheets of dough for tagliatelle and tagliolini. She transformed the old hunting lodge into a cheerful "home kitchen." The first "outside" customers were hunters who came to warm at the hearth, and who usually gave a part of their catch to Nonna Maria to cook, and an occasional fatigued archaeologist who found her good bowl of noodles a marvelous restorative. By 1910 the reclamation of the swamps was entirely successful, and a stone monument was erected in testimony to the arduous labors and steady faith of this band of Northerners.

About thirty-five years ago the present trattoria came into being just opposite the monument and on the site of the old osteria. The original emphasis was on those simple Emilian foods that the local population remembered with some nostalgia: pork chops, soft cheeses, tagliatelle, tagliolini, passatelli, and imported Lambrusco wine to wash them down. The restaurant operated with quiet success until after World War II. Then the generally more affluent Romans, each with a car—or at least a friend with a car—began to make a trip to the trattoria a favorite outing. The sea is close; the Rome Lido, a long white strip of sand largely built up with bathing establishments and resort housing, is only a mile or two away. Some stretches, beyond the pine woods, roll gently with wild hillocks interrupted by an occasional fisherman's shack and a faded blue boat turned on its side. It is just the right place for a day's excursion, with a Monumento dinner of fresh fish, now become the trattoria's specialty, on the way home.

The original old fireplace, modernized a bit, is still there, but it is no longer the only source of heat. It has taken on a new importance: it now serves for cooking all those foods that need the lick of a flame or the steady glow of live embers. The dining room and porch are unadorned but comfortable enough. Country simplicity and excellent cooking are a relief from the pretensions of the city, and have attracted such notables as Gassman, Fanfani, Saragat, and even former President Gronchi. The director Fellini comes here and eats in the kitchen—he loves the passatelli. He's a Romagnolo too. Mamma Nerina, who inherits the tradition of Nonna Maria's cooking, prepares all of the splendid dishes herself with only the help of her sister-in-law Germana, and daughter-in-law Livia. The men of the Fenati family stay out of the kitchen, but provide good culinary advice and hospitable service. Elio, Mamma Nerina's handsome, mustachioed son, who talks with a Roman accent lightly crossed with Romagnolo, performs admirably as head waiter, master of the house, and general historian.

The Monumento specialties, besides the old favorites which are retained from the Romagnolo menu, are a remarkable marine-sauced spaghetti; lightly fried Roman prawns (mazzancolle al coccio) or sole, bathed with white wine, cognac, and a good squeezing of fresh lemon; chicken in a spirited hot sauce; and cappelletti romagnoli, little stuffed pasta hats swelling with Parmesan, soft stracchino cheese, nutmeg, grated lemon peel, and beaten eggs—and at their very best when served with a sauce of simple melted butter. Some dishes are not always on the menu, but it is worth asking for them: vincisgrassi, a very rich lasagne baked en casserole; the stuffed squid, with a sauce that is excellent over spaghetti; a rice and cuttlefish sauté made according to an old Venetian formula; the rich fish soup and classic fish stew; the rare but exquisite roe and milt of sea bass, poached delicately in individual pans; and whole mullets cooked tenderly in an aromatic fish broth.

Signor Elio has kindly given me three recipes for the Monumento seafood dishes most revered by customers of long standing:

251

SPAGHETTI AL MONUMENTO

2 lbs. fresh, tiny clams, in their shells (or 1 cup, shelled)
2 lbs. fresh mussels, in their shells (or 1 cup, shelled)
½ cup olive oil, plus more as needed

3 cloves garlic, minced
1 piece dried, hot red pepper, or a dash of powdered
1 lb. spaghetti
1 or 2 stalks parsley, chopped

Put the well scrubbed clams and mussels in separate frying pans over a good flame, adding about ½ cup of water to the clams. When the shells open, remove the meat, and place in separate bowls. Strain the clam juice over the clams, the mussel liquor and a little water over the mussels, and let them stand a few minutes to settle out any remaining sand. Remove the meat, and reserve the clam (but not the mussel) liquor, straining it through cheesecloth before using it. Put the olive oil and garlic to cook in a heavy skillet, and when the garlic is just taking on a blond tinge, add the clams, mussels, and clam juice. Cover and simmer very gently, never allowing them to cook briskly. A few additional drops of olive oil will lower the temperature in the skillet, if it approaches boiling. Continue cooking for about twenty minutes. Add the red pepper, mashed or powdered. Turn the sauce over one pound of firmly cooked spaghetti, and sprinkle the chopped parsley over the top. Serves four.

CALAMARETTI AFFOGATI
(Poached Baby Squid)

per portion:

½ lb. baby squid (thumbnail size)
6 tbsp. olive oil

2 tsp. vinegar
salt and pepper
juice of ½ large lemon

Clean the tiny squid and remove skins and ink sacks. Put them in a cold skillet with 2 tbsp. olive oil and 1 tsp. vinegar, and bring to a simmer. After several minutes of cooking, drain off all the liquid. Add the rest of the olive oil and vinegar to the squid, and season lightly with salt and pepper. Simmer, covered, for five more minutes, and just before serving pour the fresh lemon juice over them.

252

NOTE: These baby squid are extremely tender and delicate, but even in Italy they are not always easy to obtain. You can substitute junior sized squid, but the cooking time must be almost doubled, and the flavor will be slightly less subtle. But still delicious.

SOGLIOLA O MAZZANCOLLE AL COCCIO
(Sole or Prawns in Wine Sauce)

per portion:

1 1-lb. sole (whole, with skin and head)	flour
	1 cup olive oil
or	1 cup white wine
1 lb. large prawns in their shells (at least three-inch size)	1 oz. (1 small jigger) cognac
	salt and pepper
	juice of ½ large lemon

Clean the sole or prawns. Remove the shells from the middle of the prawns, leaving the heads and tails intact. Flour them lightly. Put them in a skillet with cold olive oil, and bring them to fry briskly, turning from time to time so that they take on a good golden color all around. Add the wine, cognac, salt and pepper, and reduce the sauce to about four fifths over a good flame. This should take about four or five minutes. Add the fresh lemon juice, remove from the fire, and serve immediately on a hot platter. At Monumento, the sole is filleted by the waiter, after he first presents it whole, and the juices are spooned over it.

DA ANTONIO A SAN CALISTO

MOVIE crews were busy setting up giant scaffolds, klieg lights, and other sizeable paraphernalia the last time I was in Antonio's neighborhood. The small street, as lively as a country fair, and teeming with colorful passersby, is just the proper background for the typical Cinecittà production: so Roman that when you see it on the screen you may think that the set men have overdone it a bit! Flanked by a modest bar on one side, and a busy restaurant on the other, the domain of Antonio's terrace is never clearly defined. On a summer evening waiters scurry to and fro, moving the plant boxes outward, as more and more guests arrive, hooking up impossible tangles of wire to extend hanging lanterns, and manipulating tables and chairs with the skill of a troop of jugglers. Suddenly, the dining space accommodates twice the number; but before long another troop of diners arrives, and the waiters are moving the hedges again.

There was an osteria on the spot before Antonio came along. Without compromising its original unpretentiousness, he transformed it into a fine trattoria, inexpensive, popular, and specializing in fish cookery that is astonishingly good. His waiters, always a genial bunch, know your favorite dishes after a few visits, and will even remember them after a considerable absence. A few years ago two of them, Giovanni Ticconi and Adriano Cimarelli, bought the place from Antonio, who moved to the hill town of Albano. Angelino Merletti, the cook, stayed on too, and so one hopes that the honest, hearty dishes and the friendly greeting will remain unchanged for a long time to come.

Piazza San Calisto, Antonio's locale, is actually a small square running off the larger and more familiar Piazza di Santa Maria in Trastevere. As a bit of Roman verse on Antonio's wall tells you, there are two things you will find there: a church with a well inside, and across from it a spot that will satisfy every joy of your appetite. The well is the one into which the Romans threw the martyr San Calisto (although some historians say it was really San Patrizio) in the days of the Christian persecutions. The Palazzo di San Calisto across from Antonio was once the site of the Congress of Rites, the tribunal of the Holy See.

Antonio's has a big refrigerated showcase containing the day's catch of fish so that you can select the fellow that most pleases you. If your party is large, Angelino will roast you a good, big sea

254

bass, a grey mullet, or a dentex. If you prefer your fish steamed, there is a type of sea bass called ombrina that takes especially well to cooking in white wine, lemon juice, and a sprinkling of fresh parsley. The mixed fry includes crisp ringlets of squid (if you are finicky, just tell them to leave it out, but more's the pity), whitebait, shrimp, sole, and whatever other small swimmer got caught in the nets that day, encrusted in golden breading. An excellent cold seafood salad marinated in oil and vinegar dressing, a dish which Romans like as an antipasto, is one of the specialties at Antonio. Another is the spaghetti al capriccio, a tangle of noodles under a steaming tomato sauce dotted with clams, mussels, bits of squid, scampi, shrimp, and prawns that have all simmered gently in oil, garlic, and hot red pepper. Before serving, the chef tosses a bit of chopped parsley and minced raw garlic over the top.

The rospo, an ugly fish whose meat is good for stews and soups, is prized in the Venice area, however, for the delicacy of his tail. Antonio gets his supply from Ancona on the Adriatic and grills or roasts them in the traditional East-coast manner (coda di rospo). Red mullet is another specialty of the house, baked for twelve or fifteen minutes in oiled parchment cases with mushrooms and hunks of squid, oil and delicate seasonings (triglia al cartoccio).

One of the best of all ways to prepare spaghetti is with a simple sauce of clams and garlic, and here is Antonio's recipe:

SPAGHETTI ALLE VONGOLE
(Spaghetti with Clams)

½ cup olive oil
2 large cloves garlic, minced
1 lb. fresh tomatoes (or about two cups stewed plum tomatoes without too much juice)

about ½ lb. shelled clams or 2 10-ounce cans Japanese clams
parsley
salt and pepper
1 lb. spaghetti

255

Heat the oil in a large skillet, and add the garlic (at Antonio they slice it in paper-thin slivers, which is the preferable way to cut it for this recipe providing you are a real garlic lover). Add the fresh tomatoes, skinned and chopped, and cook until they reduce to a rich purée. Add the clams, parsley, salt and pepper, and simmer together several minutes longer. Cook the spaghetti in boiling salted water until just tender. Drain and turn out on a warm serving platter, pour the sauce over the top, add a generous glob of butter and a sprinkle of minced parsley. [Do not serve this dish with cheese.] Serves four.

[NOTE: If you use fresh clams, you will need about one pound. Put them, well scrubbed, with a bit of oil or water in a frying pan over high heat, and cook until all the shells open. Remove the clams from the shells and put to soak in a little strained pan juice to settle out the sand. Avoid using large, strongly flavored fellows. I find that the tiny whole Japanese clams that my grocery carries in ten-ounce cans are very delicate and sweet, as are the Italian vongole, and quite successful in this recipe. One and a half cans, drained, make about the right amount, but two cans will do no harm. At Antonio they use about another quarter pound of spaghetti for four servings, but this may be a bit large for American appetites.]

One of the most delicious of all the Italian seafood is scampi, shellfish that prosper especially well in Adriatic waters. Armed with two small pincers, the scampo is otherwise very much like a large rosy prawn, but the meat is a great deal more delicate. Sometimes growing as large as eight or ten inches, scampi in their shells fill a huge platter when prepared for a single portion. They can be boiled and sauced or grilled on the spit, but are at their very best baked in a good hot oven, as in this recipe from Antonio.

SCAMPI ALLA PESCATORA
(Scampi Fisherman's Style)

6 to 8 scampi per portion	bread crumbs
salt	olive oil
pepper	

Split the scampi in halves, keeping the shell, head, and feet attached. Remove the black vein that runs down the back, rinse in cold water. Place shell side down in an oiled baking dish. Season with salt and pepper, then sprinkle bread crumbs over the scampi. Anoint generously with olive oil and bake in a very hot oven about fifteen minutes, or until the bread crumbs are golden brown.

[NOTE: Scampi in their shells look very large, but yield a small amount of meat for their size. If you substitute good-sized prawns, four to six may make an equivalent portion. If you like garlic, mince a little into the bread crumbs before spreading on the scampi. You can also use half the amount of oil, and dot the scampi liberally with butter.]

RISTORANTE CORSETTI

Now one of a chain of three busy seafood restaurants in the Rome area, Corsetti began over forty years ago as a simple osteria dispensing wines from the neighboring country hills. Filippo Corsetti, the founder, came to the capital from nearby Velletri with his young bride, Jolanda. He was a poor man, yet in one sense, rich enough: he possessed an excellent knowledge of the wines grown in the Roman hill towns, and he was able to obtain them in quantity from his own village. Faced with the immediate necessity of providing for his family, he set up his osteria in the square of San Cosimato in Rome's old quarter, Trastevere. This was in 1922. His efforts met with immediate success, owing in part to an unusual publicity scheme. He sent into the most crowded quarters of the city wine carts loaded down with full casks. On their sides, chalked in high white letters, one read "da Pippo a S. Cosimato il genuino vino dei castelli romani centesimi 2 al litro"—"from Pippo's in S. Cosimato genuine wine from the Roman castelli 2 centesimi a litre." His name and his wine be-

257

came famous and his business thrived. Four sons and many patrons later, with the clientele steadily increasing, the tavern added new rooms, and its destiny was decided by the inclusion of a kitchen to serve fried fish.

Although the tavern-restaurant closed its doors during the war, its reputation was so firmly established that its old clients flocked back when it reopened immediately on the cessation of hostilities. Filippo's four sons aided their father in his work and learned the business under a paternal supervision that was strict but tempered with good will. In spite of his death in 1948, they went on to develop the successful small firm into a large enterprise. Alberto, Armando, Antonio and Alfredo organized small fishing fleets in the Adriatic and Tyrrhenian seas to insure a fresh daily supply for their restaurants, now three in number. Besides the original locale, which preserves Mamma Jolanda's characteristic seafood specialties, there is a second restaurant near the Rome Lido at Torvajanica on the sea; the third and latest addition, Vecchia America, is a modern establishment with orchestra and dancing, in the E.U.R. section near the Palazzo dello Sport. The original canteen at the San Cosimato location has recently been revived as a gay pizzeria, complete with spirited music and dancing. Though Mamma Jolanda is not on the scene, having moved to the seaside restaurant which is now entirely under her direction, skill in the kitchen runs in the family, and an able niece, Fernanda, has taken over Mamma Jolanda's duties in Trastevere.

The Piazza San Cosimato cannot boast of the formal beauty of many of Rome's squares, but it does not lack character. Every morning for countless years the tenth century church of San Cosimato at one side of the piazza has formed the backdrop for a scene of pleasant but utter confusion, a hustle and jumble, a clatter and bumping, a babble and din of grand proportions. Vendors move in, stalls appear out of carts, the ground, the air. Suddenly the sleeping grey space awakens to a hundred colored fruits and vegetables, aromatic cheeses, red meats and silver fish, swinging salamis, dipping scales, waving arms, every inch of air alive, every foot of space a patch of color. And every evening the magic transformation is gone, the stalls and produce and clamor abruptly disappear without a trace.

Corsetti's summer terrace is a part of this piazza, expansive and accommodating—like so many outdoor dining rooms whose only walls are portable flower boxes or flexible screens. The indoor rooms present a pleasant arrangement, and the display of fish near the main entrance is inviting. From some tables you can see into the kitchen, and watch a woman working at the endless cutting of fruit for the macedonia, or spitting giant prawns in readiness for the fire.

The specialties are zuppa di pesce, a half portion of which will feed a family of three for a week; riso alla pescatora, a rice-seafood mixture that offers serious competition to many pasta favorites; and fish in a vast and glorious assortment, from the simplest in bianco—poached in a bouillon with or without wine and herbs—to the intriguing in cartoccio—baked with vegetables and assorted seafood in a sealed paper envelope. For dessert there is a house specialty, the coppa, either of nut ice-cream or a luscious pastel tower of assorted flavors. The intriguing, many-page menu lists a good number of foods other than fish.

Mamma Jolanda graciously gave me the recipe for her famous zuppa di pesce, which calls for a number of fish that we do not find in American waters, or sell in American markets. For these, except for the moray and shark, we can find reasonable substitutes, but for the many years of experience that season Mamma Jolanda's cooking there is no ready replacement. Her recipe calls for "cappone, murena, martino, scorfano, squadro, palombo, calamari, polpo, cozze, vongole," and "scampi." It is the blending of textures and diverse flavors that gives this dish its distinctive character.

259

MAMMA JOLANDA'S ZUPPA DI PESCE
(Mamma Jolanda's Fish Soup)

1 small sweet red pepper
2 small sweet green peppers
3 or 4 cloves garlic
olive oil
2 glasses dry white wine
octopus (a few slices)
1 cup squid in pieces
5 lbs. assorted fresh fish with the heads (such as red snapper, cod, whiting, mackerel, flounder, sea bass, eel)

½ cup cooked tomatoes
pepper
parsley
1 lb. mussels and/or small clams in their shells
12 scampi
12 or more squares French bread
butter

Slice the peppers into narrow strips. Mince 2 or 3 cloves of garlic, reserving the other. Fry together gently in olive oil for about five minutes. Add two glasses of white wine, a few slices of octopus, and one cup of squid cut in pieces (both previously cleaned, skinned, and boiled at least ½ hour—or more if necessary—to tenderize them). To the water reserved after boiling the squid and octopus, add the heads of the fish you will use, and simmer to make a good broth. Reserve. To the first mixture, add the cooked tomatoes, fresh ground pepper, some chopped parsley, the mussels and clams in their shells (scrub well first), the scampi in their shells [and, although not in Mamma Jolanda's aquarium, lobster cut in chunks is an excellent ingredient]. Simmer this mixture for about 15 minutes. Then add the fish broth and about 5 lbs. of assorted fresh fish cut in chunks. Cook another 15-20 minutes until everything is just cooked through. Rub the squares of French bread with a cut clove of garlic, and fry in butter; or toast, buttered, in the oven. Place two or three squares in each bowl, pour the broth over them, and arrange the fish and shellfish in the dish. Sprinkle with freshly minced parsley and serve immediately. Serves six.

6. Tuscan Specialties and Game

TUSCANY produces the best beef in Italy, and Tuscan restaurants always offer thick cuts of T-bone steak grilled over charcoal. Game cookery, stuffed pasta, bean dishes, and robust pot roasts are other Tuscan favorites. Chianti is the traditional wine to go with these foods, and Roman-Tuscan restaurateurs can supply it in quantity. Three non-Tuscan restaurants which prepare especially fine game dishes, Ernesto, Al Pompiere, and Da Palozzo, are described in other sections of this book.

261

FONTANELLA is in the center of the city, just across from the old book and print market, one of Rome's most enticing open-air exhibits. Stacks of weathered books, yellowed lithographs and etchings, maps, funny old postcards, an assortment of copper pots, candelabra of brass, antiquities of iron and glass, and a fine jumble of small merchandise from coins and necklaces to odd buttons, catch the fancy of browsers. Occasionally one of the stalls produces a real Piranesi, or an old Chinese painting of more than passing interest.

Next to the market looms the impressive Palazzo Borghese, with its fine Renaissance courtyard. It was once the residence of the Circolo della Caccia (the Hunt Society), complete with a handsome restaurant and liveried pages. Unfortunately the stand-ard of cooking didn't match the other splendors, and the titled gentry of this exclusive society began to slip across the way for a good dinner at the newly opened Fontanella. When Roman café-society realized that numbers of princes and dukes frequented the simple restaurant, they came to rub shoulders. Nowadays Romans of all ranks keep the spot so full and lively that it is always good to phone ahead for a reservation.

Fontanella's Tuscan cooking is perhaps the choicest of its kind in Rome, its beef selected in the North, its Chiantis produced in Fontanella vineyards. Although their restaurant is only a dozen years old, Tosella and Osvaldo Falsi, the owners, are old restau-rant hands. Before starting Fontanella they were associated for many years with Il Buco, another Florentine-style establishment. During the hunting season all kinds of game birds and beasts enrich the Fontanella menu. The pastes are exceptionally light and the sauces animated. Among the best are buttery egg noodles, pappardelle, dressed with a fine hare sauce. The polenta here is excellent and the right foil for game entrées. There is always

262

grilled Tuscan-style chicken and T-bone steak (a bit tougher than American beef, but the flavor is splendid). Fontanella serves an unusual duck, this one cooked with olives instead of oranges, and a special salad of raw mushrooms and fresh truffles, guaranteed to tickle any jaded palate.

Osvaldo gave me his secret for cooking steaks in the approved Florentine manner: Bistecca alla Fiorentina Cotta con Fuoco di Legna is a T-bone, weighing about one pound for each person. It is seasoned well with salt and pepper, and grilled over a very hot fire made of the woods of chestnut, cypress, and grape vines.

Another specialty is Osvaldo's agnolotti, ravioli-like filled pastes. Here is his recipe:

AGNOLOTTI ALL'OSVALDO

1 lb. pasta (made with 4 cups flour, 3 eggs; see recipe, p. 164)
1 onion, minced
2 tbsp. butter
¼ lb. veal
3 oz. chicken breasts
3 oz. lean pork
2 or 3 slices prosciutto (fat and lean, but lean prevailing)

1 very small lamb's brain, boiled (if large, use half; should be 3 or 4 oz.)
⅛ whole nutmeg
pepper
1 cup grated Parmesan cheese
2 egg yolks
salt, if necessary
butter and grated cheese, or any preferred sauce

Put the onion to cook in a frying pan with the butter, and sauté until golden and limp. Add the veal, chicken breasts, and pork all cut in large pieces. Brown well, and when they are nearly ready add the slices of prosciutto cut up into dice. These must cook just briefly, lest they impart too salty a flavor to the filling. Add the lamb brain to the browned mixture and cook together a few minutes. (To prepare, soak in cold water with vinegar. Then trim off the membranes; put to boil with salt and about 2 tbsp. vinegar to 2 cups water; when the water comes to a boil, lower flame and simmer about 8 minutes; leave in the water until ready to use.) Pass the filling through a meat grinder two or three times, reducing it to the finest consistency. Add the nutmeg, freshly grated, a good dash of pepper, the grated Parmesan cheese, and the egg yolks. Mix together until well blended. Taste, and add salt if necessary.

Roll out the pasta into two sheets, one slightly larger than the other. On the smaller sheet distribute the filling, by the teaspoonful, at intervals of one and a half to two inches. Cover with the larger sheet of pasta, letting it drape loosely between the mounds. Cut out each agnolotto with a pastry cutter, and pinch the edges together. The paste must be used as soon as it is made so that it will not be too dry to seal together. Set out the cut agnolotti on towels to dry. If not to be used the same day, store in the refrigerator with floured wax paper or Saran between the layers, or with a good sprinkling of finely ground corn meal between pasta and paper. When ready to cook, boil in abundant salted water until just tender. Remove with a perforated spoon, dress immediately with butter and cheese, or any desired sauce. Makes about 150 agnolotti. Osvaldo says the recipe will serve six, but eight can manage on it very nicely.

CHIANTI

In the entrance and along the wall of this small restaurant there is a dazzling display of pheasants, thrush, rabbits, bursting ripe fruits and gaudy vegetables, brilliant in their multi-colored finery, an augury of the merriment, as well as of the culinary variety, to be found across the threshold. Bright hues, Florentine straw matting, and a number of mounted game birds and wild beasts decorate the inner walls. There is a gay dining tavern downstairs, and a wandering house guitarist. In the summer louvered windows let in the breeze, but for those who prefer the unadulterated outdoors, there are sidewalk tables. The spirited cooking and bustling scene attract a cross-section of visitors and Roman citizenry: politicians, writers, artists, journalists, and any number of other cheerful personalities.

About twenty meters from the doorstep of the restaurant rises

264

the lofty Porta Pia, a structure that has witnessed its share of the city's history. Executed by Michelangelo in 1561, it derives more fame from the fact that it is the gate through which the Bersaglieri entered Rome to end the reign of the Popes in 1870. Commemorative stones that mark the actual scene of conquest lie somewhat to the left of the arch, and nearby is the Historical Museum of the Bersaglieri (Museo Storico dei Bersaglieri). Just outside the gate stands a monument to these troops.

The history of Chianti is much simpler. For the fifty-five years that it has been in operation it has remained in the same family, handed on from father to son. Ernesto and Mario, the genial brothers who now watch over the business, carry on with a tradition of equally careful attention to their kitchen and to their guests. They take particular pains to point out the day's special catch, but are just as ready to cast a proprietory vote against an order for a specialty that is not up to par that day. So heed their advice and you will fare very well indeed.

The Chianti antipasti include sausages and prosciutto made from wild boar, and ham that is smoked by the Chianti chefs. The restaurant is renowned for Tuscan meat, beefsteaks alla fiorentina (T-bones) grilled over charcoal, and for the quality and freshness of its fish. They form the backbone of a menu that changes not only with the hunting season but with the luck of the hunter. When he has had a good day, the menu will be as rich as the woods and fields. You'll find wild duck in an excellent orange sauce; wild boar in a piquant sweet and sour gravy; pheasant dressed with a spicy topping and served with polenta; grilled or stuffed squab; a variety of small succulent birds cooked on the spit; winey marinated hare; and partridge, goose, woodcock, and dove roasted brown and juicy. The risotto here is cooked with game, and the pasta specialty, lasagne, depends on the availability of wild hare for its robust sauce. Mario and Ernesto have given me their recipe, and even with the substitution of ordinary rabbit, it produces a sprightly dish.

265

PAPPARDELLE SULLA LEPRE
(Egg Noodles with Hare Sauce)

1 hare	3 tbsp. tomato paste
3 tbsp. olive oil	salt and pepper
1 carrot	rosemary
1 onion	2 lbs. lasagne
2 cloves garlic	2 tbsp. butter
giblets of the hare, and other giblets of game or fowl	Parmesan cheese
1 glass red Chianti (or other dry red wine)	

Bone the hare completely. Brown the bones in a skillet with the olive oil, and the carrot, onion, and garlic, all minced. After about ten minutes, add the minced giblets of the hare, and of other game such as pheasant or partridge, or turkey or chicken [the more giblets, the more savory the sauce]. When the bones are well browned, add the meat of the hare ground coarsely in a meat grinder or cut in small dice, one glass of red Chianti, the tomato paste, salt and pepper, and a good sprinkling of rosemary. Simmer for three hours. Cook two pounds of lasagne in abundant salted water at a racing boil, just until tender; drain, mix in two tablespoons of butter until melted, turn out on a warm serving dish, and cover with the sauce. Accompany with grated Parmesan cheese. Serves 6.

Chianti has a knowing way with mushrooms. They appear, sliced and sautéed, on the cold buffet among the boned chicken, red and green slashes of stewed peppers, casseroles of beans and tubes of pasta, plump rice-filled tomatoes. Porcini, large brown-capped wild mushrooms, are best of all dabbed with garlic and oil and roasted until the edges are almost crisp, the texture still firm, and the meat juicy. The ovoli, egg-shaped plants that display a startling orange or scarlet skin, are at their best raw in this Chianti salad. When the white truffle is in season, Chianti adds it for those who can afford such a treat.

INSALATA DI OVOLI E TARTUFI
(Salad of Wild Mushrooms and Truffles)

1 cup ovoli (amanita Cae- sarea) in thin slices	oil
⅓ cup carrots, in thin slices	vinegar
⅓ cup celery, in thin slices	salt and pepper
⅓ cup Swiss cheese, in thin slices	1 fresh white truffle (optional)

Clean the mushrooms and slice them razor thin. Peel the carrot and slice into slivers about the length of a matchstick and as thin as possible. Cut the celery into matchstick pieces. Cut the Swiss cheese into thin slivers about the same size as the carrots. Put all these slices together in a bowl. Mix two parts of oil to one part of vinegar, about ⅓ cup altogether, add salt and pepper, stir well, and pour over the other ingredients. Toss lightly. Put a layer of thinly sliced fresh white truffles from Albi over the top. Makes one large portion.

[If you can't tell a mushroom from a toadstool, substitute the cultivated variety for the ovoli. Select firm, white mushrooms, with the caps still well attached to the stems. If the under ribbing shows and the cap stands away from the pedestal, it is a sign that the mushroom is getting old. You can substitute canned white truffles for fresh, but the flavor will be markedly weaker. Chianti leaves them out altogether when they're out of season.]

MARIO

THE Via della Vite is a narrow avenue that runs between the Piazza di Spagna area and the Corso. Into it opens the rear entrance, and various subdivisions, of that infinitely mysterious organization, the Post Office. To anyone who has ever tried to mail a package from Rome, the Via della Vite is indeed unforgettable—that is, if he ever got that far. For there is a kind of game played by all of the clerks in the building to conceal the fact that this is the hiding-place of the parcel post division. Besides, there is no such formation as a line in Italy, and it takes the strategy of a quarterback and the stamina of a Marine just to get up to a window to ask directions in the first place. Then, under the contemptuous stares of all those still behind you, you will be unceremoniously dismissed by the clerk because you are in the wrong place, and furthermore your package is not wrapped in the approved fashion. Fortunately, rewrapping can be accomplished in a little store in the front of the Post Office proper, where two young ladies hold court behind a desk cluttered with shears, cord, scraps of brown paper, and globs of sealing wax. Their writhing audience beseeches, whines, wheedles, shouts, pokes, and jostles, but this has not the slightest effect on their studied slow motion. If hunger should set in, you lose nothing by taking time out for a leisurely lunch at Mario's, and rejoining the battle just where you left off. When your turn finally comes, you must tell the wrapping clerk whether this is special delivery, insured, or (and this will lose you considerable face) a simple mailing. The first two categories command respect, and their wrapping procedures are consequently much more demanding. The "insured, special delivery" is the monarch of packages. After its numerous folds and counterfolds have been held in by a complex of knots that any sailor would envy, out come a lighted candle and sealing wax to guarantee that every overlap and seam shall remain inviolate. The final precaution is a series of lead seals attached through the rigging. Once the package is ready, it is just a matter of attacking the Post Office again to find out where and how to mail it.

Mario Mariani, the proprietor of the restaurant up the street, is what you might call a Post Office buff. He is very thankful for his proximity to that institution, not only for the steady stream of tired refugees, but also for his own sacks of mail. Foreigners who have enjoyed his hospitality—their number was especially large during the Olympics—have written to him from all over the world. His postcard correspondence alone has totaled more than twelve hundred messages in the last two years, and he is the kind of person who likes to answer! "Simpatico," the Italians call him, and strangers obviously agree.

His small Tuscan restaurant has been in operation since 1960. Before that he worked in Roman hotels and restaurants for twenty years. He came from a farm in Tuscany which his parents still operate, and which is the source of many of the country products that he offers. He imports almost everything Tuscan on the menu, like the sausage of wild boar (salsiccia di cinghiale) from Siena, and an exceptional pork salami peppered with fennel seeds (finocchiona toscana) from Florence. His two simple and pleasantly disordered rooms are typical of cozy trattorias everywhere, but the profusion of Chianti flasks stamps the place as Tuscan. There are straw-covered chairs from Garfagnana, and splashes of carnival color on the tables of the inner room. There is a garland on the ceiling, woven of laurel, myrtle, red peppers, tomatoes, plaits of onions, pigtails of garlic, and pendulums of sausages and salamis. Baskets of fruit fill every spare corner, and the inevitable wine flasks hang even among the myrtle leaves from the ceiling.

Mario likes to cook with a passion—"Always have, even when I was a small boy"—and he spends every morning in the restaurant kitchen, after he finishes the marketing. One of the best of Mario's antipasti is a dish of broad beans and caviar; his recipe for this excellent, improbable combination will be found below. As part of the mixed antipasto, he often whips up a cloudlike omelette enfolding a melange of vegetables, country-style: tomatoes, zucchine, eggplant, peppers, onions, and the like. It is greatly to be preferred to his other version, which may appeal to Tuscan appetites but frankly not to mine. I find the lightness of pure egg superior to enrichments of crumbs and semolinas, no matter how subtle their flavor: whatever the gain, the air is gone, sacrificed for a heaviness reminiscent of a bride's first biscuits. But never mind, for when you order mixed antipasto, there are also

269

exceptional stuffed zucchine, marinated beans, rice-filled tomatoes, baked eggplant, and all such manner of delicately spiced
appetizers that come along. If you manage to get as far as the
soup course without having tried some form of Mario's beans,
you should remember that his specialty is bean soup Francovich,
and it is a fine change from pasta. He has kindly given me that
sturdy recipe too. Eaters of tripe will find that Mario makes his,
according to an old Roman custom, on Saturday, and according
to an old Florentine recipe that calls for tomato gravy with a
little finely ground meat sauce added to it. He serves it with homemade, country-style bread, and mounds of grated cheese. Mario
often serves pork liver that has been turned carefully on the spit.
In winter there is a spicy roast of pork; and hare, partridge, figpeckers, and thrush as well, all served up with a portion of polenta. Perhaps the best of all Tuscan entrées remains the classic
beefsteak, here cut thick and charged by the kilo.

These are Mario's instructions for thick bean soup, and beans
with caviar:

ZUPPA DEI FAGIOLI FRANCOVICH
(Bean Soup Francovich)

1 lb. dried beans	salt and pepper
3 cloves garlic	12 2-inch squares of bread
olive oil	parsley

Soak the beans in cold water overnight. Drain. Boil in a very
large kettle with a large quantity of water. Cook until the beans are
very tender, about two hours. There should be enough liquid left
to form a thick soup. Add two cloves of minced garlic that have been
sautéed in olive oil (and the oil), and salt and pepper to taste. Fry
or bake the bread squares in olive oil until they are golden, then
rub them with a bruised clove of garlic. In deep soup bowls or individual casseroles, put two toasts for each portion, and pour the
bean soup over them. Sprinkle with parsley just before serving.
Serves six.

270

FAGIOLI CON CAVIALE
(Beans with Caviar)

1 lb. dried beans	12 2-inch squares of bread
salt and pepper	parsley, chopped
olive oil	6 heaping tbsp. black caviar
3 cloves garlic	

Soak the beans in cold water overnight. Drain, and put to boil in a good quantity of water for about two hours, or until tender. There should be enough liquid left to make a bit of a sauce. Add salt very lightly, and fresh ground black pepper. Mince two cloves of garlic and sauté in olive oil until limp; add to the beans along with the oil [optional but good]. Fry or bake the bread chunks in olive oil. When lightly toasted, rub with a cut clove of garlic. Place the bread, two pieces per portion, in deep bowls, spoon the beans and their sauce over them, sprinkle with parsley, and finish with a scattering of caviar over the top. Serves six.

[NOTE: To prepare beans as a side dish, Mario follows the above procedure for boiling, adds the sautéed garlic and oil, and simmers with two cups of tomato purée, a few fresh sage leaves, and salt and pepper. He serves this dish with his pot roast.]

TOSCANA

No visitor to Rome, of whatever faith, overlooks the Vatican, but few ever have enough time to see even a small part of its treasures. A race through the basilica, the dome, the populous Sistine Chapel, and a few highlights of the galleries and museums will take all of a crowded day, and without some rest and refreshment your chances of survival are slim. The Holy City itself has no places to eat that I know of, except two small bars—one on the way to the dome, the other near the treasury. It is hard to understand why its Italian neighbors have not surrounded it with as many restaurants as they have souvenir shops. But they haven't. Therefore, it is fortunate to have so good a restaurant as Toscana in the Via Germanico, about five blocks from the entrance to the Vatican Museums.

Pietro Bruno, the Sienese proprietor, does not waste any effort on decor. The place has an old-fashioned, almost stark simplicity about it. There are large spits, and an appetizing array of food-stuffs in crocks and jars, on shelves, in cases, and behind glass refrigerator doors. In the summer the sidewalk makes a large and comfortable dining area. In 1959 the Accademia della Cucina Italiana awarded Signor Bruno its diploma for excellence of cook-ing. His specialties are Tuscan, as the name of his trattoria indi-cates, with a few other favorites added for good measure: among the best, the inevitable cannelloni, and spaghetti alla chitarra, sauced with mushrooms, peas, tomatoes, butter, and freshly grated cheese.

Signor Bruno suggests that in game season guests try the pap-pardelle alla lepre, wide egg noodles sauced with a ruddy brown hare gravy, or any of the other game dishes that appear during the cold weather. He lists them daily, depending on the catch, and points out only that he never serves the wild beasts refriger-ated and out of season. Among Toscana's other recommendations are beefsteaks, Tuscan style, and beans either in oil or simmered with sage and tomatoes, all'uccelletto. The chiantis are all genu-ine, from the approved classic zone.

Two Tuscan dishes which Toscana serves regularly are the recipes which Signor Bruno selected to give me:

CERVELLE CON ZUCCHINE
(Brains and Zucchine)

1 small brain	1 zucchina
2 beaten eggs	salt
flour	optional: 1 artichoke in halves;
salt and pepper	1 large wild mushroom; or
olive oil	2 or 3 button mushrooms

272

Trim the brain and slice in large pieces. Dip in the slightly beaten eggs, then in flour seasoned with salt and pepper. Heat the oil until it is hot in a frying pan. Add the floured pieces of brain, and pieces of zucchine prepared in the following way: cut the zucchina into strips, make a slit in each one, and sprinkle with salt. Leave for half an hour. Drain, then dip in flour only. When fresh artichokes and mushrooms are available they can either substitute for or accompany the zucchine. Slice the artichoke down the center, remove the outer leaves and choke, leaving only the edible portions. Clean the mushrooms; if large, cut in two or three pieces. Dip both artichokes and mushrooms in egg and seasoned flour. Serves one.

[NOTE: The Italians cook both calf's brains and those of the suckling lamb. Many chefs prefer to prepare the brains first by soaking them for at least fifteen minutes in cold water, sometimes changing it once or twice. Then they put them to cook well-covered with fresh water, together with an onion, a pinch of salt, a sprig of parsley, and a teaspoon of vinegar. When they boil, they are removed to a bowl of cold water until ready to use. After draining and trimming, they are dipped in the egg and flour, as above. Some cooks prefer to fry them in butter rather than in oil, and pour the pan gravy over them at the end. It is appetizing to sprinkle the golden pieces with minced parsley, and to squeeze a bit of fresh lemon over them before eating.]

POLLO FRITTO DORATO ALLA TOSCANA
(Golden Fried Chicken, Tuscan Style)

per portion:

1 quarter chicken, cut into several small pieces	flour
	salt and pepper
1 egg	olive oil

Remove the large bones. Each portion should contain several bite-size pieces of chicken. Dip in slightly beaten egg, then in flour, and sprinkle with salt and pepper. Put to fry briskly in olive oil for about fifteen minutes, turning to insure even browning. Remove and drain on absorbent paper before serving. Artichokes, mushrooms, or zucchine prepared as above make an excellent accompaniment.

THE Piazza Barberini, a crossroads that leads to the Trinità dei Monti, the railway terminal, the Via Veneto, and Tullio, is one of Rome's most frequently traveled plazas. The National Gallery in Palazzo Barberini has a well-visited collection just up the way, and the neighborhood is dotted with Bernini and Borromini churches and fountains. The Via Veneto wends its way up to the Porta Pinciana and the Villa Borghese through an embroidery of sidewalk cafés, chic shops, commodious hotels, and past the Palazzo Margherita, better known as the United States Embassy. At the Barberini end of the street there is a stark Capuchin church. In its cellars over 4,000 members of the order have at one time been interred in a patch of genuine, imported, Palestinian soil. Since there wasn't room in the small plot for such a large number of burials, older skeletons were exhumed to make way for later generations. Visitors can see the bones and skulls, which now cover five skeleton-lined chapels, their patterns adding an ironic touch of decoration to the deliberate severity that is in keeping with the Capuchin order.

Off the piazza is the Via Barberini, and the offices of the Fulbright Commission, guardian angel of visiting American scholars, who make up a small part of the faithful that return regularly to Tullio, just one street over. The three modest rooms there, which can seat eighty or ninety diners, are also generally jammed with downtown business people, who like the honest atmosphere and sound cooking. Tullio and partner Duilio, both Tuscans, opened the restaurant in 1950, and have found themselves expanding the place ever since. But they promise to keep it down to a size that is still compendious, for familiarity is certainly one of its charms.

The "girarrosto" is always in plain view. A carbon grill with a revolving spit that is the trademark of Tuscan cookery, it is handsomely laden with crackling haunches of lamb, plump Tuscan chickens, and succulent T-bones. Another of Tullio's best dishes is duck marinated in wine, and served with polenta, the classic corn meal accompaniment. That substantial Tuscan pot roast, stracotto, is also a specialty here. Tullio and Duilio make theirs by larding a good chunk of beef with a mince of bacon, garlic, carrot, and seasonings, browning it well in olive oil in a large pot crammed with carrots, celery, onions, bay leaves, mushrooms, and meat trimmings. They cover it well with red wine and beef broth once it has taken on a good rich color, and simmer it for many hours until it is tender. To go with it, they suggest either a steaming purée of potatoes, or broad beans made, according to the recipe they gave me, in the following manner:

FAGIOLI ALL'UCCELLETTO
(Beans in Tomato Sauce)

1 lb. dried beans	1 clove garlic
olive oil	a few sage leaves
1 cup stewed tomatoes, or	salt and pepper
2 cups fresh tomatoes	
skinned and cut in pieces	

Soak the beans in cold water overnight. Drain, and put to boil with abundant water for about two hours, or until the beans are tender. The water should be reduced to a thick sauce. Meanwhile, sauté the tomatoes, whole garlic, sage leaves, and salt and pepper in the olive oil until it forms a good purée. When the beans are cooked, remove the garlic, stir in the tomato sauce, and adjust the seasonings. Serves six.

Among the most wondrous of all Tuscan pastes are agnolini, traditionally stuffed with a mixture based on stracotto. Here is the classic recipe:

AGNOLINI

pasta made of 4 cups flour,
3 eggs, 1 tbsp. olive oil,
¼ cup water (see
recipe, p. 164)
½ lb. cooked stracotto, cut
into chunks (see recipes,
pp. 275 and 279)

1 large roll (French type)
soaked in the gravy from
the stracotto
¼ cup grated Parmesan cheese
2 large eggs
salt and pepper (light)
grated fresh nutmeg

sauce:

¼ lb. butter, softened

grated Parmesan cheese

Roll out the pasta into two sheets, for a filling already prepared as follows: Put the meat and bread, broken into pieces, through the food mill. Mix in the other ingredients. Add a little gravy from the stracotto if too dry. It should be a light, moist "paste." On one sheet of pasta spoon one row of filling in little mounds about 1½ inches apart and the same distance from the edge. When the first row is complete, turn the edge over the mounds, as if turning up a hem over them. With the side of the hand press firmly between each mound and along the closing edge. Cut the row of mounds away from the rest of the sheet of pasta, then cut out each individual mound with a fluted pastry cutter. Continue the process until all the filling and pasta have been used up. Cook in abundant salted water just at a simmering boil (stuffed pastes will tear apart in briskly boiling water). When they are firmly cooked, remove them with a slotted spoon and serve with lots of softened butter and a generous garnish of grated cheese. Makes 120 to 150 agnolini, enough to feed six or eight.

THE Piazza di Spagna contains probably the best known stairway in the Western world, carpeted in decent weather with loungers and footsore tourists from the bottom to the top of its one hundred and thirty-seven steps. At Easter the Spanish steps are spectacular in their finery, an avalanche of flaming azaleas. In spite of its name (after the residence of the Spanish ambassador to the Vatican) this area was long the center of the English colony. The Keats and Shelley museum, in Keats' house at the bottom of the steps, is one of the most sentimental shrines of English culture. The Brownings once lived in the neighborhood, Shelley stayed not far off, and the English church is nearby in the Via Babuino. Most lately it has been taken over by migrant Americans, most of them no doubt on their way to the American Express for mail or money.

Leading from the Piazza is the Via Condotti, lined with the swankiest boutiques in the city. Within its short confines a shopper can purchase anything from a real Western saddle to a collapsible gold champagne swizzler (with carrying case). There are products from the couturier and haberdasher, shoes to be made to order, Venetian chandeliers for house or opera house, and a collection of embroideries, jewels, and antiques that dazzle purchaser and browser alike. A block or two further along, in the neighborhood of the Via della Croce, some of the best-stocked food markets in town supply Roman cooks with everything from imported cheeses and ricotta out of season to the earliest assortment of game and the wildest array of mushrooms.

It is a blessing that in such a well-traveled neighborhood there should be such a dependable restaurant as Nino. Tucked away in the Via Borgognona, one of the complex of narrow streets off the piazza, it has been a favorite with visitors, homesick Florentines, and Romans with a penchant for Northern cooking, since it opened in 1940. Before that, in 1932, Tuscan-born proprietor Nino Guarnacci had established a restaurant in the Via Rasella, and that one is still bustling along under the direction of his brother Mario. In the Via Borgognona, Nino offers a large menu —at least a dozen soups and another dozen pastes, for example —and in particular well-cooked specialties of the Tuscan cuisine. Although there are such non-Tuscan entrées as steak tartare, baked eggplant, and poached sea bass, the house is most proud of its game cookery, its beans in oil, a golden-fried Florentine chicken, and huge T-bone steaks cut from sides of beef imported from home. In the winter there is an especially fine roast of pork, perfumed with spikes of rosemary and garlic. Nino cooks tripe tenderly in a Florentine tomato sauce scented with marjoram, and serves it blanketed with Parmesan cheese. Although Frascati and Asti Spumante are also featured, the wines are largely from Nino's own vineyards and from the best Tuscan producers. Besides the traditional table wines in straw-covered flasks, Nino has a good stock of superior vintages put up in bottles.

The classic pot roast of beef, Tuscan style, is really a multiple recipe, equally adaptable for hare, pheasant, or guinea fowl, depending on your luck in the field. Nino obligingly gave me his instructions for preparing all four, as well as the recipe for his excellent pork roast.

ARISTA DI MAIALE
(Roast Pork)

3 lb. boned loin of pork (you can substitute other, less expensive cuts, such as Boston butt)

one branch of rosemary
several cloves garlic

pesto:

rosemary
garlic

salt and pepper

278

Cut little pockets or slits in the meat and stuff with a well-minced pesto of garlic, rosemary, salt and pepper. Thread the whole branch of rosemary through the middle, where the bone has been taken out, and insert three or four cloves of garlic along with it (it is easiest to do this before securing the roast). Put the well-seasoned roast to cook in a slow-moderate oven (325°) for at least two hours, basting from time to time with the natural juices. [I prefer to add a little dry white wine to the basting liquor, and I often add fresh sage leaves along with the rosemary.] Nino serves his arista with fagioli all'uccelletto, beans simmered with tomato, garlic, and sage. Serves six.

[NOTE: If you use an unboned roast, stuff with pesto in little pockets as above, and lay the other seasonings across the top. Roasting time will be approximately one-half hour shorter for the same size roast, and it will feed four instead of six.]

STRACOTTO ALLA FIORENTINA
(Pot Roast of Beef, Florentine Style)

[May also be made with hare (lepre), pheasant (fagiano), or guinea fowl (faraona)]

5 lb. sirloin, rump, or round roast
olive oil
6 carrots, cut in dice
6 stalks celery, cut in dice
2 onions, cut in dice
beef bones and trimmings (not too fat), cut in small pieces

giblets of 2 or 3 chickens (or of the hare, pheasant, or guinea fowl, when using them), cut in dice
2 cups red wine, Chianti type
½ to 1 cup tomatoes (fresh chopped, or whole canned)

larding pesto (about 1 cup):

3 large cloves garlic
1 fistful rosemary leaves

4 slices bacon
salt and pepper

second pesto:

3 fresh sage leaves
1 clove garlic

1 anchovy
1 tsp. rosemary leaves

Cut pockets through the beef roast and stuff with the larding pesto, which has been finely minced together. Put the beef in a very large kettle or casserole, and brown it in olive oil until it has taken on a dark, rich color. Add the diced vegetables, beef bones and trimmings, and giblets. Continue browning so that the vegetables begin to take on a golden color. (It may be necessary to do the browning in two pots.) Make the second pesto by mincing the ingredients as fine as possible. Sprinkle over the browned meat and vegetables. After a few minutes of cooking, bathe the roast with two glasses of red wine. Add the tomatoes (fresh tomatoes should be peeled first), and stir the sauce so that all of the ingredients are well mixed. Cover the pot and cook gently for at least three or four hours, until the meat is very tender (it sometimes takes about five or six hours, I find, for the meat to cook tender enough to cut with a fork, which is the way it should be). During the cooking, turn the meat from time to time so that it cooks evenly. A little water can be added if necessary to bring up the level of the liquid; this will help to cook the meat more evenly. When the meat is done, remove it, and keep it warm. Skim the excess fat off the sauce. Cook the sauce over a lively flame until it is well reduced. Strain it through a sieve. Slice the meat in thick slabs, and pour some of the hot sauce over them. A five pound roast will feed eight or ten persons. The sauce is excellent over boiled pasta, and is traditionally used in this way (perhaps that is why there is so much of it).

[NOTE: If you use hare, one large animal will take about the same amount of sauce as the beef, but because of the weight in bones, the number of portions will be reduced. Figure about one-half pound per portion minimum. If you prepare pheasant or guinea fowl one bird will feed two, unless you've managed to bag a big one. The amount of other ingredients should be reduced and the cooking time cut to about two or two and a half hours (figuring about one-half hour to the pound). A young bird will cook tender sooner. The pesto is used only for larding the beef roast; it can be stuffed whole into the hare and game birds, which should then be sewed or tied closed. If you prefer, cut them into large pieces, and add the pesto to the kettle as the general seasoning, when the second pesto is added.]

7. Bolognese Specialties

SEVERAL restaurants in the Rome area offer individual dishes from the Bolognese cuisine, a cooking characterized by its richness, its meaty sauces, its melting cheeses, its creams and truffles, its green lasagne and delicately stuffed pastes, and the best salami and mortadella in the country. In Rome there is one restaurant that devotes itself to Bolognese cooking.

281

BOLOGNA, the capital of Emilia, the seat of Europe's first university, and the repository of one more leaning tower than Pisa, is perhaps most widely known for the richness and perfection of its cuisine. All over the country gourmands indulge themselves in Bolognese veal scallops and turkey breasts adorned with bubbling cheeses, ham slices, and scatterings of white Albi truffles. The meat sauce that bathes almost every type of pasta is of Bolognese origin, and the Bologna sausage, another of the region's specialties, has become unforgettable to Americans as "baloney." In Rome there is one citadel of Bolognese cooking, a restaurant that was started about forty years ago by three Bolognese immigrants, who took over the premises of an old Roman trattoria.

Dal Bolognese looks out on one of the city's busiest piazzas, a great oval at the foot of the Pincio, guarded by churches and a huge city gate, filled with fountains and a central obelisk, and endowed with a rich bulk of art and architecture. Valadier designed the piazza and the serpentine ascent that loops its way up to the Pincio and the Villa Borghese. The hand of Bernini is everywhere: he did the inner face of the gate (Michelangelo designed the other side), one of two baroque churches that mushroom out of the opposite end of the piazza, and the redesigned interiors, a great deal of statuary, and some of the tombs in the church of Santa Maria del Popolo, a kind of minor museum that stands at the piazza's north flank. Bramante and Raphael contributed to the design and decorations of the same church, and Pinturicchio, Caravaggio, del Piombo, and a series of lesser masters are represented with paintings and frescoes. The piazza is haunted by artists and lovers of culture. The Café Rosati, next door to Bolognese, is virtually the intellectual headquarters of Rome; and the restaurant has always enjoyed its own share of

282

talented patrons. Roman writers are generally great eaters as well, and generations of them, from Trilussa and Belli to Moravia, have frequented the premises.

There is an air of well being in the restaurant. Its respectable decor is pleasantly worn: a touch of dark wood, some etchings, a snow of white linen. All of the flouncier garnishes are saved for the cooking. Ettore Tomaselli, the Bolognese proprietor, has had nearly a half-century of restaurant work, almost all of it in his native city. He bought Dal Bolognese from the remaining original partner just a few years ago, when he decided to move to Rome. He brought his family along with him, and two of them are active in the business: brother Giancarlo as a partner, and Mamma Elvira as the cook.

Mamma Elvira's talents are immediately in evidence in any one of a number of rich pasta dishes. She is expert at the many-layered casserole of green lasagne, done up with authentic Bolognese ragù, and rivers of cream sauce and hot cheese. She can turn out delicate tortellini with a subtle meat stuffing and a spicy meat dressing. They come also touched only by consommé, and traditionalists can have them alla panna, cooked in cream, the way they are frequently served in Bologna. Signor Ettore has supplied the classic recipe, which is one of those below. Mamma Elvira makes tortellini di magro, stuffed with ricotta cheese, the traditional paste for the family meal in Bologna on Christmas Eve. They are perhaps the most delicate of all, and worth trying when they are on the menu. Egg noodles, called tagliatelle in the North, are served here with a brown meat gravy, a melting mound of butter, and a gentle cover of grated cheese.

Breaded veal cutlets, chicken, and turkey breasts are splendid here, fried Bolognese style under a layer of ham and melting cheese. Variations include filetted turkey breasts in a Madeira sauce, or smothered in a mushroom gravy. If you are still in the mood for something at the end of the meal, try the semifreddo, called simply Dolce Mamma. Signor Ettore's recipes include a summer-time classic that can be found all over Italy, cold veal with a tuna-"mayonnaise" topping, and the two favorites of Bolognese cuisine, veal cutlet, and tortellini in heavy cream.

VITELLO TONNATO
(Veal with Tuna Sauce)

3 lb. round or boned loin of veal
salt
1 large branch of celery
optional: white wine, onion, carrot
1 lb. canned tuna fish (choice white meat in oil)
1 small can anchovy filets, with the oil

1 hard-boiled egg yolk
1 generous tbsp. vinegar
juice of 1 lemon
¾ cup olive oil
2 heaping tbsp. capers
garnishes: hard-boiled egg white, gherkins, olives, anchovies, pimientos, etc.

Cover the roast with water and put it to boil, adding salt and a good branch of celery. Some cooks prefer a mixture of white wine and water, and the addition of a whole carrot and an onion. When the meat is tender, about an hour and a half, remove the pot from the stove. Let the meat cool in the broth. Meanwhile mix together the tuna fish, with its oil, anchovies, with their oil, hard-boiled egg yolk, vinegar, lemon juice, and olive oil, and pass them through a fine sieve (or use the blender). Reserve. When the meat is cool, remove it to a carving board and cut it in slices a little less than a quarter inch thick. Arrange these on a large oval serving platter in an overlapping pattern. Pour the tuna sauce over it, spreading it evenly, and sprinkle generously with capers. If you want to be more decorative, arrange circles or moons of egg white, slices of gherkins, olive buds, anchovy curls, slashes of red peppers, or any preferred garnishes, in patterns on the tuna. Refrigerate at least one day before serving. This makes marvelous hot-weather fare for six.

284

COTOLETTA ALLA BOLOGNESE
(Veal Cutlet, Bolognese Style)

3 slices of veal: round steak or
   loin cutlet, ¼ lb. each
1 beaten egg
bread crumbs
salt and pepper

1 large lump of butter
6 tbsp. broth
3 slices prosciutto
1 cup grated Swiss cheese and
   Parmesan cheese, mixed

Pound the veal steaks to flatten them slightly. Dip them in beaten egg, then bread crumbs. Sprinkle with salt and pepper. Melt the butter and brown the meat in it. When the veal is a good rich color all around, add the broth, and cook about fifteen minutes or until tender. Cover each cutlet with a slice of prosciutto, and mound the mixed grated cheeses on top. Cover and simmer for about five minutes or until the cheese melts and flows over the cutlets. Serves three.

TORTELLINI ALLA PANNA
(Tortellini in Cream)

1 lb. tortellini (use ½
   recipe, p. 148)
4 quarts broth

4 tbsp. butter
½ glass heavy cream
grated Parmesan cheese

Boil the tortellini gently in the broth until they are cooked through but still firm. Put the butter to melt in a large pan. Scoop out the tortellini with a slotted spoon, let the broth drain off each spoonful, and put in the pan with the melted butter. Stir gently. Add the cream, and leave about thirty seconds to heat through. Sprinkle liberally with cheese, mix carefully, and cook only until the cheese, cream, and butter amalgamate into a rich sauce. Serve at once with a little grated Parmesan over the top, and more on the side. Serves three (or four).

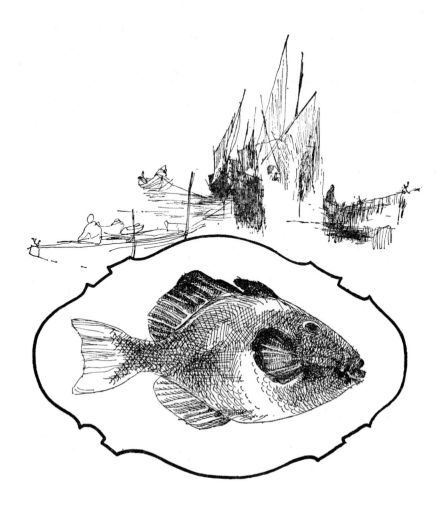

8. Venetian Specialties

VENETIANS eat seafood, polenta, quantities of rice, and calf's liver sautéed with onions. They generally drink wines from the Verona vineyards—Valpolicella, Soave, Bardolino. In Rome, the old-style trattoria Battaglia specializes in the cuisine of this region.

BATTAGLIA
(TAVERNA ANTONINA)

"THE intellectual faculties seem to have soared in an enduring exaltation under the influence of spices. Is it to spices that we owe Ariosto, Tasso, and Boccaccio? Is it to spices that we owe Titian's masterpieces? I am tempted to believe it," once wrote Alexandre Dumas.[11] It is certainly owing to spices that Venice became the opulent queen of the Adriatic, receiving cargoes from India and the East that burgeoned her coffers, and perfected the finesse of her cuisine. Until the mid-sixteenth century, the city was celebrated for the extravagance of its gastronomy, and, according to Elizabeth David, "it was the Venetians who introduced the use of forks at table (regarded at the time as an insensate luxury) and of fine glassware." [12] Despite the vicissitudes of time and history, the tradition of opulent cuisine lingers in Venice still, and the memory of the spice trade adds spirit to Venetian cooking. The large Rialto market, like Les Halles of Paris, is an awesome sight, decked out with the riches of the earth and sea. Gondolas take the place of market trucks, and also become floating stalls in quiet back canals. The artichoke vendor hawks his violet blossoms, one of Venice's prized vegetables; the fishmonger holds up the ugly rospo, of which the Venetians grill only the tail over glowing embers. There are baskets of tiny soft-shell crabs, which, breaded and fried, are a delicacy in their season. Sea snails and periwinkles are sold to and consumed in quantity by the seafood-loving Venetians.

Some twenty years ago Umberto Battaglia, whose career had

11. *Alexandre Dumas' Dictionary of Cuisine,* ed. and trans. by Louis Colman, New York, Simon and Schuster, 1958, p. 19.
12. Elizabeth David, *Italian Food,* New York, Alfred A. Knopf, 1958, p. 5.

taken him from Venice to London, to Paris, and finally to Rome, opened this modest trattoria dedicated to the cooking of his native city. He and his wife, who is an expert cook, stock their larder with all of the special products of the Venetian cuisine: butter and oil from the Veneto, beans from the great farms of Lamon that grow no other product, special corn meal as only the Venetians mill it, a whole aquarium of Adriatic mollusks and sea creatures, and a merlot, a tokay, and a cabernet from the inland hills near Venice.

Signor Umberto offers his guests a price-fixed menu which includes paste or soup, entrée and vegetable, fruits or cheese, a quartino of Frascati, and the charges for cover and service. Although this is a considerable bargain, there are some unusual dishes on the menu which make it difficult to order any way but à la carte. There is first of all a tripe soup made according to a venerable Venetian recipe, and another that combines egg noodles and those special Lamon beans. The rice at Battaglia is generally enriched with chicken livers, and the cannelloni sauced with béchamel, tomatoes, peas, and mushrooms is remarkably delicate. Calf's liver and onions, perhaps the best known of all Venetian specialties, is always featured, and Battaglia makes it well. They cook their salt cod with milk and butter and serve it with polenta, although occasionally they produce a much livelier version that harks back to the spicy cooking of their native city; it is one of the recipes that follows. If you have time to order in advance—at least half a day, but better even earlier—you can obtain a butter-soft chicken cooked for five hours in clay. The same cooking technique serves for pheasant or guinea fowl (pollo, fagiano, or faraona alla creta), although they also come cooked in the usual fashion. Small game birds are another favorite, served with a golden square of polenta. When you order roasted breast of veal or a crackling joint of abbacchio, Signor Umberto sends it garnished with excellent, small, browned potato balls.

Among the rare dishes on the menu is the salad of raw mushrooms, and here is Signor Umberto's recipe for it:

INSALATA DI FUNGHI CRUDI
(Salad of Raw Mushrooms)

½ lb. mushrooms sliced razor
  thin
½ cup olive oil

juice of 1 large lemon
salt and pepper

The mushrooms should be cleaned with a damp sponge or soft brush, then sliced vertically as thin as possible. Mix the olive oil, lemon juice, and salt and pepper. Pour over the mushrooms, and toss lightly. Let sit at least several minutes before serving. This salad will keep as long as overnight in the refrigerator, but although the flavor is still excellent, the mushrooms "cook" in the lemon juice, and lose the firmness of their texture and the purity of their color. Serves four.

BACCALÀ
(Salt Cod)

1 dried salt cod of about 2 lbs.
3 or 4 onions, chopped very
  fine
butter the size of an egg

½ cup olive oil
flour
milk
Parmesan cheese

stuffing:

parsley
12 anchovies
1 small onion

salt and pepper
several good dashes of
  cinnamon

Soak the cod overnight or longer in several changes of cold water (or put in a container under continuously running cold water). In a large kettle, sauté the onions slowly in the butter and oil. Cook until they are glossy. Cut the cod almost in half lengthwise to make a

289

cavity for the stuffing. Mince the parsley, anchovies, and onion as fine as possible, add the salt, pepper, and cinnamon, then fill the fish with this mixture. Close the two halves, in the manner of a book. Cut the fish into six equal portions, and tie these with butcher's string, or secure with toothpicks. Dip each portion in flour. When the onions are slightly golden, add the fish, turning it frequently so that it imbibes all of the onion flavor and colors evenly. After fifteen or twenty minutes, cover the fish with milk, sprinkle a little Parmesan cheese over the top, cover the pot, and cook gently for three to four hours. It should simmer very slowly, just below the boiling point. The finished baccalà can be stored in the refrigerator for later use (in the cooking liquid). When reheating, always cover the pot, or the fish may darken. Serves six.

POLENTA
(Corn Meal)

The very best Italian polenta comes from the Venice area, where it is milled to a different consistency than the average product. As a general rule, the longer you cook polenta, the better it will be; maize is not the kind of food to eat "al dente."

1 cup polenta	salt
1 quart of water (or 3 cups for Venetian type)	oil

Bring the water to a racing boil. Add the polenta, stirring as you do, and cook until it is tender and stands away from the sides of the pot when you stir. This should take at least half an hour, but three-quarters of an hour is better yet. It is necessary to stir the maize almost continuously while you cook it, to prevent lumps and insure lightness. When it is very thick and nicely tender, turn it out on an oiled marble table or counter top, or a greased cookie sheet. Spread it evenly about three-quarters of an inch thick, and let it cool. Cut it into squares (the Italians usually use a string instead of a knife). The polenta can be reheated in the oven in a buttered pan, or browned in a little butter on the top of the stove. Serves four.

290

[NOTE: The substitution of broth for water enriches this modest dish, and the addition of cheese and butter makes it into a good dough for gnocchi. Baked and sauced, they can serve as a course by themselves. Here is the recipe:]

GNOCCHI DI POLENTA
(Corn Meal Gnocchi)

polenta (see above)
3 to 4 tbsp. butter

½ to ¾ cup grated Parmesan cheese
sauce of your choice

While the polenta is still hot, mix in a few tablespoons of butter and the grated cheese, a little at a time. Spread evenly on an oiled table to cool. Cut into squares. The gnocchi can be arranged, overlapping, in a buttered baking dish, then sprinkled with cheese, and baked until brown. Often they are sauced with a gravy of tomatoes and dried mushrooms, and sprinkled with cheese. Serves four.

9. Pizzerie
Neapolitan Specialties

PIZZA is the most famous of Neapolitan recipes, but fried mozzarella sandwiches, fish soups, garlicky tomato sauces, carnival
lasagne, and spaghetti topped with clams are also favorite dishes
from the Naples area. Among the many pizzerie in Rome, here
are three of the most reliable.

THE first Tempio di Agrippa was built in 27 A.D. by Augustus' son-in-law. It was replaced by the Pantheon, just across from where there now stands another Tempio di Agrippa, a pizzeria. The Pantheon has had its ups and downs, having been sacked, pillaged, and restored countless times, and what stands today is bereft of most of the marbles, bronzes, and gilded ornaments that formerly glorified it. The vast dome, open to the elements and dependent on the light from the top of the cupola, contains the tombs of many notables: Raphael, Queen Margherita of Savoy, Humbert I, and Victor Emanuel II among them. Once consecrated, the Pantheon became officially known as the church of Santa Maria Rotonda.

Across the way, the Tempio di Agrippa pizzeria keeps late hours, and its Neapolitan-style guitarists and singers put on a lively show. They were experts, last time I was there, at concocting stornelli, the "folk song" that is created on the spot, the singer weaving an often bawdy, rhymed tale, a fortune, an adventure, about the person he is singing to. When the guitarists quiet down, one of the waiters can usually be persuaded to sing a rousing aria, with all of the requisite tremolos. Singing has been an integral part of the pizzeria's operations ever since it opened more than sixty years ago. The brothers Bianchi, who now direct the restaurant, tell me that the Maestro who launched the tenor Beniamino Gigli when he was a boy frequented this locale, and every evening he cheered the other clients by singing for them.

The Tempio di Agrippa is divided into a small restaurant above and a smaller tavern below, and there are both a regular dinner menu and a pizzeria menu. The first contains a normal assortment of Italian dishes, pleasantly cooked and appetizingly presented. Among them I have sampled a fine pollo alla diavola and a tender roast of veal. But the thing to have here, especially late

293

in the evening, is one of the specialties: a pizza, stuffed pastries called calzone, or a sizzling golden sandwich of mozzarella, and some light Italian beer. The Bianchis have given me their recipes for each of these favorites.

PIZZA ALLA NAPOLETANA
(Neapolitan Pizza)

dough:

2½ cups flour
1 tbsp. salt
1 envelope yeast

½ glass warm water
4 tbsp. olive oil
½ glass milk

garniture:

2 lbs. (or about 4 or 5) fresh tomatoes, peeled and chopped (canned may be substituted)

1 small oval of mozzarella, sliced
1 small can filleted anchovies
pepper
olive oil

Sift together the flour and salt onto a table. Make a well in the center, and add the yeast dissolved in warm water, the olive oil, and part of the milk. Gradually work the liquid into the dry ingredients, adding more milk as needed to make a soft dough. (The total amount of liquid used depends on the quality of the flour, so the amounts given are approximate.) Cover the hands with flour as you work, and knead until it forms a smooth dough. (The Bianchis recommend a half-hour, but you can obtain satisfactory results in half the time.) Shape into a ball, place in a lightly floured pan or bowl, cover with a dampened cloth or kitchen towel, and store in a warm, draft-free place for about four hours (although, again, half the time may suffice), or until it has risen to more than double its volume. Knead again for a few minutes, then reshape into a ball. Flatten the dough into a disc by patting it out, about ¼ inch thick. If you prefer to make individual pizzas, divide the dough into four parts, and make four discs. Place the disc or discs on a large, well-oiled baking sheet or flat roasting pan. Spread the surface liberally with the chopped tomatoes, slices of mozzarella, strips of anchovies (some prefer to chop these coarsely and sprinkle all about), a good grating of black pepper, and several generous spurts of olive oil. Put to bake in a very hot oven (as hot as you can make it) for ten to fifteen minutes (here, I find, the home oven may require twice as long), or until the crust is golden and the filling bubbles. Serve immediately. Makes one large, two medium, or four individual pizzas.

PIZZA AI FUNGHI
(Pizza with Mushrooms)

pizza dough (see above)
2 lbs. fresh tomatoes, chopped
1 oval mozzarella, sliced

¼ lb. mushrooms (or more)
pepper
olive oil

Proceed as for Neapolitan pizza. When the discs are ready for the filling, cover them with the fresh, chopped tomatoes, slices of mozzarella, and the mushrooms, cleaned and sliced (vertically) as thin as possible. Season with fresh black pepper, and anoint with several good dashes of olive oil. Bake in a very hot oven for ten to fifteen minutes, or longer if necessary. Serves four.

PIZZA ALLA CAPRICCIOSA
(Pizza with Mixed Filling)

same as for pizza ai funghi
(above), cutting the
amount of mushrooms by
half, and with the addition
of:

2 slices of prosciutto
1 dozen shelled mussels
1 hard-boiled egg, quartered
4 tbsp. fresh cooked (or
canned) peas

Follow the recipe for the mushroom pizza. Decorate the unbaked round by sections, one with mushrooms, one with ham slices, and one with mussels. At the center put the four spears of hard-boiled egg, and sprinkle the whole surface with peas, black pepper, and olive oil. If you prefer, arrange some of each of the ingredients on four individual sections. Bake in a very hot oven for ten to fifteen minutes, or as long as is needed. Serves four.

295

[NOTE: The addition of fresh or dried herbs such as basil, rosemary, oregano, or marjoram is good on any of the above pizzas, and sausage, salami, sweet peppers, and black olives are fine additions to the topping. One of my Roman friends has been growing stout on a pizza filled with potatoes, and she unreservedly recommends this combination. I have never tried it myself.]

CALZONE
(Stuffed Pastries)

pizza dough (see above)	pepper
1 oval mozzarella	olive oil
prosciutto or anchovies	

Roll out the pizza dough into a large sheet, and cut it into circles of about three-inch diameter. On one half of each disc put a slice or cube of cheese, and a slice of ham or two anchovies (or make some with ham, some with anchovies). Sprinkle with a little black pepper and a drop or two of olive oil. Fold the undressed edge over the filling, press the edges together firmly, and fry the half-moons in deep fat until they are golden. Drain and serve immediately. Enough for four portions.

MOZZARELLA IN CAROZZA
(Fried Mozzarella Sandwich)

3 slices bread, homemade white, or French type	flour
milk	1 beaten egg
3 large slices mozzarella cheese	olive oil

Soak the bread slices briefly in milk, but not enough to make them fall apart. On each dampened bread slice, lay one piece of mozzarella. Dip lightly in flour, then in beaten egg. Put about an inch of oil in the bottom of a skillet, and when it comes to the boiling point, fry the three sandwiches in it, turning once to brown each side evenly. Serve immediately. Serves one to three.

296

"SANT'IGNAZIO is known to all the world," says Ernesto Montelli, its Neapolitan-born proprietor. Judging from his collection of autographed pictures, now numbering close to three hundred, it is known at any rate to a good many of the world's most prominent citizens. It has been bustling along ever since Signor Ernesto and his new bride Elena opened the doors in April of 1922. Signora Elena is now the recipient of a gold medal from the Camera di Commercio di Roma ed Industria for "Faithfulness to her Work, Contribution to Economic Progress, and Thirty-Eight Years of Continuous Management."

The decor of Sant'Ignazio is cheerful, if a bit coquettish, and in summer the tables are set in the pleasant front yard of the piazza, which contains the seventeenth century church of Sant'Ignazio, of rather elaborate design, and a coterie of eighteenth century palazzi. The name of one of the narrow streets that joins the square here, the Via del Burrò, is really a contraction of the French "Bureaux," says Signor Ernesto, a "remembrance of the French military occupation of 1800."

There are many restaurant specialties, including pizza, and guests receive a printed list that defines a good dozen and a half of them. The pastes include a veal-filled cannelloni, and spaghetti with garlic and clams or mussels. Veal simmered in tomato sauce with a strong garlic flavor is typical of Neapolitan cookery, and scampi or Roman mazzancolle come with a peppy sauce of oil and vinegar, garlic, anchovies, and coarsely ground black pepper. Signor Ernesto has showered me with recipes, all of them house favorites, of which there are five given below. I do not repeat his directions for pizza alla Napoletana, only because that recipe has already been given elsewhere, but I cannot overlook his final word on the subject: "Però la vera pizza napoletana deve essere cotta in forno a legna," "However, the true Neapolitan pizza must be cooked in a wood-burning oven." This will help to explain why it is impossible to obtain the same kind of pizza at home as in the pizzeria. Here are some of the other recipes from Sant'Ignazio:

FEGATINI DI POLLO
(Chicken Livers)

¼ lb. butter

1 lb. chicken livers

sage leaves

salt and a little pepper

½ glass dry white wine

Melt the butter in a small skillet. Add the chicken livers, a few fresh sage leaves (or a sprinkling of dry, powdered sage), salt, and a light sprinkling of pepper. Cook for about ten minutes, turning from time to time so that the livers brown evenly. Add the white wine, cook a few minutes longer over a lively flame to reduce the sauce, and serve at once in a hot serving platter. Serves four.

RICCIARELLE ALLA CAMPAGNOLA

olive oil

2 cloves garlic, finely minced

2 filets anchovies, cut up

½ cup dry (white) vermouth

¼ cup dry white wine

½ lb. mushrooms, cut into thin slices

1 cup fresh tomatoes, cut up (canned may be substituted)

salt and pepper

1 lb. ricciarelle (curlicues of pasta: if unobtainable, use spaghetti)

chopped fresh parsley

Heat the oil in a heavy saucepan. Add the garlic and anchovies. When they are colored, add the vermouth, and cook over a lively flame for a few minutes. Add the white wine, then the mushrooms, and continue cooking slowly until they are tender. Then add the tomatoes, and salt and pepper to taste. Simmer until they form a

298

thick sauce. Cook the ricciarelle in a large kettle of racing salted water. When just done, drain and return to the same cooking vessel. Mix in the simmering sauce, stir until evenly distributed, and serve covered with chopped parsley on a warmed platter. Serves six.

[NOTE: I prefer to add the mushrooms with the garlic and anchovies, brown, then add the vermouth and white wine, and finally the tomatoes.]

MACCHERONI ZITA ALLA SORRENTINA
(Macaroni Casserole)

sauce:

3 tbsp. butter	1 cup fresh, chopped tomatoes
½ onion, chopped	(or canned)
½ glass dry (white) vermouth	salt and pepper

1 lb. macaroni (maccheroni di Zita No. 30), broken into five parts	4 fistfuls grated Parmesan cheese
1 lump butter	1 large oval mozzarella cheese, cut in slices

Make a sauce by melting the butter, browning the onion in it over a good flame, adding the vermouth, and cooking for two minutes. Then add the tomatoes, season with salt and pepper, and cook over a low flame slowly for at least a half hour. When the sauce is of a good consistency, put the macaroni to boil in a good quantity of salted water until they are just tender. Drain them, and return to the pot, adding half of the sauce and a good lump of butter. Mix well together. Turn half of the pasta into a baking dish (preferably oval), dress with several spoonfuls of sauce, dust with about two handfuls of grated Parmesan cheese, and spread with half of the slices of mozzarella cheese. Cover with the second half of the pasta, and the sauce and cheese as above. Put in a hot oven for about five or ten minutes, until the mixture bubbles and the cheese melts, and serve in the baking dish. Serves four to six.

⅔
PISELLI FRESCHI AL PROSCIUTTO
(Fresh Green Peas with Ham)

Signor Montelli says that according to the "sistema del Ristorante S. Ignazio," the secret of keeping fresh peas a good green color is to cook them in salted, boiling water of generous quantity—like pasta—and to take them off the flame before they are quite done. They should be drained (retain some of the water) and added immediately to some chopped onions and butter which have been browned in a copper skillet. Add a few drops of the liquid in which the peas cooked, sprinkle with sugar and slivers of cooked prosciutto. Simmer just long enough for the flavors to mix and the peas to finish, and turn out into a large serving platter, "in a way so that they have space and are not crowded. Many Romans cook their green peas by adding them raw to the skillet of butter and onions. And what is the result?" sighs Signor Ernesto, "the peas become yellowish." [2 lbs. fresh peas, one onion, and about ¼ lb. of cooked ham will provide the ingredients for four green portions.]

⅔
MELANZANE ALLA SICILIANA
(Eggplant Stuffed Sicilian Style)

per portion:

1 medium eggplant	½ fresh tomato, chopped (or
5 or 6 black olives	canned)
10 capers	pepper
½ anchovy	*no* salt
	olive oil

Wash the eggplant, and cut it in two lengthwise, but do not remove the purple skin. In a well-oiled baking dish, line up the split eggplants, one next to the other. Make two long cuts on each, and stuff into them a mixture of the following ingredients: the black olives, pitted and chopped (the chef at Sant'Ignazio always uses olives of Gaeta); about ten capers; the anchovy, washed well of salt; the fresh tomato, chopped; and black pepper. Sprinkle any remaining filling over the top. Splash the eggplants well with olive oil, and put to cook in a hot oven. To test their doneness, insert a fork.

When it comes out "without resistance," as Signor Ernesto puts it, the eggplants are ready. It takes around an hour, but the size and temperature will alter the cooking time.

RISTORANTE - PIZZERIA LACAPRICCIOSA

DURING the early and somber days of World War II, Enea Dante Santerini launched his business career by opening a small pizzeria in Rome. Because of the times, he didn't have much of a success, but in spite of everything he stuck it out. When the troops of liberation began to crowd the city, he began to find customers. At about the same time he started serving a variation on Neapolitan pizza, which he called pizza capricciosa. He soon obtained a "patent" on both the name and the recipe, which is now known all through Italy and is indexed and described in Italian cookbooks as a standard part of the cuisine. It certainly was the turning point in Signor Santerini's career. The pizzeria now includes a large restaurant that features specialties of Signor Santerini's province of Romagna. Umberto and Sergio Santerini, his sons, have joined the staff, and the list of faithful pizza-eaters includes figures from the theatre, films, television, opera, politics and journalism. If the person biting into that pizza next to you looks like Anita Ekberg or Sophia Loren, it probably is.

In the summer the sidewalks and streets in front of Roman eating places suddenly fill with tables, screens, potted plants, and other dining accessories, and the Largo dei Lombardi in front of Capricciosa is no exception. But the street here is so wide that the outdoor dining terrace is bisected by a stream of traffic. Your

301

waiter may come dashing between the Fiats and Vespas, balancing his tray like a tightrope walker with a parasol. Somehow he always manages to negotiate the vehicular stream and bring a full course dinner safely to guests seated on the other side.

Among the restaurant's specialties, the green lasagne baked with meat sauce, cheese, and béchamel, the ravioli filled with spinach and ricotta, the little stuffed rings of tortellini or the little stuffed hats of cappelletti are typical of the cooking of Romagna. All the pastes are made on the premises. Another regional dish that Capricciosa features is turkey breasts fried golden and served with melting cheese and ham. The kitchen turns out particularly good mozzarella in carrozza, sandwiches of cheese dipped in egg and flour and fried in hot oil until they are crunchy. Crostini, bread slices baked with a cover of cheese and a sauce of melted butter and anchovies, are a classic dish on Roman menus, but Signor Santerini has added a Romagnolo touch to his crostini alla Capricciosa, a sauce of butter, ham, fresh peas, and sliced mushrooms. The menu lists six varieties of pizza, but the most famous in this location is pizza Capricciosa. Here is the recipe from its originator:

PIZZA CAPRICCIOSA

dough:

2 cups flour	¼ cup tepid water
1 tbsp. salt	¼ cup cold water
1 envelope yeast	4 tbsp. oil

filling:

olive oil	12 shelled mussels
1 large mozzarella cheese	1 hard-boiled egg
8 or more tbsp. tomato purée	basil, oregano, marjoram
2 tbsp. sliced mushrooms	fresh grated black pepper
2 or 3 slices prosciutto	

Dough: Sift together the flour and salt onto a table top or into a large bowl. Make a well in the center. Dissolve the yeast in the tepid water, and pour into the well, along with part of the cold water (add the rest as needed) and four tablespoons of olive oil. Work the flour into the liquid until a good dough is formed. Knead until smooth. Form into a small round, sprinkle lightly with flour, and place in a bowl covered with a cloth in a warm, draft-free spot for two hours or more, or until the dough doubles its size. Knead again for a few minutes, then roll or pat out to the desired size. This makes two medium or one very large pizza.

Filling: Spread the dough generously with olive oil. Over this make a layer of chips of mozzarella cheese, and spoon thick tomato purée over the cheese. Mentally divide the pizza into four quarters. On one quarter spread the thinly sliced mushrooms; on the second, long strips of prosciutto; dot the third with the mussels; leave the fourth portion as it is. Divide the egg into three spears, and place in the center of the pizza. Sprinkle various spices according to taste over the top: basil, oregano, marjoram. Grind fresh black pepper over all, and slosh liberally with olive oil. Bake in a very hot oven until the crust is flaky and the filling bubbly.

For mussels, you can substitute small clams, minced clams, anchovies, or flakes of tuna fish, but this is no longer the classic pizza Capricciosa.

MOZZARELLA IN CARROZZA
(Fried Mozzarella Cheese Sandwich)

for each sandwich:

2 slices of bread	flour
milk	beaten egg
1 slice mozzarella cheese	olive oil

The bread should be of a fairly firm consistency. French bread is good, or any homemade-type white bread. Dip each slice lightly in milk. Place a slice of mozzarella between two dipped slices of bread, flour lightly on both sides, dip in an egg beaten frothy, and fry until golden in bubbling hot olive oil, turning once. Serve immediately.

RAVIOLI DI SPINACI E RICOTTA
(Spinach and Cheese Ravioli)

pasta:
(see recipe, p. 164)

filling:

½ cup cooked, chopped
  spinach
½ cup ricotta cheese
½ cup grated Parmesan
  cheese

2 eggs
salt and pepper
nutmeg

sauce:

butter and grated Parmesan
  cheese, or meat sauce and
  grated Parmesan cheese

Divide the finished dough into two equal parts and roll out into two thin sheets, one slightly larger than the other. It is important to work quickly once the sheets are rolled out so that they do not become too dry. Place a teaspoonful of the filling at regular intervals —about two finger-widths apart—on the smaller sheet of pasta. Cover loosely with the other sheet, allowing it to drape down between the mounds of filling. Cut between the mounds with a pastry-cutter or floured knife, making even squares. Press the edges firmly together with the fingers, and store in a single layer in a floured tray or platter until ready to cook.

FILLING: Mix together the chopped spinach (which should be well drained of any cooking moisture), the ricotta and Parmesan cheese, the eggs, salt and pepper, and a good grating of nutmeg.

COOKING: Boil the ravioli in abundant salted water for about five minutes. They rise when they are cooked. Drain in a colander or take out with a large slotted spoon. Serve with generous lumps of soft butter and a good sprinkling of Parmesan cheese over the top, or with a few spoons of meat sauce and grated cheese. Serves six.

[NOTE: If the sheets of pasta begin to dry out before you finish distributing the filling, it is necessary to brush with beaten egg between the mounds before putting on the covering sheet. Otherwise they will not press together securely.]

CROSTINI ALLA PROVATURA
(Baked Cheese Toasts with Anchovies)

butter

2 or 3 slices of bread per portion

provatura or mozzarella cheese

1 tbsp. butter per portion

2 chopped filets of anchovy per portion

Spread a baking dish generously with butter. Place slices of bread in the dish, slightly overlapping or side by side. On each slice of bread place one slice of mozzarella. Put to bake in a 450° oven for eight to ten minutes or until the cheese melts and the toasts brown on the edges. While the crostini are baking, melt one tablespoon of butter with two chopped anchovies for each portion. Pour over the baked crostini and serve immediately.

[NOTE: Some cooks prefer to butter each slice of bread before putting on the mozzarella. Others fry the toasts on one side in hot olive oil, put fried side up in the baking dish, and proceed as above. If the anchovies you use are very salty, it is best to rinse them under cold water before chopping them.]

CROSTINI ALLA CAPRICCIOSA
(Baked Cheese Toasts with Ham, Peas, and Mushrooms)

Prepare crostini in the oven (as above). Pour over them a sauce made of one tablespoon of butter melted with one tablespoon of cooked fresh or canned peas, one tablespoon sliced, sautéed mushrooms, one slice of ham cut into small pieces, for each portion.

305

10. Atmosphere

ROME itself lends considerable atmosphere to the most unassuming places, but a few restaurants are famous for their very special settings. Pancrazio, etched out of the ruins of Pompey's Theatre, couldn't be more historic; Tre Scalini, right in the Piazza Navona, has one of the loveliest summer dining terraces in the city; and Da Meo Patacca, a boisterous mixture of local color and artful contrivance, couldn't be more rollicking.

306

Two thousand years ago Pompey ordered the construction of a monumental theatre, capacious enough to seat more than 27,000, and built splendidly of marble in emulation of Greek theatres he had seen and envied. On its Eastern flank stood the Porticus of Pompey, which contained the Curia, a chamber for the convenience of the Senators, and the inadvertent scene of Caesar's demise at the hands of Brutus and Cassius. The gigantic statue of Pompey, at the foot of which the bloody Caesar supposedly expired, now stands in the Palazzo Spada, one of half a dozen neighboring palaces that are significant monuments of the Renaissance. They include also the Palazzo Farnese, now the French Embassy, which was designed by Sangallo the Younger and Michelangelo, and the Palazzo della Cancelleria, the depository of the chains of St. Peter and parts of the Cross. In the same neighborhood, the Campo dei Fiori is one of the city's liveliest markets, though in grimmer days it was used for executions. Pompey's Theatre survived from its completion in 52 B.C. until the sixth century.

When you dine downstairs at Pancrazio, you can eat in rooms built in the excavations of the ancient theatre, among remnants of some of the original columns, stones, vaults, and decorations. The reconstruction and embellishments have been handled with care and good taste. Pancrazio has added one coffered ceiling, a few new urns, appropriate light fixtures, clay-red table cloths, and of course such construction materials as were needed to transmute the former grand entry hall into two of the most remarkable dining rooms in Rome. The head of a lion, a small sarcophagus, and several amphorae were dug up among the ruins, and now add to their adornments. Beyond the larger of the two downstairs rooms is an area of further excavation. A door that has now been partly dug out indicates that there is yet another level below, which, I am sure, the restaurant personnel will gladly show to interested amateur archeologists, except during peak business hours. The upstairs dining areas include a grand salon with rose marble columns, high ceilings, and classic statuary, newly built for parties, banquets, and festivities. There is outdoor dining in the summer, although the downstairs rooms are just as cool, and more inviting than the terrace. No matter which you choose, be sure to take a turn through the lower reaches before you leave.

Signor Pietro Macchioni, the present owner, tells me that before his father Pancrazio took over the operation in 1920 there had been a restaurant on the spot for over a hundred years. Sor Pietro, as the waiters call him in traditional Roman style, offers his guests a very good selection of Italian cooking—twenty-seven different pastes and soups, and a good three dozen main courses the last time I was there! To begin with there are pizzas, crostini, and several rice dishes: with chicken livers in a light broth, with mixed seafood, or with a touch of saffron in the style of Milan (recipe below). Those who choose pasta will find a whole range of stuffed delicacies: tortellini, agnolotti, and cappelletti; and such riches as baked cannelloni, the Abruzzi specialty maccheroni alla chitarra, and bubbling casseroles of lasagne. Pancrazio provides an ample choice of fish, fresh from the grill, infused with wine and herbs in a mixed casserole, fried crusty brown, or delicately steamed with lemon, oil, and parsley. Veal turns up in many guises; the best of these and the house specialty is zingarella al funghetto, for which Sor Pietro kindly gave me his recipe. In summer heat, the galantine of chicken is light and tempting, and all year round there are classic Florentine beef steaks.

Here are the recipes for Milanese rice, and "gypsy girl" veal smothered in mushrooms.

308

RISOTTO ALLA MILANESE
(Rice Milanese Style)

3 small Italian sausages,
   sliced
2 tbsp. butter
2 tbsp. olive oil
1 onion, minced
2 cups rice
saffron powder

salt and pepper
3 cups or more rich chicken
   broth, heated
½ cup dry white wine
grated Parmesan cheese
dabs of butter

Brown the sausages in the butter and oil, add the onion, and sauté until glossy. Add the rice, and stir well until it is coated with the oil and butter mixture. Add a dash of saffron and a light seasoning of salt and pepper. Add the hot chicken broth one ladle at a time, cooking over a vigorous fire and stirring well with each addition. After all the broth has been added, cook a few minutes over a high flame, then add the white wine. Stir well, cover, and turn the flame down very low. Simmer until all the liquid is absorbed. The Italians prefer their rice, like their pasta, al dente, and they cook this dish about twenty or twenty-five minutes, so that the rice is creamy but still firm to the bite. However, different qualities of rice have different cooking times, and not everybody likes his rice on the verge of tenderness. Besides this, the amount of liquid varies depending on rice and cooking time, so you may need to alter the amount of broth. The best rule is to test the rice after twenty minutes, and finish the cooking to your taste, adding liquid if necessary. When the rice is cooked, add a generous quantity of Parmesan cheese— at least ¼ cup—mix well, and cook over low heat a few minutes. Turn out into warm plates. Top with dabs of butter and more cheese. Serves four.

ZINGARELLA AL FUNGHETTO
(Veal with Mushrooms)

1 lb. choice, boneless veal (milk-fed and as white as possible), in 4 equal slices
flour
olive oil
2 tbsp. butter
½ cup dry white wine
several fresh sage leaves

4 slices prosciutto, cut in julienne
1 lb. mushrooms, sliced and sautéed in garlic and oil
4 fresh tomatoes, peeled and chopped
salt and pepper
parsley

Pound the four veal slices with a meat mallet. Flour them lightly and set to cook in a skillet with a little oil over a lively fire. When they are just beginning to take on a golden color, drain off the olive oil, and add two tablespoons of butter, the white wine, a few sage leaves, and the slivers of prosciutto. Cook briskly until the sauce is reduced by half. Add the cooked mushroom slices, fresh tomatoes, and salt and pepper. Continue cooking over a good flame until the sauce is almost creamy and thick. Serve with a sprinkling of finely minced parsley over the top. Serves four.

TRE SCALINI

"PIAZZA NAVONA, the most Roman piazza of Rome, the most ancient and the most original, seems to reflect in itself the rise and the growth of the new city on the ruins of the old." [13]

Follow any one of the several small streets that wander into the Piazza Navona, and its beauty and energy will burst abruptly

13. Translated from Luigi de Gregori, *Piazza Navona prima d'Innocenzo X*, Rome, Fratelli Palombi (n.d.), p. 7.

upon you. It is a long oval set among handsome earth- and clay-colored palaces, crowned with roof gardens rambling with greenery. The west side is dominated by a great baroque church dedicated to Sant'Agnese. Borromini designed the Renaissance façade of the church. Bernini, his fellow architect, sculptor, and closest rival, designed the commanding fountain facing it: a gigantic configuration representing the rivers Danube, Nile, La Plata, and Ganges, with a Roman obelisk towering above. At either end of the piazza are smaller fountains, one by Bernini, the other much more recent.

In Roman times the Emperor Domitian dedicated this circus to bouts and competitions. It was here that the young Christian girl Agnese, having spurned the attentions of a prominent Roman, was punished by being exposed naked. Her hair grew miraculously to cover her. She later escaped death at the stake when the flames did not burn her, but finally she was beheaded.

By the seventeenth century, the stadium was converted to water sports, at least in the dog days of August, when on Saturdays the whole place was flooded and the crowds came to dip and splatter as if it were the sea itself. The picture on Tre Scalini's menu shows the water-filled piazza, a scene which continued well into the nineteenth century.

It is the Christmas season that attracts special attention in modern times; the Piazza Navona is the heart of the Romans' celebration. A carnival prevails until January 6th, and the nougat and ribbon candy makers rule supreme. The piazza is filled with booths that sell dazzlements for the children, toys, souvenirs, and seasonal ornaments. Shepherds from outlying areas come into the plaza to play on their melancholy pipes and native recorders in front of the crèche. On Epiphany Eve the Befana, a witch from whom Italian children get their toys, takes off on her broom and makes her distributions, which marks the occasion for wild celebration in the piazza. At midnight the noise is unbelievable and it is almost perilous to roam through the surging crowds.

311

Tre Scalini, named for its three entrance steps, commands a fine perch on one side of the piazza. It is certainly best to dine here in the summer, for the experience on a balmy evening of a leisurely dinner in this extraordinary setting cannot be marred— not even by a number of tourist buses, an army of sightseers, or a bunch of Italian high-livers and American colonists who make their headquarters at the neighboring Tre Scalini bar. From a box seat you can enjoy the splash of fountains and the clatter of the horse carriages, and ponder over the specialties that Luigi Ciampini, Tre Scalini's owner, recommends. His father began operating the restaurant here in 1932, joined later by his sons. Mamma did all the cooking, but now she just supervises. The current chef has been with the family for over a dozen years. His specialties are two: cannelloni and bauletto (the stuffed veal recipe below). The bar is famous for an ice cream confection that the Ciampinis invented, according to Luigi, and you can have it for dessert in the restaurant. It is the gelato tartufo, rich chocolate ice cream with a surprise cherry in the middle, riddled generously with solid chocolate slivers, and topped off gloriously with a fluff of whipped cream. It is perhaps wise, if you plan to finish with this, to start with something like ham and melon instead of cannelloni. I have enjoyed the roast abbacchio here, and have asked for its recipe, along with the Ciampinis' instructions for stuffing veal rolls. The menu also includes chicken, broiled, roasted, or sautéed Roman style with peppers and tomatoes, sweetbreads braised in tomato sauce, roast beef with a garnish of fresh spinach, and baked eggplant between layers of sauce and melted cheese. In the summer there is vitello tonnato, and cold mixed meats. Although the dessert list is larger than usual here, everyone should try the chocolate tartufo at least once. Here are the Tre Scalini recipes:

ABBACCHIO ARROSTO
(Roast Baby Lamb)

Make a number of incisions in the meat, and stuff these with spears of garlic, tiny sprigs of rosemary, and small strips of prosciutto [or bacon]. Salt and pepper the roast and place it in a baking pan. Before roasting in a moderate oven, pour over it a generous wetting of olive oil, and dot with a few dabs of butter. Bake until brown and crisp, basting with the pan juices from time to time, and with ½ cup of dry white wine about ten minutes before it is finished. Tre Scalini uses suckling lamb, which you can perhaps obtain from an Italian butcher in your area. Otherwise, use leg of lamb, cooking no more than thirty minutes to the pound, unless you prefer the lamb rarer. At Tre Scalini they serve their abbacchio with browned potato wedges, and it is the perfect accompaniment.

BAULETTO TRE SCALINI
(Stuffed Veal Rolls, Tre Scalini)

1 lb. veal cut into 8 equal slices
1 tbsp. butter
8 slices prosciutto
1 oval mozzarella cheese, cut in eight slices
8 or 16 spears asparagus, depending on size
toothpicks
1 lump of butter
½ cup veal gravy or broth
optional: ½ cup sliced, sautéed mushrooms
optional: dry white wine or Marsala

Pound the veal flat. In a pan that can later go in the oven, brown the veal quickly in the butter until it is a good color. Cover each piece of veal with one slice of prosciutto, one slice of mozzarella and a spear or two of asparagus. Roll up each veal package and secure with toothpicks. Return to the pan and put in a moderate-hot oven to roast just until the cheese begins to melt (this shouldn't take very long). Then add a lump of butter to the baking pan, spoon the gravy or broth over the meat, and return to the stove or oven just long enough to serve bubbling hot. Scrape the pan juices and sauce over each veal roll. You can top with sliced mushrooms, sautéed sepa-

313

rately with butter and garlic. You can also add a bit of white wine or
Marsala along with the broth or gravy. Note: The Italian prosciutto
is generally salty enough to season the meat sufficiently, but you may
prefer to add a light sprinkling of salt. Serves four.

DA MEO PATACCA

DA MEO PATACCA has more atmosphere, both authentic and contrived, than any place in Rome. It is a carnival, an antique shop,
and a country inn combined. The parking attendant, in costume,
directs traffic from horseback. At any moment the musicians,
strolling about with a great deal of commotion, may receive a chal-
lenge from a soprano planted in a second-story window, and a
singing duel ensues. A bunch of neighborhood gamins, perched on
an old winecart just outside of the dining area, burst into rollicking song, accompanying themselves on homemade instruments.
The restaurant's eighteenth century setting is largely bucolic, the
tables and benches on the cobblestones all around it heavily rus-
tic. There are lights and garlands and flying lanterns, cascades of
garlic, dry corn, and red peppers, and meandering vendors hanging on to great soaring clusters af balloons. Old carts and carriages
are scattered on the fringes, and just across the piazza a contin-
gent of Trasteverini drape on the benches of a bottiglieria to
drink wine and stare at the antics. (They provide a guaranteed
snatch of local color for the diners; Da Meo Patacca owns the
bottiglieria, too.) Almost all of the restaurant personnel parade
about in costumes, join in a folk song or two, jig a bit of a taran-
tella, or follow the band in a noisy march around the piazza. The
neighbors put up with the general din and racket because, I am
told, most of them have relatives employed there.

314

If you are disappointed that there are few finds left at the Sunday morning Flea Market, it is just that Da Meo Patacca's proprietor has probably got there first. The inside rooms of the place display a wondrous assortment of statuary, portraiture, and high class junk juxtaposed with great good humor and imagination. There are also giant spits that send their flames licking at suckling pigs, baby lambs, or skewered birds; and grapes, gaudy peppers, crates of apples or peaches are stacked in a glass show case refreshed by a trickle of cool water. The ladies' room has floral designs in unexpected places, and if you peep through a main-floor grate near the bar you can see fathoms down into the dark, cold cellars.

As if all of this happily contrived setting were not sufficient, the Trastevere area surrounding the place is naturally spirited. It has been the popular seat of Roman individuality since the Middle Ages. There is a good deal of shouting. Instant mobs spring up at the least provocation. Shabby houses sometimes reveal a chicken or two scurrying across the floor. Doorways are filled with wrinkled old people leaning on their canes and watching the normal commotion, and with cushiony women who dwarf the cane stools they settle on to shell the peas for the family dinner. Neighborhood youths wisecrack and jostle as they strip off their shirts and duck under the stream of a public water spout.

The Piazza De' Mercanti angles off of the larger Piazza di Santa Cecilia, overshadowed by the great, second century church of Saint Cecilia, the site of her house and her martyrdom. This Roman gentlewoman refused to worship idols, and was rewarded for her Christian perseverance by being locked up in her calidarium to be scalded alive. (There are remains of these baths and some of the original steam pipes off a corridor near the sacristy of the church.) She miraculously escaped, only to be beheaded, but even then she did not finally succumb for three days. She is widely revered as the patron saint of music, and is credited with the invention of the organ. I am surprised that Da Meo Patacca has overlooked installing one in her honor.

In the summer of 1963, during the Trastevere Festival of Noantri, the restaurant's proprietors dedicated a life-size bronze replica of Sor Capanna to the city of Rome. Sor Capanna was a famous Trastevere minstrel, a blind singer and composer of stornelli, which are a kind of spontaneous folk song. His name is coupled with those of the poets Trilussa and Belli, all of them having contributed to a literature founded on Roman dialect. Since Da Meo Patacca is a stronghold of stornelli singers, the gift was most appropriate. The bearded painter and sculptor Harry Jackson, commissioned to construct the memorial, is a folk singer in his own right. The dedication of the Sor Capanna bronze, heralded by an avalanche of publicity, and fortified by the announcement that the wife of the United States Ambassador would do the unveiling, erupted into complete chaos. The evening before, and in the midst of a cocktail party for the press, two white-uniformed policemen served an order demanding the removal of the statue (by now well anchored in a concrete base) because the Lazio Commission for Fine Arts had not given its approval. After some soap-opera shenanigans on both sides, the ceremonies went ahead on schedule—Madame Ambassador arriving in a horse-drawn rig, and Sculptor Jackson turned out in full cowboy regalia. But a day later, down came Sor Capanna. At this writing the statue is still entwined like Laocoön in the serpentine folds of Roman bureaucracy.

The boss of Da Meo Patacca is Remington Olmstead, a gigantic American who distinguished himself at UCLA by playing both on the football team and in the operetta. The latter was the start of a career in the theatre, and by the late Thirties he had moved from Hollywood to New York, where he eventually landed the role of Jud's understudy in "Oklahoma!". When the London company of that musical formed, Remi became the first-string Jud. At the end of the run, friends convinced him to pursue

316

voice studies in Italy, where he arrived shortly thereafter by motorcycle. Since he had little money, he settled in the working-
man's quarter, Trastevere, which he liked so much that he has
never left it. He married an Italian gentlewoman named Diane
Varé, and four years ago they launched Da Meo Patacca. It was
the spirit of high-living that appealed to Remi when he named
the restaurant: Meo Patacca is supposed to have been a legendary
con man who lived hereabouts in the Middle Ages, and had a
roisterous good time on other people's money. ("Patacca" has
several possible meanings, the cleanest of which in Roman dialect
is "swindle.")

The place is not all atmosphere. Chef Dino Menicatti, an old
friend of Remi's, is a Florentine who knows a good deal about
cooking, and in particular the art of roasting on a spit. Before
Remi opened Da Meo Patacca, Dino worked in several of Rome's
fine Tuscan and game restaurants. He directs a large operation
with a success that could well be the envy of many a less demanding kitchen. The menu, literally over a yard long, and unrolled
by necessity with the gesture of a town-crier, is largely Italian and
written in the Romanesco jargon of Trastevere. Here and there
a dish like onion soup, "fondù à la Borguignone," or roasted corn
on the cob sneaks in among the fettuccine and mixed Roman
salad. There is also Irish coffee and French champagne. People
find it amusing to order as hors d'oeuvres giant radishes and a
peppery oil for dipping with the bawdy name ravanelli ar cazz'im-
perio. Bruschette, Roman garlic breads, are another delicious way
to spend the time it takes to cook the pasta. The smoked mountain ham from the Abruzzi is especially good, and comes with the
proper summer accompaniment of fresh figs or melon. The specialties from the spit are crunchy and highly flavored: juicy Umbrian piglet with a crackling skin, Roman abbacchio, pig's liver,
scampi, and chicken. If you have difficulty making up your mind,
there is a mixed platter which contains a little of everything.
The only disappointment I find is the corn, roasted dry and tough

317

each time I have tried it. I understand that you can have it boiled instead, with a good gob of fresh butter melting over it, and this should be more successful.

Dino has given me several recipes, including this one for roasting a suckling pig.

PORCHETTINI UMBRI AR GIRAROSTO
(Umbrian Suckling Pig on the Spit)

1 suckling pig of about 28 to 29 pounds	a whole fennel or two, including the leaves
several heads of garlic	salt and pepper
a bouquet of rosemary (several large branches)	

The combined seasonings should be enough to stuff the pig. Chop the garlic, rosemary, and fennel together coarsely, and mix in a good quantity of salt and freshly ground pepper. Stuff this in the cavity of the pig, and tie the pig with cooking string so that the filling is tightly enclosed. Put to cook on a rotating spit over a good charcoal fire (it has to cook for about three and a half hours without burning to a crisp). Do not baste, as the pig bathes in its own fat and juices. Serves twenty-five to thirty.

ANITRA CO' LA SARSA
(Duck with Sauce)

1 duck weighing 2½ to 3 lbs.	1 onion, chopped
olive oil	1 stalk celery, chopped
salt and pepper	1 carrot, chopped
rosemary (two or three sprigs)	1 cup dry red wine, Chianti type
sage (three or four leaves)	

Put the duck in a roasting pan together with a little olive oil, the seasonings, and the vegetables. Roast in a 375° oven until the vegetables begin to color well and the duck starts to brown. Pour over it a cup of red Chianti, and continue cooking until the duck is tender

318

(with this size Italian duck it takes about an hour, but ducks seem to vary). When the duck is roasted, remove from the pan and keep warm. Skim off any excess fat, and pass the sauce through a fine mill. Cut the duck in quarters, return it to the roasting pan, cover with the sauce and heat through before serving. Dino likes to serve steaming rice as an accompaniment, with a generous ladle of sauce poured over it. Serves four.

[NOTE: I think the sauce is improved by the addition of all the giblets except the liver to the roasting pan along with the vegetables and seasonings. At Da Meo Patacca the giblets find their way, I am sure, into the excellent sauce that covers the fettuccine.]

In the hunting season, the menu is rich with wild boar, hare, pheasant, and quail. Here is Dino's recipe for the last, which you can also make in a heavy frying pan if you don't have a revolving spit.

DU' QUAJE COR CROSTONE
(Quail with Bread Crusts)

per portion:

2 quail	two thick slices of firm bread
2 thin but wide slices of bacon	(French type)
fresh sage leaves	olive oil
salt and pepper	

Wrap the bacon across the back of the quail in such a manner that the skewer will keep it in place when the birds are spitted. Sprinkle a liberal amount of salt and freshly ground black pepper in the cavity of each bird, and stuff with fresh sage leaves. Cut the bread about 1½ inches thick, to a size that will fit neatly between the birds (French rolls serve well for this purpose). Alternate the bread chunks and the birds on a skewer, and set to turn over a charcoal fire, basting frequently with abundant olive oil. If you use a skillet instead, the procedure is the same, but it is necessary to turn the skewer frequently so that the birds will cook evenly. Average cooking time is thirty minutes, but it depends on the size of the birds.

AROSTO MISTO A LA SPIEDO
(Mixed Roasts from the Spit)

The restaurant version of a Roman mixed grill includes a hunk of spitted baby lamb, chicken, pig's liver, pork sausage, and a crackling cut of piglet. For a family barbecue, select any two of the meats and roast them along with a pork sausage on a revolving spit over a good charcoal fire. The lamb should be pierced with spikes of garlic and rosemary (cut a pocket near the bone), well salted and peppered, and basted with oil or butter along with its own fat. The chicken should be seasoned with salt and pepper inside and out, and stuffed with garlic cloves and sage leaves or a few branches of rosemary. The pork liver must be cut into chunks, seasoned with salt and pepper, then carefully wrapped in bacon cut as thin as possible (one piece around one way, another to close the other sides). Alternate it with bread chunks and laurel leaves on the skewer, taking care that the bacon is firmly in place. Baste the bread with oil as it cooks (about ten minutes).

This dish is always served on Monday at Da Meo Patacca:

PORPETTINE DE MANZO CON LI FACIOLI
(Meatballs with Beans)

2 lbs. ground beef	3 beaten eggs
1 piece stale white bread (French or homemade type), soaked in water, then squeezed out	1¼ cups grated Parmesan cheese
parsley	salt and pepper
2 cloves garlic	olive oil
	¼ cup dry white wine
	2 cups stewed tomatoes

Put the beef, bread, parsley, and garlic through the food mill, or chop well together. Add the eggs, cheese, salt, and pepper, and mix well. Shape into small hamburgers or rounds about the size of a golf ball. Put to brown in a skillet with hot olive oil, turning so that they color evenly. Bathe them with about a quarter cup of white wine, simmer a few minutes, and add the stewed tomatoes. Cook, covered, over low heat for about three-quarters of an hour to an hour. Makes about two dozen golf ball size, one dozen hamburger size; serves six.

NOTE: This same meat mixture goes into the making of meat loaf, polpettone. It is decorative to fill the loaf with whole, hard-boiled eggs. Cook it in the oven slowly for an hour and a half.

At Da Meo Patacca the meatballs come with a serving of boiled broad beans cooked in a sauce of garlic, olive oil, sage, tomatoes, salt and pepper. (For six people, one pound of beans, soaked overnight, boiled approximately two hours or until tender, added to the half-cooked sauce.)

CIPOLLETTE AGRODORCE
(Sweet and Sour Pearl Onions)

2 lbs. of the smallest pearl
   onions you can find
½ glass vinegar
¼ cup olive oil
½ glass dry white wine

¼ cup wine vinegar
salt and pepper
2 tbsp. sugar
2 laurel leaves

Put the onions (in their skins) in a large pot with hot water to cover and a half glass of vinegar. Bring to a boil and simmer about five minutes. Drain and cool. Peel off the skins. Put in a baking dish with all of the other ingredients, mix well, and cook in the oven at 400° for an hour. Serves six. [These are even better after a day or so, and would be just the thing to replace the tired creamed onion on Thanksgiving tables.]

BRUSCHETTA
(Garlic Toast)

Cut French bread or heavy homemade white bread into large thick slices. Put to toast on the grill or in the oven. When both sides are a good color, rub immediately with a cut clove of garlic, sprinkle with salt, and place on a dish. Pour good olive oil liberally over them, and eat at once, while they are still hot.

321

IV

GLOSSARY

Italian-English

English-Italian

DIRECTORY
OF RESTAURANTS

GLOSSARY

Italian-English

abbacchio: suckling lamb (Rome)
acciughe: anchovies in oil
aceto: vinegar; sott'aceto:
    preserved in vinegar
acqua: water; acqua minerale:
    natural sparkling mineral water
affettato: cold cuts
affogato: steamed
affumicato: smoked
aglio: garlic
agnello: lamb
agnolotti: pasta with meat filling
agro: sour
agro-dolce: sweet and sour
aguglie: garfish
albicocche: apricots
alici: anchovies in salt
allodole: larks
amarena: sour cherry
amaretti: macaroons
amaro: bitter

amburghese: hamburger
ananasso: pineapple
anguilla: eel
anguria: watermelon (Northern
    Italy)
animelle: sweetbreads
anitra: duck
antipasti: appetizers or hors
    d'oeuvres
aragosta: spiny lobster
arancia: orange
aranciata: orangeade, or
    carbonated orange drink
aringhe: herring
arista: spitted or oven-roasted
    pork
arrosto: roast
arsella: cockle (Genoese)
arzilla: ray
ascé: hamburger
asparagi: asparagus

325

GLOSSARY

baccalà: dried, salted cod
bacon: bacon
banane: bananas
barbabietole: beets
barbo, barbio: red mullet
barchette: flaky pastry boats, usually containing a fish preparation
basilico: basil
battuto: base for soups, stews, meats, sauces, and vegetables; made of onion, celery, parsley, carrot, garlic, and sometimes prosciutto, sautéed in oil
bauletto: veal rolls filled with cheese, simmered in sauce
beccaccia: woodcock
beccaccino: snipe
beccafichi: figpeckers
bel paese: soft, mild cheese
besciamella: béchamel, or basic white sauce
(in) bianco: pasta with butter and Parmesan; a sauce without tomatoes; steamed or boiled
bicchiere: glass
bieda: chard
boldro: angler or frogfish
biscotti: cookies, biscuits
bistecca: beef or veal steak; alla fiorentina: T-bone, grilled or broiled
bollito: boiled
braciola di maiale: pork chop; —— di manzo: rib steak
branzino: striped bass

brasato: braised roast
broccoletti di rape: leafy plant with broccoli-like, long-stemmed flowering heads; in U.S., Chinese broccoli, Gai Choy, is closest equivalent; mustard or turnip greens come from the same family, can be used as substitute
broccoli: broccoli
brodetto: fish soup
brodo: broth
bruschetta: toasted bread seasoned with garlic and oil
buccia: skin or peel
budino: pudding; blood pudding
bue: beef
burro: butter
burro di noccioline: peanut butter

caccia, cacciagione, selvaggina: game
(alla) cacciatora: hunter style: usually cooked with some combination of garlic, parsley, sage, bay, or other spices, oil, vinegar, white wine, celery, onions, anchovies
cacciucco: fish stew, a specialty of Livorno
caciocavallo: cow's milk cheese similar to provolone
caffè: coffee; caffè corretto: coffee with grappa; caffè espresso: strong, black coffee; caffè latte: half hot milk, half coffee

326

calamari, calamaretti: squid

caldo: hot

(a) calo: to pay for wine by the amount consumed

calzone: flaky pastry envelope with minced chicken, meat or fish, and vegetables

canapè: small open-faced sandwich

canestrello: small scallop-like bivalve

cannella: cinnamon

cannelloni: pasta squares rolled around filling (usually meat), covered with sauce (tomato, cheese, béchamel) and baked

cannoli: crisp pastry tube filled with sweetened ricotta, chocolate, and candied fruits

cannuccia: drinking straw

cappelletti: filled, hat-shaped paste

capellini: long, thin noodles, usually served in broth

capitone: large eel

caponata: eggplant hors d'oeuvre

capperi: capers

cappone: seahen or gurnard

cappuccina, barba di; insalata ——: salad of small herbs

cappuccino: coffee and hot aerated milk

capretto: kid

capri(u)olo: venison, roe buck

caramelle: candies

carciofi: artichokes; alla giudia: deep fried in oil; alla manticiana: grilled; alla romana: stuffed with garlic, parsley, and mint, and steamed in wine; fondi di ——: bottoms

cardi: stalk-like vegetables of the thistle family, cardoons

carne: meat; carne macinata: ground meat, hamburger

carote: carrots

carrozza, mozzarella in: a crusty fried sandwich of mozzarella dipped in batter

carpa: carp

casalingo, casereccio: homemade

cassata: frozen Sicilian sweet

casseruola: deep metal cooking pot

castagne: chestnuts

caviale: caviar

cavoletti di bruxelles: Brussels sprouts

cavolfiore: cauliflower

cavolo: cabbage

ceci: beans (garbanzo)

cedron: citron

cefalo: common grey mullet

cerfoglio: chervil

cernia: grouper, like sea bass

certosino: mild, soft, spready cheese

cervello: brains

cervo: venison

cespo (d'insalata): lettuce

cetrioli: cucumbers

cetriolini (sott'aceto): gherkins

327

GLOSSARY

(alla) Chantilly: with whipped
cream

china: quinine

chiodo di garafano: clove

cialda: wafer, waffle; *cialdone:*
horn-shaped wafer; *panna e
cialdone:* whipped cream with
wafers

ciambella: ring-shaped cake,
often coffee cake

cicoria: chicory, sometimes
dandelion

ciliege: cherries

cinghiale: wild boar

cioccolato: chocolate

cipolle: onions

cipolline: pearl onions

ciriole: small eels

cocco: coconut

cocomero: watermelon (Rome)

coda (di bue): oxtail; *alla vaccinara:* oxtail cooked in a rich
tomato sauce

coltello: knife

condimenti: condiments

condito: seasoned; *insalata condita:* salad with dressing;
insalata scondita: salad without dressing

coniglio: rabbit

conserva: conserve (generally
tomato paste)

contorni: vegetables accompanying main course

coppa: head cheese, a fatty pork
cold cut; also cup or bowl
(of dessert or ice cream); *coppa
mista:* cup of ice cream of
assorted flavors

coratella: liver, lights, giblets,
heart

cornetti: croissants, crescents

coscetto, cosciotto, coscia: leg

costatella, costoletta, cotoletta:
chop

costato: rib steak

cotechino: highly spiced pork
sausage

cotogno: quince

cotto: cooked

cozze: mussels

crema: custard; *crema caramella:*
custard with caramel glaze

crema di: cream of (with soups)

crema di latte: coffee cream

crêpes: pancakes

crescione: water cress

croccante: crispy

crosta; crostata; crostatina: crust;
pie crust; tart

crostini: croutons, bread cubes,
or triangles of toasted bread;
in Florence spread with a pâté
of chicken livers, anchovies
and capers; —— *alla provatura,*
bread slices baked with melted
cheese and served with
anchovy sauce

crudo: raw

cucchiaio, cucchiaino: large
spoon, small spoon

cuore: heart

cuscus, cuscussù: a complicated southern dish of Arabian origin, generally containing meat and semolina

dadini: cubes or croutons
datteri di mare: sea-dates, like mussels
(al) dente: (pasta or rice) cooked firmly
dentice: dentex, similar to pompano
dolce: sweet
dolci: sweets, cakes
dorato: golden brown, sometimes breaded
dragoncello: tarragon

entrecote: rib steak
erbe: herbs
erbetta: parsley (Rome)
escarola: escarole

fagiano: pheasant
fagioli: kidney beans, white beans
fagiolini: string beans
farcito: stuffed
farina: flour; —— *d'avena:* oatmeal; —— *gialla:* cornmeal; —— *di riso:* rice flour
fava: broad bean
fegato: liver; *alla veneziana:* liver sautéed with onions
fegatini di pollo: chicken livers; *alla salvia:* with sage
(ai) ferri: grilled

fette, fettine: slices
fettine dorate: fried bread, southern style
fettuccine: thin egg noodles; *alla romana:* with butter and Parmesan cheese
fichi: figs
filetto: filet
finocchio: fennel
fiocchi di granturco: cornflakes
focaccia, fogaccia: pizza crust
fondi di carciofi: artichoke bottoms
fonduta: fondue
fontina: medium tangy cheese
forchetta: fork
formaggio: cheese
forno, al forno: roasted or baked
fragole: strawberries
fragoline dei boschi: tiny wild strawberries
fragoline di mare: baby octopi
frappè: frappé
frattaglie: interior organs and minor parts, such as giblets, tail, marrow, heart, etc.
freddo: cold
fresco: fresh, uncooked, raw
friggere: to fry
fritella: fritter or doughnut; fried squares of cheese-filled pasta
frittata: omelette
fritto: fried
fritto misto (alla romana): mixed fried foods: brain, artichokes, liver, veal steaks, heart, sweet-

329

breads, etc.; also mixed fried
fish

frittura di pesce: fried fish

frullato di frutta: thick mix of
fruit, milk, sugar and crushed
ice, blended by machine

frutta: fruit; —— *di stagione:*
fruit in season

frutti di mare: mixture of
shellfish

funghi: mushrooms

galantina: galantine

gallina: hen

gamberi, gamberetti: shrimp

gelato: ice cream

ghiaccio: ice; *ghiacciato:* iced

gianduia: chocolate cream

gnocchi: "dumplings" made from
flour, semolina, potatoes, corn
meal, spinach, ricotta, baked
with cheese and butter, or
boiled and served with sauce

gobbi: stalk-like vegetables of the
thistle family, cardoons

gorgonzola: blue-green veined
cheese

grancevola: crab

granelli (d'agnello): testicles
(lamb)

granita: water-ice; —— *di caffè:*
of coffee; —— *di limone:* of
lemon; —— *di fragole:* of
strawberries; —— *con panna:*
topped with whipped cream

granturco: corn

(alla) gratella: grilled

gratinato: au gratin

grattugiato: grated

(alla) griglia: broiled or grilled

grissini: bread sticks

groviera: Swiss cheese

guanciale: bacon (Rome)

imbottito: stuffed

indivia: endive (escarole type);
—— del Belgio: Belgian endive

insalata: salad; capricciosa, mista,
misticanza (Rome): mixed
salad; cappuccina, barba di:
salad of small herbs; verde:
green salad; russa: cooked
vegetables with mayonnaise

intingolo: gravy, sauce, spicy dish

involtini: thin veal slices rolled
around prosciutto, sage leaves,
carrots, mozzarella (or other
variations) and sautéed in
broth &/or wine

lamponi: raspberries

lardo: lard

lasagne: broad flat noodles;
timballo di, al forno: baked
in layers of sauces and cheese

latte: milk

lattuga: lettuce

lauro: laurel or bay

legumi: vegetables, in general
those with pods or shells

lenticchie: lentils

330

lepre: hare; —— in salmì: marinated in wine and herbs

lesso: boiled

lievito: yeast

limonata: lemonade

limone: lemon

lingua (di bue): tongue (beef)

liquori: liquors, cordials or liqueurs

littoridina: periwinkles

lombata: loin

lombatine: loin chops

luccio: pike

lumache: snails

maccheroni: macaroni

macedonia (di frutta): fruit cocktail with maraschino or white wine, served for dessert

maggiorana: marjoram

magro: lean

maiale: pork

maionese: mayonnaise

mandarino: tangerine

mandorla: almond

manteca: cheese and butter loaf

manzo: beef

(alla) marinara: mariner style

marinato: marinated

maritozzi: sweet buns sometimes filled with whipped cream

marmellata: jam, marmalade, preserve

martino: angler

mascarpone, mascherpone: soft cream cheese

mazzancolle: very large prawns (Rome)

medaglioni: medallions

melagrana: pomegranate

melanzane: eggplant

mele: apples

mele cotte: baked apples

melone, popone: melon, generally cantaloupe; prosciutto e melone: ham and melon antipasto

menta, mentuccia (Rome): mint

meringhe: meringue

merlano: whiting

merli: blackbirds

merluzzo: cod

messicani: stuffed veal parcels, usually in sauce

midollo: marrow

miele: honey

mille foglie: short flaky pastry

milza (di bue): spleen

minestra: soup

minestre: soup &/or pasta course

minestrone: vegetable soup with pasta or rice

Monte Bianco: Mont Blanc, a puréed chestnut and whipped cream dessert

molecche (Venice): tiny soft-shell crabs

monachine: bullfinches

more: blackberries

mortadella: large spiced baloney

moscardino (Genoa): very tiny octopus

331

GLOSSARY

mostarda: mustard
mozzarella: soft, mild cheese used
    in pizza; —— in carrozza:
    fried mozzarella sandwich
muggine: common grey mullet
murena: moray

nasello: hake
nespole: medlar pears
nocciole: hazelnuts
noccioline americane: peanuts
noce moscata: nutmeg
noci: walnuts

oca: goose
odori: herbs
olio: oil; all'olio: in oil
olive: olives; nere: black olives;
    verdi: green olives
ombrina: croaker
omelette: omelette
orata: red snapper, bream
origano: oregano
ortolano: ortolan
orzo: barley
ossobuco: shin-bone of veal,
    cooked with the marrow
ostriche: oysters
ovoli: (amanita Caesarea) wild,
    orange-scarlet mushrooms

pagliata, pajata: a kind of tripe,
    tubular and very succulent
palombacci: game pigeons
palombo: smooth hound shark

pan di Spagna: spongecake
pancetta (di maiale): bacon
pane: bread; —— in, a, cassetta:
    packed, sliced bread; —— di
    segale, di merano, nero, or
    tedesco: rye bread; ——
    integrale: whole wheat bread
pane tostato: toast
panettone: cake studded with
    candied fruit peel, a Milanese
    specialty
panforte: a hard Sienese cake of
    finely ground nuts and candied
    citron
pangiallo: traditional Roman
    Christmas cake, of nuts,
    spices, citrus peel, raisins
panini: rolls
panna montata: whipped cream
pappardelle: lasagne
parmigiano: Parmesan cheese
passatelli: Bolognese pasta made
    by forcing egg-cheese-bread-
    crumb dough through sieve,
    and poaching in broth
passera: plaice
pasta: dough of flour and water
    used to make noodles, spa-
    ghetti, etc.; —— all'uovo:
    dough of flour, water and eggs;
    pasta asciutta: pasta served
    in any form except soup;
    pasta per dolci, pasticcio:
    dough for pastries
pastella: batter for frying

332

pastina: small noodles (or paste in other shapes) for soup

patate, patatine: potatoes; —— arroste: roast potatoes; —— fritte: fried potatoes; —— novelle: new potatoes; purè di ——: mashed potatoes

pecorino: hard sheep-milk cheese, rather sharp, widely used in Rome

pepe: black pepper

peperoni: green peppers; —— gialli: sweet red peppers; —— sott'aceto: peppers preserved in vinegar; —— sott'olio: peppers dressed with oil

peperoncini: dried, usually crushed, hot red peppers

pere: pears

pernice: partridge

persico: bass

pescatrice: angler or frogfish

pesce: fish

pesce spada: swordfish

pesche: peaches

pesto: a Genoese specialty of fresh basil, Parmesan cheese, garlic, and sometimes pine nuts or walnuts, ground in olive oil, used on spaghetti or in minestrone

pettirossi: robins

petto di: breast of

pezzi, pezzetti, pezzettini: pieces, small pieces, bits

(a) piacere: cooked to your pleasure

(alla) piastra: cooked on the griddle

piatti: dishes, courses; —— freddi: cold dishes; —— caldi: hot dishes

piccante: spicy; salsa piccante: ketchup or spicy sauce in general

piccione: squab

pilaw: pilaf

pimiento: sweet red pepper

pinoli: pine nuts

piselli: peas; —— al prosciutto: peas, ham and onion; seppie coi piselli alla romana: peas and cuttlefish stewed in white wine, oil, and garlic

pizza: pie; leavened dough baked with a covering of mozzarella, tomato, oil, garlic, oregano, mushrooms, anchovies, sausage, peppers, prosciutto, hard-boiled eggs, mussels, etc., or any combination

(alla) pizzaiola: with tomato sauce, generally seasoned with garlic and oregano

polenta: cooked corn meal, often served with meat sauce or with game

pollame: poultry

pollo: chicken; —— alla diavola: grilled or broiled chicken

333

polpette, polpettini: meatballs
polpetti: baby octopi
polpettone: meat loaf
polpo: octopus
pomodoro: tomato
ponce, poncino: punch
popone: melon
porchetta: roasted whole suckling pig, filled with spices, often served sliced at festas on crusty bread or rolls
porcini: (Boletus edulis) large field mushrooms
porro: leek
prezzemolo: parsley
prosciutto: ham; —— cotto: cooked, boiled ham; —— crudo: cured ham; —— e melone: ham and melon antipasto
provatura: a cheese of buffalo milk, very fresh and soft, similar to mozzarella
provola: buffalo cheese, sometimes smoked
provolone: smoked, semi-hard cheese from buffalo's or cow's milk
prugne: prunes, fresh plums
punch: punch
puntarella: spiky salad green, usually served with an anchovy, oil and garlic dressing
purè: purée

quadrucci: small squares of pasta, used in broth
quaglie: quail

rabarbaro: rhubarb
radicchio: red salad plant
radici: radishes
rafano: horse-radish
ragù: meat sauce; stew
rane: frogs
rapa: turnip
ravanello: radish
ravioli: pasta envelopes stuffed with meat &/or vegetables, sometimes ricotta
razza: ray
ribes: currants
riccio: sea urchin
ricotta: cottage cheese
rigaglie di pollo: giblets (of chicken)
rigatoni: thick tubular pasta
ripieno: stuffing; as an adjective, filled
riso, risotto: rice, rice dish
ristretto: consommé
rognone, rognoncini: kidneys
rosbiffe: roast beef
rosmarino: rosemary
rospo, coda di rospo: angler or frogfish
rughetta: a European herb known as "rocket plant," the small, piquant leaves of which are used in salad; popular in Rome

salame: salami

sale: salt

salmì, in salmì: marinated in wine and herbs

salmone: salmon

salsa: sauce; besciamella: béchamel or white sauce; —— di pomodoro: tomato sauce; —— verde: green sauce, a blend of parsley, capers, anchovies, garlic, gherkins, onion, salt and pepper, ground to a fine paste and added to oil and vinegar; generally served cold with meat

salsicce: pork sausage

saltimbocca alla romana: thin veal slices, fresh sage leaves, and prosciutto, skewered together and sautéed in oil/butter and Marsala

salvia: sage

(al) sangue: rare (of meat)

San Pietro: John Dory

sarde, sardine: sardines

savoiardi: lady fingers

scaloppine: thin slices of veal sautéed in oil/butter, sometimes with Marsala, mushrooms, etc.

scampi: Norway or Danish lobsters, a type of large prawn

scarola: escarole

schienali: "marrows" or cords of the backbone, like brain

sciroppo: syrup

scondito: unseasoned

scorfano: scorpion fish, like rockfish

sedano: celery

selvaggina: game

selvatico: wild

semi: seeds

semifreddi: mousses, frozen puddings

semolino: semolina, a very good quality of flour

semola: bran

senape: mustard

seppie: cuttlefish

sfinge: doughnuts or cream puffs

sgombro: mackerel

soffritto: base for soups, stews, meats, sauces, vegetables; of sautéed onions, celery, carrots, parsley, oil, garlic, and sometimes prosciutto

sogliole: sole

sorbetto: ice cream (sherbet type)

sottaceti: pickles

spaghetti: spaghetti

sparagi: asparagus

spezie: spices

spezzato: cut in pieces, such as spezzato di vitello, veal stew

spiedino, spiedo, allo spiedo: spit, spitted, roasted on a spit

spigola: striped bass

spinaci: spinach

spremuta: fruit drink, squash;

335

—— di arancio: orangeade;
—— di limone: lemonade

spuma: whip

spumone: spumone, a frozen pudding of puréed fruit or other base, and whipped cream

squadro: angel shark

(di) stagione: in season

starna: partridge

stoccafisso: stockfish; prepared dried cod, usually served with oil, anchovies, walnuts, and black olives

storione: sturgeon

stracchino: soft, mild cheese

stracciatella: broth containing a mixture of egg, semolina, and grated cheese

stracotto: pot roast

strutto: lard

stufatino: meat and vegetable stew

stuzzicadenti: toothpick

succo: juice

sufflè: soufflé

sugo: gravy or sauce

supplì: hot rice balls filled with meat, mozzarella, and sometimes tomato sauce

susine: plums

tacchino: turkey

tagliatelle: flat egg noodles

tamarindo: tamarind, a fruit with acid pulp used in preserves, but most commonly as a thirst-quenching drink

tarocco, tarocchi (also torocco): blood orange(s)

tartelette: flaky filled pastry, served as antipasto

tartufo: truffle; —— nero: black truffle; —— bianco: white truffle; —— di mare: clam-like shellfish

tè, thè: tea

tegame: frying pan; al tegame: cooked in the pan

tellina (Tuscany): cockle

testa: head; —— di maiale: pig's head; —— di vitello: calf's head

timballo: casserole, mold

timo: thyme

tonno: tuna fish

topinamburo: Jerusalem artichoke

tordi: thrushes

torrone: nougat

torta: cake

tortellini: small stuffed rings of pasta served in broth or sauce

totani: cuttlefish

tramezzino: small sandwich

trancia: slice

trenette: shoelace-thin noodles, usually served al pesto

triglia: red mullet

trippa: tripe

trota: trout

uccelletti, uccellini: small birds; uccellini scappati, uccelletti matti: rolled veal birds

(in) umido: stewed in a gravy, usually with tomato and herbs

uova: eggs; —— alla coque: boiled eggs; —— sode: hard boiled eggs; —— fritte: fried eggs; —— in camicia, affogate: poached eggs; —— strapazzate: scrambled eggs

uva: grapes

uva secca, uvetta: raisins

vaniglia: vanilla

vermicelli: very thin spaghetti

vermut: vermouth

vincisgrassi: variation of baked lasagne, layered with cheeses, and meat sauce

vino, vini: wine, wines; bianco: white wine; rosso: red wine; da tavola, comune, locale, nostrano: local or table wine

vini passiti: sweet dessert wines made from dried grapes

vitello: milk-fed, very young veal

vitellone: young beef

vongole: clams

wiener, wurstel: hot dog or small sausage

Yoga: pulpy fruit juice (a brand name)

zabaglione, zabaione: egg yolks, sugar, and Marsala whipped frothy over low heat

zafferano: saffron

zampa: foot

zampone: highly spiced pork sausage, encased in the skin of the forefeet (a specialty of Modena)

zeppole (di San Giuseppe): cream puff type sweets eaten on St. Joseph's Day in Rome

zucca: pumpkin

zucchero: sugar

zucchine: squash

zuppa: soup; —— di pesce: fish stew; —— inglese: custard pudding and cake; trifle

GLOSSARY

English-Italian

almond: mandorla

anchovies: acciughe (in oil),
   alici (in salt), but used
   interchangeably

angler fish: boldro, martino,
   pescatrice, rospo

appetizers: antipasti

apples: mele; —— cotte (baked)

apricots: albicocche

artichokes: carciofi; —— alla
   giudia (deep fried in olive oil);
   —— alla romana (stuffed with
   garlic, parsley and mint,
   and steamed in wine); fondi
   di —— (bottoms)

asparagus: asparagi, sparagi

bacon: bacon, pancetta (di
   maiale), guanciale (Rome)

baked: al forno

baloney-type sausage: mortadella

bananas: banane

barley: orzo

*base for soups, stews, meats,
   sauces:* battuto, soffritto

basil: basilico

bass: branzino, persico, spigola

batter (for frying): pastella

bay: lauro

beans: ceci (garbanzo), fagioli
   (kidney or white), fagiolini
   (string), fava (broad)

béchamel sauce: besciamella

beef: bue, manzo; vitellone
   (young beef)

beefsteak: bistecca (beef or veal
   steak); —— alla fiorentina
   (T-bone, grilled or broiled)

Belgian endive: indivia del Belgio

beets: barbabietole

birds: uccelletti, uccellini (game);
   uccelletti matti, uccellini
   scappati (veal birds)

biscuits: biscotti

bitter: amaro

blackberries: more

blackbirds: merli

blood pudding: budino

boar: cinghiale

boiled: bollito, lesso

brains: cervello

braised roast: brasato

bran: semola

bread: pane; fettine dorate (fried, southern style); —— in cassetta (packaged, sliced bread); —— di segale, di Merano, nero, tedesco (rye bread); grissini (bread sticks); —— integrale (whole wheat)

bream: orata

breast (of): petto (di)

broccoli: broccoli

broiled: alla griglia, alla gratella, ai ferri

broth: brodo; pastina in —— (with noodles); ristretto (consommé); stracciatella (containing a mixture of egg, semolina, grated cheese)

brown (glazed, sometimes breaded): dorato

Brussels sprouts: cavoletti di bruxelles

bullfinches: monachine

buns: maritozzi (sweet, sometimes filled with whipped cream)

butter: burro

cabbage: cavolo

cake: torta; ciambella (ring-shaped, sometimes coffee cake); panforte (hard Sienese cake of finely ground nuts and candied citrus); panettone (cake or brioche studded with candied fruit peel, a Milanese specialty); pangiallo (in Rome the traditional Christmas cake, made with raisins, nuts, citrus peel, and spices)

calf's head: testa di vitello

candies: caramelle

cantaloupe: melone, popone

capers: capperi

carp: carpa

carrots: carote

casserole, mold: timballo

cauliflower: cavolfiore

caviar: caviale

celery: sedano

chard: bieda

cheese: formaggio; gorgonzola (blue); groviera (Swiss); manteca (cheese and butter loaf); mozzarella (soft, pizza cheese); parmigiano (Parmesan); provolone (smoked, semi-hard)

cherries: ciliege; amarene (sour)

chervil: cerfoglio

chestnuts: castagne

chicken: pollo; —— alla diavola (grilled or broiled)

chicken livers: fegatini di pollo

chicory: cicoria

chocolate: cioccolato; gianduia (rich chocolate cream)

chop: costatella, costoletta, cotoletta

cinnamon: cannella

citron: cedron

clams: vongole

clove: chiodo di garafano

coconut: cocco

cockle: arsella (Genoese); tellina (Tuscan)

cod: merluzzo; baccalà (dried, salted)

coffee: caffè; —— corretto (with grappa); —— espresso (strong, black); caffè latte (half milk, half coffee); cappuccino (coffee and aerated milk)

cold: freddo

cold cuts: affettato

condiments: condimenti

conserve, generally tomato paste: conserva

consommé: ristretto

cooked: cotto

cooked to your pleasure: a piacere

cooked firm (pasta or rice): al dente

cookies: biscotti

cordials: liquori

corn: granturco; fiocchi di granturco (cornflakes)

cornmeal: farina gialla; polenta (cooked, often served with meat sauce, or as accompaniment to game)

cottage cheese: ricotta

crab: grancevola; molecche (tiny, soft-shell, Venice)

cream: crema; —— di (cream of, with soups); —— di latte (coffee cream); chantilly,

panna montata (whipped cream)

cream cheese: mascarpone, mascherpone

cream puffs: sfinge

crisp: croccante

croaker: ombrina

croissants: cornetti

croutons: crostini, dadini

crust: crosta, crostata (pie crust), crostatina (tart)

cubes: dadini

cucumbers: cetrioli

cup: tazza

currants: ribes

custard: crema; —— caramella (with caramel glaze)

custard-cake: zuppa inglese

cutlet: costoletta, cotoletta

cuttlefish: seppie, totani

dandelion: cicoria

Danish lobsters: scampi

dates (fruits) of the sea: datteri di mare (similar to mussels)

dentex: dentice (similar to pompano)

desserts: dolci

dishes: piatti; —— caldi (hot dishes); —— freddi (cold dishes)

dough: pasta; —— all'uovo (egg dough); —— asciutta (served cooked in any form except soup); —— per dolci, pasticcio (dough for pastries)

341

doughnuts: fritelle, sfinge, zeppole (di San Giuseppe)

duck: anitra

"dumplings": gnocchi (made from flour, spinach, ricotta cheese, potatoes, corn meal, semolina; baked with butter and cheese, or boiled and sauced)

eel: anguilla; ciri(u)ola (small); capitone (large)

egg flip: zabaglione, zabaione (egg yolks, sugar, Marsala, whipped over low heat)

egg noodles: fettuccine, pasta all'uovo, tagliatelle

eggplant: melanzane; eggplant hors d'oeuvre: caponata

eggs: uova; —— alla coque (boiled); —— fritte (fried); —— in camicia, affogate (poached); —— sode (hard boiled); —— strapazzate (scrambled)

endive: indivia (escarole type); —— del Belgio (Belgian endive)

escarole: escarola, scarola

fennel: finocchio

figpeckers: beccafichi

figs: fichi

filet: filetto

fish: pesce

fish soup or stew: brodetto, cacciucco (Livorno), zuppa di pesce

flour: farina; —— di riso (rice flour)

fondue: fonduta

foot: zampa

fork: forchetta

frappé: frappè (thick mix of fruit, milk, sugar, crushed ice, blended by machine)

fresh: fresco

fried: fritto; —— misto alla romana (mixed fried foods: brain, artichokes, liver, veal steaks, heart, sweetbreads, etc.); fritto misto (or frittura) di pesce (mixed fried fish)

fritter: fritella

frogfish: boldro, pescatrice, rospo (or coda di rospo)

frogs: rane

fruit: frutta; —— di stagione (in season)

fruit cocktail: macedonia di frutta

fruit juice: succo di frutta, Yoga (brand name)

fry (mixed): fritto misto, frittura di pesce (fish)

frying pan: tegame; al —— (cooked in the pan)

galantine: galantina

game: caccia, cacciagione, selvaggina

garfish: aguglie

garlic: aglio

342

gherkins: cetriolini (sott'aceto)

giblets: rigaglie di pollo

glass: bicchiere

goose: oca

grapes: uva

grated: grattugiato

(au) gratin: gratinato

gravy: sugo, intingolo, umido
   (stew, stewed, usually with
   tomato and herbs)

griddle: piastra

grilled: (alla) griglia, (in)
   gratella, ai ferri

ground meat: carne maccinata

grouper (like sea bass): cernia

gurnhard (seahen): cappone

hake: nasello

ham: prosciutto; —— cotto
   (cooked, boiled); —— crudo
   (cured); —— e melone (ham
   and melon antipasto)

hamburger: carne maccinata,
   amburghese, ascé

hare: lepre; —— in salmì
   (marinated in wine and herbs)

hazelnuts: nocciole

head: testa; —— di maiale (pig's
   head); —— di vitello (calf's
   head)

head cheese: coppa

heart: cuore

hen: gallina

herbs: erbe, odori

herring: aringhe

homemade: casalingo, casereccio

honey: miele

hors d'oeuvres: antipasti

horse-radish: rafano

hot: caldo

hot dog: wiener, wurstel

hunter style: alla cacciatora

ice: ghiaccio; iced: ghiacciato

ice cream: gelato; coppa mista
   (cup of assorted flavors);
   cassata (Sicilian ice cream-
   cake); sorbetto (sherbet-type)

ices: granita; —— di caffè (of
   coffee); —— di limone (of
   lemon); —— di fragole (of
   strawberries); —— con panna
   (topped with whipped cream)

jam: marmellata

Jerusalem artichoke: topinamburo

John Dory: San Pietro

juice: succo

ketchup: salsa piccante

kid: capretto

kidney beans: fagioli

kidneys: rognone, rognoncini

knife: coltello

lady fingers: savoiardi

lamb: agnello; abbacchio
   (suckling lamb, Rome)

lard: lardo, strutto

larks: allodole

lasagne: lasagne, pappardelle;
   lasagne al forno, timballo

343

di ——, vincisgrassi (baked in layers with cheese, sauce, meat, etc.)

laurel: lauro

lean: magro

leg: coscetto, cosciotto, coscia

lemon: limone

lemonade: spremuta di limone, limonata

lentils: lenticchie

lettuce: cespo d'insalata, lattuga; radicchio (red salad plant)

leek: porro

liqueurs, liquors: liquori

liver: fegato; —— alla veneziana (sautéed with onions); coratella (liver, lights, giblets, heart)

(chicken) livers: fegatini di pollo; —— alla salvia (with sage)

lobster (spiny): aragosta

loin: lombata; lombatine (loin chop)

macaroni: maccheroni

macaroons: amaretti

mackerel: sgombro

marinated: marinato; in salmì (in wine and herbs)

mariner style: alla marinara

marjoram: maggiorana

marmalade: marmellata

marrow: midollo

marrow-bone (veal shin): ossobuco

mayonnaise: maionese

meat: carne; —— maccinata (ground mcat, hamburger)

meat balls: polpette, polpettini

meat loaf: polpettone

medallions: medaglioni

medlar pears: nespole

melon (generally cantaloupe): melone, popone; prosciutto e melone (ham and melon)

meringue: meringhe

milk: latte

mineral water: acqua minerale

mint: menta, mentuccia (Rome)

Mont Blanc (puréed chestnuts and whipped cream): Monte Bianco

moray: murena

mousses: semifreddi

mullet: cefalo, muggine (common grey); barbo, barbio, triglia (red)

mushrooms: funghi; porcini (boletus edulis, large field mushrooms); ovoli (amanita Caesarea, orange-colored wild mushrooms)

mussels: cozze

mustard: senape, mostarda

noodles: capellini (long, thin, usually in broth); fettuccine, pasta all'uovo, tagliatelle (egg noodles); fettuccine alla romana (with butter and Parmesan cheese); pastina (small noodles or other shapes for soup); trenette (shoelace-thin, usually served al pesto)

nougat: torrone

nutmeg: noce moscata

oatmeal: farina d'avena

octopus: polpo; polpetti, fragoline di mare, moscardino (Genoa), (tiny octopi)

oil: olio; all'olio (in oil)

olives: olive; —— nere (black); —— verdi (green)

omelette: frittata, omelette

onions: cipolle; cipolline (pearl onions)

orange: arancia; tarocco, tarocchi (blood oranges)

orangeade: spremuta di arancia, aranciata

oregano: origano

ortolan: ortolano

oxtail: coda (di bue); —— alla vaccinara (cooked in a rich tomato sauce)

oysters: ostriche

pancakes: crêpes

paste, pastes: pasta, paste; agnolotti, cappelletti, ravioli, tortellini (stuffed pastes); cannelloni (stuffed, baked in sauce); quadrucci, pastina (small, in broth); rigatoni (large, tubular); vermicelli, capellini (fine)

Parmesan cheese: parmigiano

parsley: prezzemolo, erbetta (Rome)

partridge: starna, pernice

pastries: barchette (flaky, boat-shaped, usually filled with fish mixture); tartelette (flaky, filled pastries, served as antipasto); calzone (envelope filled with minced chicken, meat or fish, and vegetables); mille foglie (very short, flaky pastry for vol-au-vents, etc.); cannoli (crisp tube filled with sweetened ricotta, chocolate, candied fruits)

peaches: pesche

peanut butter: burro di noccioline

peanuts: noccioline americane

pears: pere

peas: piselli; —— al prosciutto (peas, ham and onion); seppie coi piselli alla romana (peas and cuttlefish stewed in white wine, oil, garlic)

peel: buccia

pepper: pepe (black); peperoni (sweet green); peperoni gialli, pimiento (sweet red); peperoni sott'aceto (preserved in vinegar); peperoni sott'olio (preserved in oil); peperoncini (dried, usually crushed, hot red peppers)

perch: cernia

periwinkles: littoridina

pheasant: fagiano

345

pickles: sottaceti
pie: pizza
pieces, small pieces, bits: pezzi,
    pezzetti, pezzettini
(suckling) pig: porchetta (roasted
    whole, filled with spices, served
    sliced at festas in sandwich
    form)
pigeons: palombacci (game);
    piccione (squab)
pig's head: testa di maiale
pike: luccio
pilaf: pilaw
pineapple: ananasso
pine nuts: pinoli
plaice: passera
plums: susine, prugne
pomegranate: melagrana
pork: maiale; braciola di
    —— (pork chop); cotechino,
    zampone (Modena), (pork
    sausage); arista (spitted or
    oven-roasted); cotiche (pork
    rind)
pot: casseruola (usually deep,
    metal)
pot roast: stracotta
potatoes: patate, patatine;
    —— arroste (roast); —— fritte
    (fried); —— novelle (new);
    purè di —— (mashed)
poultry: pollame
prawns (Rome): mazzancolle
    (large)
preserves: marmellata
prunes: prugne

pudding: budino; semifreddi
    (mousses, frozen puddings)
pumpkin: zucca
punch: ponce, poncino, punch
purée: purè

quail: quaglie
quince: cotogno
quinine: china

rabbit: coniglio
radishes: ravanelli, radici; rafano
    (horse-radish)
raisins: uva secca, uvetta
rare (of meat): al sangue
raspberries: lamponi
raw: crudo, fresco
ray: arzilla, razza
rhubarb: rabarbaro
rib steak: entrecote, costato,
    braciola di manzo
rice: riso, risotto; supplì (hot rice
    balls filled with meat,
    sometimes mozzarella and
    tomato sauce)
rice flour: farina di riso
roast: arrosto; al forno (roasted
    or baked)
roast beef: rosbiffe
robins: pettirossi
roe buck: capri(u)olo
rolls: panini
rosemary: rosmarino
rye bread: pane di segale, di
    Merano, —— nero,
    —— tedesco

346

saffron: zafferano

sage: salvia

salad: insalata; —— capricciosa, mista, misticanza (Rome), (mixed); barba di cappuccina, insalata cappuccina (salad of small herbs, Rome); insalata verde (green); —— russa (cooked vegetables with mayonnaise)

seasoned: condito; insalata condita (salad with dressing); insalata scondita (salad without dressing)

salami: salame

salmon: salmone

salt: sale

sandwich: tramezzino; canapè (open-faced); mozzarella in carrozza (hot cheese sandwich, dipped in batter, fried)

sandwich (packaged) bread: pane in cassetta

sardines: sardine (small), sarde (large)

sauce: sugo (also gravy), salsa; besciamella (white sauce); salsa di pomodoro (tomato sauce); salsa verde (green sauce: parsley, capers, anchovies, garlic, gherkins, onion, salt, pepper, oil, vinegar; usually accompanies cold meat); salsa piccante (ketchup; spicy sauce); pesto (fresh basil, Parmesan cheese, garlic, oil, sometimes pine or walnuts, finely ground, used on pasta or in minestrone; Genoese); ragù, alla bolognese (meat sauce); alla pizzaiola (with tomato sauce, generally seasoned with garlic and oregano)

sausage: salsicce, cotechino; zampone (Modena, highly spiced pork sausage encased in skin of forefeet)

scorpion fish: scorfano (like rock fish)

sea dates: datteri di mare (like mussels)

seahen (gurnard): cappone

(in) season: di stagione

sea urchin: riccio

seeds: semi

semolina: semolino

shark: squadro (angel); palombo (smooth hound)

shellfish: frutti di mare

shrimp: gamberi, gamberetti

skin: buccia

slice: trancia, fetta, fettina

smoked: affumicato

snails: lumache

snapper: orata (red)

snipe: beccaccino

sole: sogliola

soufflé: sufflè

soup: zuppa, minestra; minestre (soup &/or pasta course)

sour: agro

spaghetti: spaghetti

347

GLOSSARY

spices: spezie
spicy: piccante
spinach: spinaci
spit, spitted, roasted on a spit:
    spiedo, spiedino, allo spiedo
spleen: milza
spongecake: pan di Spagna
spoon: cucchiaio (large),
    cucchiaino (small)
squab: piccione
squash: zucchine (vegetable);
    spremuta (fruit drink)
squid: calamari, calamaretti
steamed: affogato
stew: spezzato, stufatino, ragù
stockfish: stoccafisso
straw: cannuccia
strawberries: fragole; fragoline dei
    boschi (tiny, wild strawberries)
string beans: fagiolini
stuffing: ripieno
stuffed: ripieno, imbottito, farcito
sturgeon: storione
sugar: zucchero
sweet: dolce
sweet and sour: agro-dolce
sweetbreads: animelle
sweet red pepper: pimiento,
    peperoni gialli
sweets, cakes, desserts: dolci
Swiss cheese: groviera
swordfish: pesce spada
syrup: sciroppo

tamarind: tamarindo
tangerine: mandarino

tarragon: dragoncello
T-bone steak, grilled: bistecca
    alla fiorentina
tea: tè, thè
testicles: granelli (usually
    d'agnello, of lamb)
thrushes: tordi
thyme: timo
toast: pane tostato
tomato: pomodoro
tomato paste: conserva
tongue: lingua
toothpick: stuzzicadenti
trifle: zuppa inglese
tripe: trippa (honeycomb);
    pagliata, pajata (tubular,
    especially full-flavored)
trout: trota
truffle: tartufo; —— nero (black);
    —— bianco (white)
tuna fish: tonno
turkey: tacchino
turnip: rapa

unseasoned: scondito

vanilla: vaniglia
veal: vitello; bauletti (rolls filled
    with cheese, simmered in
    sauce); involtini (rolls filled
    with prosciutto, sage, carrots,
    mozzarella, other variations,
    sautéed in broth or wine);
    messicani (veal parcels stuffed
    with meat mixture, usually in
    sauce); saltimbocca alla

348

romana (thin veal slices, fresh sage leaves, prosciutto sautéed in butter/oil and Marsala); scaloppine (thin veal slices sautéed in butter/oil, sometimes with Marsala, wine, mushrooms, etc.); uccellini scappati, uccelletti matti (rolled veal birds)

vegetables: legumi (in general those with pods or shells); contorni (accompanying an entrée)

vegetable soup: minestrone (with pasta or rice)

venison: cervo, capri(u)olo

vermouth: vermut

vinegar: aceto; sott'aceto (preserved in vinegar)

wafer, waffle: cialda; cialdone (horn-shaped); panna e cialdoni (whipped cream with wafers)

walnuts: noci

water: acqua; acqua minerale (sparkling mineral water)

water-ice: granita

water cress: crescione

watermelon: cocomero (Rome); anguria (Northern Italy)

whip: spuma

whipped cream: panna montata, Chantilly, latte miele (in Milan)

white sauce: besciamella

whiting: merlano

wholewheat bread: pane integrale

wild: selvatico

wine, wines: vino, vini; —— rosso (red); —— bianco (white); —— da tavola, comune, locale, nostrano (local or table wine); —— passiti (sweet dessert wines)

woodcock: beccaccia

yeast: lievito

349

Directory of Restaurants

1. ALFREDO ALLA
   SCROFA
   (*Characteristic*)
   Via della Scrofa 104
   65 01 63

2. ALFREDO
   ALL'AUGUSTEO
   (*Characteristic*)
   Piazza Augusto Imperatore 30
   68 16 72
   68 31 23

3. ALFREDO A
   TRASTEVERE
   (*Characteristic*)
   Piazza Santa Maria
      in Trastevere 13–14
   58 20 26

4. ANGELINO A
   TOR MARGANA
   (*Di Moda*)
   Piazza Margana 37
   68 13 28

5. ANTONIO A
   SAN CALISTO
   (*Seafood*)
   Piazza San Calisto 7
   58 60 61

6. AUGUSTEA
   (*Characteristic*)
   Via della Frezza 5
   68 46 28
   68 40 81

351

7. BATTAGLIA (TAVERNA
   ANTONINA)
   (*Venetian*)
   Via Colonna Antonina 48
   68 37 17

8. DAL BOLOGNESE
   (*Bolognese*)
   Piazza del Popolo 1
   38 02 48

   CAMILLUCCIA
   (see Palazzi)

9. CAMINETTO
   (*Characteristic*)
   Viale Parioli 89
   80 39 46

10. DELLA CAMPANA
    (*Characteristic*)
    Via della Campana 18
    65 52 73

11. CAPRICCIO
    (*Elegant, Expensive*)
    Via Liguria 38
    48 92 54
    46 33 70

12. LA CAPRICCIOSA
    (*Pizza*)
    Largo dei Lombardi 8
    67 40 27
    67 55 39

13. CASINA VALADIER
    (*Elegant, Expensive*)
    Pincio
    67 34 69
    67 20 83

14. CELESTINA
    (*Characteristic*)
    Viale Parioli 184
    87 82 42

15. CHECCHINO AL
    MATTATOIO (dal 1887)
    (*Characteristic*)
    Via Monte Testaccio 30
    (Piazza Mattatoio)
    57 38 09

16. CHECCO ER
    CARRETTIERE
    (*Old-Style*)
    Via Benedetta 13
    58 70 18

17. AL CHIANTI
    (*Tuscan and Game*)
    Via Ancona 17
    86 10 83

18. COMPARONE
    (*Characteristic*)
    Piazza in Piscinula 47
    58 62 49

352

19. CORSETTI
    (*Seafood*)
    Piazza San Cosimato 27
    50 90 09
    58 63 11

20. DA MEO PATACCA
    (*Atmosphere*)
    Piazza de' Mercanti 30
    58 61 98

21. ERNESTO
    (A SS. APOSTOLI)
    (*Characteristic*)
    Via del Vaccaro 1
    67 38 97

22. LA FONTANELLA
    (*Tuscan and Game*)
    Largo Fontanella di Borghese
    68 38 49

23. GALEASSI
    (*Characteristic*)
    Piazza Santa Maria in
       Trastevere 3
    50 37 75
    50 98 98

24. GEORGE'S
    (*Elegant, Expensive*)
    Via Marche 7
    48 45 75

25. DA GIGGETTO
    (*Old-Style*)
    Via Portico d'Ottavia 21/a
    56 11 05

26. GIGGI FAZI
    (*Di Moda*)
    Via Lucullo 22
    46 40 45
    47 89 28

27. GIOVANNI
    (*Characteristic*)
    Via Marche 19
    48 92 66

28. HOSTARIA DELL'ORSO
    (*Elegant, Expensive*)
    Via Monte Brianzo 93
    56 42 21
    56 42 50

29. IMPICCETTA A
       TRASTEVERE
    (*Old-Style*)
    Via dei Fienaroli 7
    58 82 94

    MARGUTTA
       (see Taverna Margutta)

30. MARIO
    (*Tuscan and Game*)
    Via della Vite 64
    68 38 18

353

31. MARIO AL LARGO
       PALLARO
       (PALLARO MARIO)
    (Old-Style)
    Largo del Pallaro 15
    65 14 88

    MEO PATACCA
       (see Da Meo Patacca)

32. AL MONUMENTO
    (Seafood)
    Ostia Antica
    60 280 21

33. AL MORO
    (Characteristic)
    Vicolo delle Bollette 13
    68 31 59

34. NINO
    (Tuscan and Game)
    Via Borgognona 11
    67 56 76

    ORSO
       (see Hostaria dell'Orso)

35. OTELLO ALLA
       CONCORDIA
    (Old-Style)
    Via della Croce 81
    67 11 78

36. PALAZZI
       (CAMILLUCCIA)
    (Elegant, Expensive)
    Via della Camilluccia 355
    34 05 78
    34 06 15

    PALLARO MARIO (see
       Mario al Largo Pallaro)

37. DA PALOZZO
    (Old-Style)
    Via Padova 1
    Genzano
    from Rome: 07– 93 962 13

38. PANCRAZIO AL
       BISCIONE
    (Atmosphere)
    Piazza del Biscione 92–94
    56 12 46

39. SILVANO PARIS
    (Characteristic)
    Piazza di San Calisto 7/a
    58 53 78

40. PASSETTO
    (Di Moda)
    Via Zanardelli 14
    65 05 69
    65 36 96

354

41. PASTARELLARO
(*Characteristic*)
Via di San Crisogono 33
58 08 71

42. PIPERNO A MONTE
CENCI
(*Old-Style*)
Via Monte de' Cenci 9
65 06 29

43. HOSTARIA AL
POMPIERE
(*Di Moda*)
Via di Santa Maria de'
Calderari 38
65 696 41

44. RANIERI
(*Di Moda*)
Via Mario de' Fiori 26
67 15 92

45. AL RE DEGLI AMICI
(*Characteristic*)
Via della Croce 33 b
67 53 80
68 31 19

46. ROMOLO A PORTA
SETTIMIANA
(*Characteristic*)
Via di Porta Settimiana 8
58 82 84

47. PIZZERIA
SANT'IGNAZIO
(*Pizza*)
Piazza Sant'Ignazio 169
67 10 58

SILVANO PARIS
(see Paris)

48. TAVERNA MARGUTTA
(*Old-Style*)
Via Alibert 16
67 07 68

49. TEMPIO DI AGRIPPA
(*Pizza*)
Piazza della Rotonda 14
65 56 43

50. TOSCANA AL
GIRARROSTO
(*Tuscan and Game*)
Via Germanico 56
31 47 18

51. 31 [TRENTUNO] AL
VICARIO
(*Di Moda*)
Via degli Uffici del Vicario 31
67 22 51

52. TRE SCALINI
(*Atmosphere*)
Piazza Navona 30
56 13 12

DIRECTORY OF RESTAURANTS

53. TULLIO
   (*Tuscan and Game*)
   Via San Nicolò da
      Tolentino 26
   47 85 64

54. VINCENZO
   (*Old-Style*)
   Via della Lungaretta 173
   58 53 02

AL VICARIO
(see Trentuno)

INDEX TO OTHER RESTAURANTS AND CAFFÈ

Bars and Caffè:
al "cavallino rosso" 11, 27
Alemagna 12–13
Babington's English
   Tearoom 14
The Café de Paris 11
Café Greco 13–14
Canova 14–15
Carpano 11
Doney's 10, 11
Giolitti 13
Golden Gate 11
Gran Caffè Berardo 11
Greco Café 13–14

Hassler-Villa Medici
   Garden 15
l'Hungaria 11
Löwenbrau 14
Manhattan Café 27
Peru 14
Raimondi 14
Roma 14
Rosati 11, 282–83
Rugantino's 27
Strega 11
Tearoom 14
Vienna Beer Garden 26
Wiener Bierhaus 26

Restaurants:
da Amato 28
American 27
Apuleius 24
Arabian 27
Austrian 26

Baths of Caracalla 19
Belvedere delle Rose 22
la Biblioteca 23
Brazilian 28
il Buco 262
Casina della Rose 22

Cavalieri Hilton (la Pergola) 19, 22

Cencio al Parolaccio 24–25

China Garden 28

Chinese 27–28

la Cisterna 24

the Colony 27

Culla del Lago (Castelgandolfo) 23

Domus Aurea 19

Elio Cabala (Marino) 22

les Escargots 26

il Fedelinaro 19

Fontanone 26

Foreign 26–28

Forum Hotel Roof Garden 19

French 26

il Fungo 19

German 26

Grand Hotel Villa Fiorio 22

Hassler-Villa Medici Rooftop Terrace 19

Hong Kong 28

Hungarian 26

Jewish 26, 210–13, 214–16

Kosher 26

Libyan 27

Luau 27

the Madison House 27

Manhattan Café 27

Moulin Rouge 26

Negma, Taverna 27

Norcina 25

the Old Vienna 26

el Patio Andaluz 28

la Pergola Roof Garden (Cavalieri-Hilton) 19, 22

la Piazzetta 24

il Piccolo Budapest 26

la Pistamentuccia (Genzano) 23

Polynesian 27

Rugantino's 27

Rupe Tarpea 22

Russian 26

Samovar 26

Shanghai 27

la Siesta 23

Spanish 28

Taverna Negma 27

Tenenbaum's Kosher Restaurant 26–27

Tientsin 28

il Tinello 28

Tokay 26

Ulpia 19

la Vigna dei Cardinali 22

Villa dei Cesari 23–24

Villa Fiorio (Frascati) 22

la Villetta 51

INDEX OF RECIPES

Index of Recipes

Abbacchio: alla Cacciatora 168; Arrosto 107; Arrosto 313; Brodettato 151; *see also* Lamb
Acciughe Ripiene 53
Agnolini 276
Agnolotti all'Osvaldo 263
Anchovies, Fresh Stuffed 53
Anchovy Dip 33
Animelle al Prosciuto 154
Anitra co'la Sarsa 318
Antipasti: *see* Hors d'Oeuvres
Aperitif Renato Torti 77
Apples, Baked 234
Arista di Maiale 278
Arosto Misto a la Spiedo 320
Artichokes: in Roman Fry 139; Jewish Style 214; Raw, with Sauce 105; Roman Style 215
Asparagus, in Roman Fry 140

Baccalà 289; Spinati, Filetti di 212, 214
Bagna Cauda 33
Bauletto Tre Scalini 313

Bean Soup Francovich 270
Beans: and Macaroni 180; Broad, in Sauce 321; Fava, Roman Style 179; in Tomato Sauce 275; Macaroni and Chick Peas 180; with Caviar 271; with Pork Rind and Ham Bone 196; *see also* Facioli, Fagioli
Béchamel: Crocchette di Latte 140; Croquettes 140; Sauce 108, 164, 208, 238
Beef: Braised 178; Meatballs 321; Meat Loaf 321; Pot Roast 152; Pot Roast, Florentine Style 275, 279; Stew 210; T-Bone Steak, Broiled 263
Besciamella: *see* Béchamel
Bistecca alla Fiorentina Cotta con Fuoco di Legna 263
Bocconcini 151; di Vitello con Peperoni 185
Boiled Meats 170, 237
Bollito Misto 170, 237
Bolognese Sauce 229, 238

361

INDEX

Braciola di Maiale con li Broccoli Strascinati 181

Brains: and Zucchine 272; Fried 322; Fried Milanese Style 233; in Brown Butter 232; in Roman Fry 139

(er) Brasato de Bove 178

Broccoli: Sautéed 150; Strascinati 181

Bruschetta 321

Bucatini alla Amatriciana 142

Cake: and Custard 71; Chocolate 73

Calamaretti Affogati 252

Calf's Liver: in Mixed Roman Fry 139; Venetian Style 49

Calzone 296

Cannelloni: 108, 164, 208, 238

Capellini Maria Luisa 175

Caponata 64

Capretto: Arrosto 194; Brodettato 151

Capriolo alla Cacciatora 168

Carciofi: alla Giudia 214; alla Romana 215; al Pinzimonio 105; *see also* Artichokes

Carni: *see under kind*

Cauliflower, in Roman Fry 140

Cervella, Cervelle: al Burro Nero 232; con Zucchine 272; Dorate 232; Dorate alla Milanese 233

Cheese; Crostini alla Capricciosa 305; Crostini alla Provatura 305; Fonduta alla Piemontese (Fondue) 69; Frittellini di Ricotta 140; Mozzarella in Carozza (Fried Sandwich) 296, 303; Mozzarella, in Roman Fry 140; Ricotta and Spinach Gnocchi 138; Ricotta, in Roman Fry 140; Toasts with Anchovies 305; with Ham, Peas, and Mushrooms 305; Zucchine Flowers, Stuffed with 190

Chestnut Purée: Dessert 72; Vegetable 59

Chicken: alla Diavola 103; Baked in Parchment 130; Fried, Tuscan Style 273; in Vinegar 173; Livers, Sautéed 298; Maximilian 161; Rita 60; Roman Style 233

Chickpeas and Macaroni 180

Chocolate: Cake 73; Sauce 235

Cipolle al Forno 129

Cipollette Agrodorce 321

Cod, Codfish, Salt 212, 214, 289

Coda alla Vaccinara 111

Coffee Mousse 235

Consommé 171

Contorni: *see* Vegetables, *also under kind*

Corn Meal: 290; Gnocchi 291

Costolette: di Pollo al Cartoccio 130; di Vitello al Cartoccio 130

Cotoletta alla Bolognese 285

Cozze: alla Marinara 163; Gratinate 170

Crema Caramella 156

Crêpes 174

Crespelle 174

Crochette di Latte 140

Croquettes: Béchamel 140; Crochette di Latte 140; Frittelline di Ricotta 140; Potato 140; Rice 42; Ricotta Cheese 140; Supplì al Telefono 42

Crostini: alla Capricciosa 305; alla Provatura 305

Croutons, Garlic, in Roman Mixed Fry 140

Custard: Cake 71; Caramel Glazed 156

Cuttlefish: in Tomato Sauce 213; Stewed 213; with Peas 213

362

Desserts (Sweet): Cake, Chocolate 73; Cake, Custard 71; Chestnut Purée 72; Chocolate Cake 73; Coffee Mousse 235; Crema Caramella 156; Custard-Cake 71; Custard, Caramel-Glazed 156; Gelato di Vaniglia 234; Granita (all flavors) 12; Ice Cream, Vanilla 234; Ices 12; Mont Blanc, Monte Bianco 72; Mousse, Coffee 235; Pere Bella Elena 233; Semifreddo al Caffè 236; Semifreddo Semi-Valadier 245; Torta Emma Servi 73; Trifle 71; Vanilla Ice Cream 234; Zabaglione 245; Zuppa Inglese 71

Dischi Volanti alla Trasteverina 195

Dolci: see Desserts

Drinks, Mixed: Aperitif Renato Torti 77; Negroni Cocktail 76–7; Punch alla Livornese 14

Duck with Sauce 318

Dumplings: see Gnocchi

Egg Dough 108, 164, 238; with Spinach 228

Egg Noodles: see Pasta

Egg "Tripe" 153

Eggplant: Baked with Cheese and Meat Sauce 190; Baked with Cheese and Tomato Sauce 189; Hors d'Oeuvre 64; Stuffed Sicilian Style 300

Eggs: Florentine 227; Frittata alla Burina 120; Frittata di Pasta 57; Omelette Country Style 120; Pasta Omelette 57; Poached in Soup 35; Shreds for Soup 35; "Tripe" 153; "Trippa" di Uova 153; Uova alla Fiorentina 227

Facioli 320–1

Fagioli: all'Uccelletto 275; con Caviale 271; con le Cotiche e le Ossa di Prosciutto 196; see also Beans

Fava Beans Roman Style (Romana) 179

Fegatini di Pollo 298

Fegato alla Veneziana 49

Fettuccine all'Alfredo 127

Fieno alla Postarola 130

Fiori di Zucchine Ripiene 190

Fish and Shellfish: Acciughe Ripiene 53; Anchovies, Fresh Stuffed 53; Anchovy Dip 33; Baccalà 289; Baccalà, Filetti di, Spinati 212, 214; Bagna Cauda 33; Calamaretti Affogati 252; Cod, Codfish, Salt 212, 214, 289; Cozze alla Marinara 163; Cozze Gratinate 170; Cuttlefish, in Tomato Sauce 213; Cuttlefish, Stewed 213; with Peas 213; Frittura di Mare 225; Insalata di Frutti di Mare 118; Mazzancolle al Coccio 253; Mullet Baked in Parchment 166; Mussels, Baked 170; Mariner Style 163; Orata 179; Prawns in Wine Sauce 253; Red Snapper in Tomato Sauce 179; Salad, Mixed Shellfish 118; Scampi: "al Gratin" 205; alla Moro 102; alla Pescatora 256; Baked 205; Fisherman's Style 256; Giganti alla Piastra 122; on the Griddle 122; Seafood Casserole 144; Fry 225; Salad 118; Seppioline: Affogati 213; con Piselli 213; in Umido 213; Sogliola: ai Ferri 107; al Coccio 253; "Orso," Filetti di 225; Sole, Grilled 107; in Wine

Fish and Shellfish (*continued*)
Sauce 253; Orso Style, Filets of 225; Soup 206, 260; Squid (Baby), Poached 252; Tegamino alla Pescatora 144; Triglia al Cartoccio 166; Zuppa di Pesce 206, 260; *see also* Pasta, Risotto
"Flying Saucers" Ravioli 195
Fondue, Piedmontese Style 69
Fonduta alla Piemontese 69
Formaggi: *see* Cheese
Fowl: *see under kind*
Fragoline all'Aceto 105
Frattaglie: *see under kind*
Frittata: alla Burina (Rurale) 120; di Pasta 57
Frittellini di Ricotta 140
Fritto Misto alla Romana 139
Frittura di Mare 225
Fruit: Apples, Baked 234; Compote 193; Fragoline all'Aceto 105; Macedonia di Frutta 193; Mele Cotte 234; Pears, Baked 234; with Ice Cream and Chocolate Sauce 233; Pere Bella Elena 233; Strawberries with Vinegar 105
Frutta: *see* Fruit
Funghi: Crudi, Insalati di 62, 289; Ovoli e Tartufi, Insalata di 267; Porcini al Forno 104; Trifolati 136; *see also* Mushrooms

Game: *see under kind*
Game Birds Grilled over Charcoal 219
Garlic Croutons 140
Garlic Toast 321
Gelati (Ice Creams): *see* Desserts
Gnocchi: Corn Meal 291; di Patate 136; di Polenta 291; di Semolino 137; Potato 136

Spinach 137; Spinach and Ricotta 138; Verdi, I 137; Verdi, II 138
Granita: di Caffè, di Fragole, di Limone (Coffee, Strawberry, Lemon) 12
Green Sauce 237
Guinea Fowl, Pot Roast 279

Hare: in Wine Sauce 220; Pot Roast 279; Sauce for Egg Noodles 266
Hors d'Oeuvres (Antipasti): Anchovy Dip 33; Artichokes, Raw, with Sauce 105; Bagna Cauda 33; Bruschetta 321; Caponata 64; Carciofi al Pinzimonio 105; Croquettes, Rice 42; Crostini: alla Capricciosa 305; alla Provatura 305; Eggplant 64; Garlic Toasts 321; Insalata di Frutti di Mare 118; Passanella 219; Peperoni (Sott'Aceto, Sott'Olio) 63; Peppers, Toasted (in Oil, in Vinegar) 63; Pomodori al Riso 201; Rice Croquettes 42; Salad of Mixed Shellfish 118; Seafood Salad 118; Squash, Stuffed 135; Supplì al Telefono 42; Toasts: Garlic 321; with Cheese and Anchovies 305; with Cheese, Ham, Peas, and Mushrooms 305; Tomatoes, Stuffed 201; Zucchine Ripiene 135: *see also* Beans, Fish and Shellfish, Onions, Salads

Ice Cream, Ices: *see* Desserts
Insalata: di Frutti di Mare 118; di Funghi Crudi 62, 289; di Ovoli e Tartufi 267; *see also* Salads
Involtini di Vitello 186

Kid: Braised 151; Roast 194

Lamb: Braised 151; Hunter's Style 168; Roast 107, 313; *see also* Abbacchio
Lasagne: *see* Pasta
Lepre in Salmì 220
Liver: Calf's, in Roman Fry 139; Chicken 298; Venetian Style 49

Macaroni, Maccheroni: *see* Pasta
Macedonia di Frutta 193
Maiale: *see* Pork
Manzo: *see* Beef
Mazzancolle al Coccio 253
Meat: *see under kind*
Meat Balls (with Beans) 321
Meat Loaf 321
Meat Sauce 152; Bolognese Style 229, 238
Meats, Boiled 170, 237
Melanzane: alla Parmigiana 189; alla Romana 190; alla Siciliana 300; Caponata 64
Mele Cotte 234
Minestrone 192
Mont Blanc, Monte Bianco 72
Mornay Sauce 227
Mousse, Coffee 235
Mozzarella: Cubes, in Roman Fry 140; in Carozza 296, 303; Sandwich (Fried) 296, 303
Mullet Baked in Parchment 166
Mushrooms: Baked 104; Raw, in Salad 62, 267, 289; Sautéed 136; Wild 62, 104, 136, 267, 289
Mussels: Baked 170; Mariner Style 163

Neapolitan Pizza 294
Negroni Cocktail 76–7

Omelette: *see* Eggs
Onions: Roast 129; Sweet and Sour 321
Orata 179
Ossibuchi con Funghi 132
Ostrica di Vitello 123
Ovoli e Tartufi, Insalata di 267
Oxtail, Stewed 111

Paillard George's 243
Pancakes 174
Pappardelle sulla Lepre 266
Passanella 219
Pasta: Agnolini 276; Agnolotti all'Osvaldo 263; all'Uova 108, 164, 238; Bucatini alla Amatriciana 142; Cannelloni 108. 164, 208, 238; Capellini Maria Luisa 175; Consommé with Pasta Shreds 35; Dischi Volanti alla Trasteverina 195; e Ceci 180; e Facioli 180; Egg Dough 108, 164, 238; with Spinach 228; Egg Noodles 127; Haystack of 130; with Hare Sauce 266; Fettuccine all'Alfredo 127; Fieno alla Postarola 130; "Flying Saucers" Ravioli 195; Frittata di 57; Green Dough 228; Hare Sauce for Egg Noodles 266; Lasagne: Casserole 228; Pasticciate 228; Macaroni: and Beans 180; and Chickpeas 180; Casserole 299; with Tomato and Bacon Sauce 142; Maccheroni Zita alla Sorrentina 299; Minestrone with Pasta 192; Omelette 57; Pappardelle sulla Lepre 266; Pesto with 158; Ravioli: di Spinaci e Ricotta 304; "Flying Saucers" 195; Spinach and Cheese 304;

Pasta (*continued*)

Verdi 138; Ricciarelle alla Campagnola 298; Rigatoni: all'Ammiraglia 120; alla Norcina 124; con la Pagliata 112; del Pastarellaro 156; George's 242; Moda del Vicario 176; Pork Butcher's Style 124; with Giblets 112; with Seafood 120; Sauces for: *see* Sauces; Soup: Consommé with Pasta Shreds 35; Vegetable with Pasta 192; Spaghetti: alla Carbonara 102; alla Moro 102; alla Pescatora 167; alle Vongole 255; all'Impiccetta 201; al Monumento 252; with Bacon, Cheese, and Egg 102; with Caviar 39; with Clams 255; with Clams and Mussels 252; with Seafood 167; with Tuna, Mushrooms, and Giblets 201; Spaghettini al Caviale 39; Spinach and Egg Dough 228; Stracciatella 35; Tortellini: alla Panna 285; Augustea 147; in Cream 285; with Mushrooms and Peas 147; Vegetable Soup with Pasta 192; Verde 228

Pastries, Stuffed with Cheese, Ham, Anchovies 296

Patate Arroste 107

Pears: Baked 234; with Ice Cream and Chocolate Sauce 233

Peas, Green, with Ham 209, 300

Peperonata 185

Peperoni: Sott'Aceto 63; Sott' Olio 63

Peppers: Stewed 185; Toasted (in Oil, in Vinegar) 63

Pere: Bella Elena 233; Cotte 234

Pesci: *see* Fish and Shellfish

Pesto 158

Pheasant, Pot Roast 279

Piccioncino Glassato con Funghi 143

Pig (Suckling) Umbrian, on the Spit 318

Piselli Freschi al Prosciutto 209, 300

Pizza: ai Funghi 295; alla Capricciosa 295, 302; alla Napoletana 294; Dough 294, 302; with Anchovies, Cheese, and Tomatoes 294; with Mixed Filling 295, 302; with Mushrooms 295

Polenta: 290; Gnocchi di 291

Pollame: *see under kind*

Pollo: all'Aceto 173; alla Diavola 103; alla Massimiliano 161; alla Rita 60; alla Romana 233; Fritto Dorato alla Toscana 273; *see also* Chicken

Polpettone 321

Pomodori al Riso 208

Pomodoro Passato 184

Porchettini Umbri ar Girarosto 318

Porcini al Forno 104

Pork: Arista di Maiale 278; Braciola di Maiale con li Broccoli Strascinati 181; Chop, with Broccoli 181; Pig (Suckling) on the Spit 318; Porchettini Umbri ar Girarosto 318; Roast 278

Porpettine de Manzo con li Facioli 320

Pot Roast: Beef 152, 275, 279; Guinea Fowl 279; Hare 279; Pheasant 279; Tuscan Style 275, 279; Veal 152

Potato: Croquettes 140; "Dump-

lings" 136; Gnocchi 136; in Roman Fry 140; Roast 107
Prawns: in Wine Sauce 253; with Rice 247; *see also* Scampi *under* Fish and Shellfish
Punch alla Livornese 14
Purè di Castagne 59

Quaglie alla Giuseppe 143
Quail: in the Style of Giuseppe 143; with Bread Crusts 319 (Du') Quaje cor Crostone 319

Ravioli: *see* Pasta
Red Snapper in Tomato Sauce 179
Ricciarelle alla Campagnola 298
Rice: Croquettes 42; Fisherman's Style 167; Milanese Style 309; Stuffed in Tomatoes 208; with Prawns 245; with Sausage, Fagiano Style 41; with Scampi 245; with Seafood and Tomato Sauce 204
Ricotta: *see* Cheese
Rigatoni: *see* Pasta
Risotto: alla Certosina 245; alla Fagiano 41; alla Milanese 309; alla Pescatora 167, 204
Roasts: Abbacchio 107, 313; Anitra co'la Sarsa 318; Arista 278; Capretto 194; Du' Quaje cor Crostone 319; Duck with Sauce 318; Kid 194; Lamb 107, 313; Misto a la Spiedo 320; Mixed from the Spit 320; Pig (Suckling) Umbrian, on the Spit 318; Porchettini Umbri ar Girarosto 318; Pork 278; Pot Roast: Beef 152, 275, 279; Hare, Guinea Fowl, Pheasant 279; Tuscan Style 275, 279; Veal 152; Quail with Bread

Crusts 319; Stracotto 275, 279; Suckling-Pig à la Flaccus 46
Rognoncino Flambé 226
Roman Fry 139

Salad: Mushrooms: and Truffles 267; Raw 62, 289; Wild 62, 267, 289; Shellfish 118; *see also* Insalata
Salsa: Besciamella 108, 164, 208, 238; Bolognese 229, 238; Cioccolata 235; Piccante 238; Verde 237; *see also* Sauces
Salt Cod 212, 289
Saltimbocca alla Romana 115
Sandwich, Fried Mozzarella 296, 303
Sauces: Anchovy 33; Bagna Cauda 33; Béchamel 108, 164, 208, 238; Bolognese 229, 238; Chocolate 235; Dip for Raw Vegetables 105; Green 237; Meat 152, 229, 238; Mornay 227; Orange for Semifreddo 246; Pesto 158; Pinzimonio 105; Pomodoro Passato 184; Spicy 238; Sugo d'Umido 152; Tomato 108, 184
Scaloppina Carlaccia 174
Scaloppine 146
Scampi: *see* Fish and Shellfish
Seafood: *see* Fish and Shellfish
Semifreddo: al Caffè 236; Semi-Valadier 245
Semolina "Dumplings" 137
Semolino, Gnocchi di 137
Seppioline: *see* Fish and Shellfish
Shellfish: *see* Fish and Shellfish
Soffritto 229
Sogliola, Sogliole: *see* Fish and Shellfish
Sole: *see* Fish and Shellfish

Soubise 175

Soup: Bean Soup Francovich 270; Consommé 171; with Egg Shreds 35; with Poached Egg 35; Fish Soup 206, 260; Minestrone 192; Stracciatella 35; Vegetable with Pasta 192

Spaghetti, Spaghettini: see Pasta

Spicy Sauce 238

Spinach: and Egg Dough 228; and Ricotta Gnocchi 138; Gnocchi 137

Squab, Glazed, with Mushrooms 143

Squash, Italian, Stuffed 135

Squid (Baby) Poached 252

Steak: T-Bone Broiled 263; Veal, with Artichokes 243

Stew: Beef 210; Oxtail 111; Veal 210

Stracciatella 35

Stracotto: alla Fiorentina 275, 279; di Fagiano, di Faraona, di Lepre 279; see also Pot Roast

Strangolapreti 138

Strawberries with Vinegar 105

Stufatino 210

Suckling-Pig à la Flaccus 46

Sugo d'Umido 152

Supplì al Telefono 42

Sweetbreads: in Mixed Roman Fry 139; with Ham 154

T-Bone Steak, Broiled 263

Tegamino: alla Pescatora 144; di Frattaglie 145

Toasts: Garlic 321; Tomato 219; with Cheese and Anchovies 305; with Cheese, Ham, Peas, and Mushrooms 305

Tomato Sauce, Stewed 184

Tomatoes Stuffed with Rice 208

Torta Emma Servi 73

Tortellini: see Pasta

Trifle 71

Triglia al Cartoccio 166

Tripe, Roman Style 152

Trippa alla Romana 152

"Trippa" di Uova 153

Truffles: Salad of, with Wild Mushrooms 267

Uccellini: Scapati 115; sul Carbone 219

Uova: see Eggs

Vanilla Ice Cream 234

Variety Cuts: see under kind

Variety Meats, Casserole of 145

Veal: Baked in Parchment 130; Bauletto 313; Birds 115; Bocconcini 151; con Peperoni 185; Boiled 171; Costolette di Vitello al Cartoccio 130; Cotoletta alla Bolognese 285; Cutlet, Bolognese Style 285; in Bollito Misto 171; in Fritto Misto 139; Involtini 186; Kidney, Flamed 226; Loin, Boiled 171; Ossibuchi 132; Ostriche 123; "Oysters" 123; Paillard 243; Pancakes, Stuffed with 174; Pot Roast 152; Rognoncino Flambé 226; Rolls 186; Rolls, Stuffed 313; Saltimbocca alla Romana 115; Scallops 129; Scallops (Roman Fry) 139; Scaloppina Carlaccia 174; Scaloppine 146; Shins with Mushrooms 132; Steaks with Artichokes 243; Stew 210; Stufatino 210; Tidbits 151; Tidbits, with Peppers 185; Uccellini Scapati 115; Vitella Caminetto 129; Vitello Tonnato 284; with Mushrooms

310; with Spicy Sauce 221; with Tuna Sauce 284; Zingarella 221; al Funghetto 310; *see also* Brains, Sweetbreads

Vegetables: Artichokes: in Roman Fry 139; Jewish Style 214; Raw, with Sauce 105; Roman Style 215; Asparagus 140; Broccoli, Sautéed 136; Broccoli Strascinati 181; Caponata 64; Carciofi: al Pinzimonio 105; alla Giudia 214; alla Romana 215; Castagne, Purè di 59; Cauliflower, in Roman Fry 140; Chestnuts, Purée of 59; Cipolle al'Forno 129; Cipollette Agrodorce 321; Eggplant: Baked with Cheese-Meat Sauce 190; with Cheese-Tomato Sauce 189; Hors d'Oeuvre 64; Stuffed, Sicilian Style 300; Fava Romana 179; Fiori di Zucchine Ripiene 190; Funghi: Crudi, Insalata di 62, 267, 289; Porcini al Forno 104; Trifolati 136; Insalata: *see* Insalata; Melanzane: alla Parmigiana 189; alla Romana 190; alla Siciliana 300; Mushrooms: Baked 104; Ovoli 267; Porcini 104; Raw 62, 267, 289; Salad 62, 267, 289; Sautéed

136; Wild 62, 104, 136, 267, 289; Onions: Roast 129; Sweet and Sour 321; Patate Arroste 107; Peas, Green, with Ham 209, 300; Peperonata 185; Peperoni 185; Sott'Aceto 63; Sott'Olio 63; Peppers: Stewed 185; Toasted (in Oil, in Vinegar) 63; Piselli Freschi al Prosciutto 209, 300; Pomodori al Riso 208; Porcini al Forno 104; Potatoes, Roast 107; Purè di Castagne 59; Salad: *see* Insalata; Soup with Pasta 192; Squash, Stuffed 135; Tomatoes, Stuffed 208; Zucchine: Flowers, Stuffed 190; in Roman Fry 140; Ripiene 135; Tuscan Style 272

Venison Hunter's Style 168

Vitella, Vitello: *see* Veal

Zabaglione 245

Zingarella: al Funghetto 310; di Vitello 221

Zucchine: Flowers, Stuffed 190; in Roman Fry 140; Ripiene 135; Tuscan Style 272

Zuppa: alla Pavese 35; dei Fagioli Francovich 270; di Pesce 206, 260; Inglese 71; *see also* Soup